AF323426

*Incredible! Because it's credible. What is absolutely remarkable about Jehane Ragai and Tamer Shoeib's book is that a textbook (!) draws us in so. It accomplishes this by imagined tales of artistic authentication that are exciting both as human stories and as detailed, documented accounts of scientific detection that teach! The theatrical staging of the scientific detective work, and the factual credibility (and limits) of the scientific techniques applied — remarkably clearly laid out in a voluminous endnotes section — intertwine in this book in a unique way. And sometimes, just as in the real world, the evidence and the experts disagree — the decision is left in your hands. I think that many young people reading this adventurous book will be drawn to become art analysts.*

**Roald Hoffmann**, Nobel Prize in Chemistry (1981) and Writer

*Truly engaging and captivating,* Technical Art History, *reads like a detective story. The authors, through their passion, scientific competence, and teaching experience, skillfully describe the fundamental role of science in authenticating works of art — so instrumental in fighting the growing battle against forgery and in providing a future to our cultural heritage.*

**Maurizio Seracini**, Diagnostician of Italian Art and Founder of the Center for Interdisciplinary Science for Art, Architecture, and Archaeology at the University of California, San Diego

*Drs. Ragai and Shoeib make a potentially arcane subject matter accessible and engaging. It is not necessarily difficult to capture public attention and imagination with stories of art fraud and art crime. But imagination is not proof. This text explains — in clear prose that "decodes" technical terminology — how to prove that fakery or forgery has occurred. The authors do so, moreover, by skillfully stitching their scientific analysis into the stories themselves, which brings both the art and the investigations to life.*

*This text is a welcome contribution to the field. As practitioners of "art law," we understand the challenge of narrating these complicated cases for judges and juries. The first step, of course, is that the lawyer must understand the scientific methodology and the evidence for him or herself. Drs. Ragai and Shoeib have written with non-scientific audiences in mind, which allows this technical handbook to stand out. This text will be appreciated and enjoyed by anyone who is interested in understanding not only the "science of art," but also the "art of science."*

**Bill Charron & Megan Noh**, Co-Chairs of the Art Law Group at Pryor Cashman LLP, New York

*Brimming with intelligence and wit, this highly readable volume strikes a perfect balance between educational tool and practical guide on art authentication by way of forensic inquiry. Cleverly presenting nine imaginary case studies of increasing complexity, Ragai and Shoeib illustrate a wide variety of scientific techniques used to detect fakes and affirm genuine works of art. In today's high stakes global art market, where fakes and forgeries abound with alarming frequency, this book is essential for the serious art professional, student, and other stakeholders who may or may not have a scientific background.*

*Written in a lively and engaging style, and with utmost clarity, Technical Art History draws us into a maze of scientific experiments to explore one of the art world's most pressing questions — "Is it authentic?". The reader is transformed into art sleuth, solving one case after another, by following the authors' step-by-step methodology.*

*In the field of art authentication, this book is the real deal.*

**Judith B. Prowda**, Sotheby's Institute of Art

*Jehane Ragai and Tamer Shoeib's* Technical Art History: A Journey Through Active Learning *is an excellent resource to train the next generation of art experts in both the academic and the museum world. Clear, compelling case studies provide a much needed introduction to the myriad technical research methods available to help determine whether a painting is authentic or not. Well-informed and very accessible, this book is highly suitable for sparking fruitful collaborations across disciplinary boundaries. In the perpetual arms race between art experts and forgers, carefully integrated multidisciplinary approaches, such as the ones advocated in this book, are absolutely indispensable.*

**Anna Tummers**, University Lecturer Early Modern Art and Theory, Leiden University Centre for the Art in Society. Author of *The Eye of the Connoisseur: Authenticating Paintings by Rembrandt and His Contemporaries*, Amsterdam University Press and Getty Publications (2011)

*Ragai and Shoeib have accomplished an extraordinary feat by writing a technical book that is highly readable, engaging, and instructive.* Technical Art History: A Journey Through Active Learning *provides students and art professionals with essential information on art analysis for authentication that is crucial to being competent in today's art market.*

**Linda Selvin**, Executive Director, Appraisers Association of America

Fusion of Art and Science

# Technical Art History

## A Journey Through Active Learning

Fusion of Art and Science

# Technical Art History

## A Journey Through Active Learning

**Jehane Ragai**
**Tamer Shoeib**

*The American University in Cairo, Egypt*

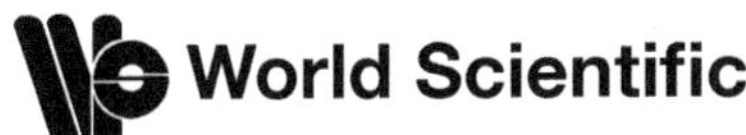



NEW JERSEY · LONDON · SINGAPORE · BEIJING · SHANGHAI · HONG KONG · TAIPEI · CHENNAI · TOKYO

*Published by*

World Scientific Publishing Europe Ltd.

57 Shelton Street, Covent Garden, London WC2H 9HE

*Head office:* 5 Toh Tuck Link, Singapore 596224

*USA office:* 27 Warren Street, Suite 401-402, Hackensack, NJ 07601

**Library of Congress Cataloging-in-Publication Data**
Names: Ragai, Jehane, author. | Shoeib, Tamer, author.
Title: Technical art history : a journey through active learning /
    Jehane Ragai, Tamer Shoeib, The American University in Cairo, Egypt.
Description: New Jersey : World Scientific, [2021] | "Fusion of art and science." |
    Includes bibliographical references and index.
Identifiers: LCCN 2020053072 (print) | LCCN 2020053071 (ebook) |
    ISBN 9781786349392 (hardcover) | ISBN 9781786349408 (ebook for institutions) |
    ISBN 9781786349415 (ebook for individuals)
Subjects:  LCSH: Painting--Expertising--Case studies.
Classification: LCC ND1635 .R34 2021 (ebook) | LCC ND1635 (print) | DDC 759--dc23
LC record available at https://lccn.loc.gov/2020053072

**British Library Cataloguing-in-Publication Data**
A catalogue record for this book is available from the British Library.



> **Disclaimer:**
> These stories are works of fiction. The incidents, names, and characters portrayed in this work are the products of the authors' imagination. Any resemblance to actual persons, events, or localities is purely coincidental.

For any available supplementary material, please visit
https://www.worldscientific.com/worldscibooks/10.1142/Q0276#t=suppl

Desk Editors: Aanand Jayaraman/Michael Beale/Shi Ying Koe

Typeset by Stallion Press
Email: enquiries@stallionpress.com

# Foreword

## Art in the Age of Technical Investigation

In 2011, Martin Kemp, an art history professor from the University of Oxford, ran an experiment in which fourteen people, none of them art experts, were shown genuine Rembrandt paintings as well as fake "Rembrandt" paintings (derivative works, copies after Rembrandt, and the like) while undergoing brain scans. A painting was shown to them and they were told it was by Rembrandt. Another painting was shown to them and they were told it was a fake. By measuring the pleasure centers of the brain, Kemp concluded that "the way we view art is not rational." Being told a work was authentic (whether or not it actually was) activated pleasure centers when it was shown, which was not the case when the viewer was told it was inauthentic (even if it was actually the real deal). It's all about anticipation. If you're poured a glass of wine and told it's a 1955 Lafite, you'll enjoy it much more than if you're told it's a 2015 Trader Joe's wine-in-a-box, whichever it truly happens to be.

This was a groundbreaking experiment, though it was small in scale. Kemp is a revolutionary figure in the study of art, not only as the leading Leonardo da Vinci specialist, but also because he came from a science background and brought with him the tools of a "hard scientist's" trade — a CSI approach to art history's mysteries. While "soft sciences" have long been used to help better understand art (from Freud's analysis of Michelangelo's *Moses* statue to my *The Art of Forgery*, which was a psychological study of forgers), hard science is a latecomer to the field. The union of art and neuroscience is a very new field, promoted by the likes of Kemp and Nobel laureate Eric Kandel, who published a book on how the human mind deals with abstract art.

To this illustrious and groundbreaking list we must add the authors of this important book, Jehane Ragai and Tamer Shoeib.

I first came across Ragai's work in her previous book, *The Scientist and the Forger*. My interest in the history of forgery was always anecdotal — I'm an art historian, and so the "hard sciences" were always mysterious to me, important but existing in some ether that I would likely never understand with any depth. The scientific texts that I'd encountered while researching for the course I teach every summer as part of the ARCA Postgraduate Program in Art Crime and Cultural Heritage Protection were always tough for me to get through. They were, essentially, written for peer scientists, penned by conservators addressing other conservators, and full of arcane-looking equations, acronyms, and abbreviations that made my head spin. I might have just set them aside and, as a defense mechanism, thought to myself "that's not important to me," but I could tell perfectly well that it was important. My approach to telling the history of art crime through anecdotes was only going to be informed storytelling if I didn't grasp the techniques at play that helped forgers fool experts, and let experts unmask forgers.

This is why I am grateful to Ragai and Shoeib, for they take hard science and put it into digestible case studies, explaining rather than assuming that readers are familiar with discipline-specific jargon. This is a book for students. When it comes to sciences (especially my high school nemesis, chemistry) I am most definitely still a student.

This book is cleverly divided into nine invented, but entirely plausible, case studies that allow the authors to lay out, step-by-step and ideally-situated-for-students, investigations into art cases that must be cracked through technical analysis. It focuses on how forensic investigation can lead to authentication. Or, as happens more often, can lead to red flags that suggest that something is amiss. Forensic analysis by conservators rarely provides specific attributions (a test to determine the exact identity of the artist who created the work). It is best at pointing out anachronisms or inconsistencies that suggest that the object was problematic or was tampered with. It could be a forgery (which criminologists define as a wholesale new work, made from scratch, or a fraudulent imitation of something else) or a fake (a pre-existing work that is altered in some way to make it appear to be something else). Such red flags do not automatically mean that there is criminality afoot. The 2020 exhibition of Jan van Eyck's *Adoration of the Mystic Lamb,* after a five-year restoration, revealed vast amounts of over-painting (as much as 10% of the surface) that historians had been examining as original van Eyck elements — none appear to have been the work of criminals, but all of over-enthusiastic restorers of generations past. Finding a radioactive isotope in a bottle of 19th century wine — an isotope that only existed on Earth after atomic testing in 1945 — does not mean that the bottle is fake. It could be an original 19th century wine that was topped up with a post-1945 wine, as is customary at high-end vineyards. But such findings clue us in that a closer look is needed, one that we would be unlikely to ever take without the discoveries of technical analysis. We art historians would have continued to believe that Van Eyck's *Mystic Lamb* in the center of his painting looked like a lamb with four ears (and not like the humanoid sheep-face that has been revealed as the original, the second set of ears pentimenti of Van Eyck's original under-painting).

The very idea that art could be investigated by scientists is not new and dates back to the Wacker Van Gogh trial in 1928. Art dealer Otto Wacker claimed to be selling some Van Goghs on behalf of a noble Russian family that wished to remain anonymous. This would've been fine, except that the two leading Van Gogh scholars, Jacob Baart de la Faille and H. P. Brenner, could not agree on which of the "Wacker Van Goghs" if any were original. In fact, not only did they disagree among each other, but they kept changing their own minds — de la Faille published one opinion on them in one monograph and switched in a later one. Wacker was on trial accused of selling forged Van Goghs, and the two expert connoisseurs on the witness stand could not agree. So the judge summoned a tie-breaker, someone whose opinion felt more objective. He was a chemist called Martin de Wild. He tested the oil paint in the Wacker Van Goghs and compared their chemical components to paint in certainly authenticated Van Goghs. The Wacker paintings all contained resin and pulverized lead mixed into the oil paints — this would have sped up the drying process — and authenticated paintings never contained these ingredients. De Wild's findings sealed Wacker's fate. He was convicted of fraud. (He appealed and, during the appeal trial, more evidence came to light that his whole family were forgers, and his sentence was increased). Thus, Martin de Wild became the first CSI art detective, and the godfather to all those who followed, and to the book you hold in your hands.

This book looks set to guide the next generation of technical art analysts, and has already informed me, a so-called expert in art crime who is very grateful to Ragai and Shoeib for explaining the science in such a lucid and interesting manner.

Dr. Noah Charney
Professor of Art History
Founder of ARCA, the Association for Research
into Crimes against Art

# Preface

Competent scientific investigation is playing a markedly more vital role in the detection of forgery in paintings. While not aspiring to supplant the connoisseur and art historian, science serves to integrate, support, and, when necessary, disprove conclusions reached without technical examination.

The alarming rate at which forgeries are multiplying and the astounding expertise behind them has resulted in the imperative need to equip students and professionals dealing with the field — either directly or tangentially — with knowledge of the long-established and the most recent scientific techniques. The fact that no textbook dealing with technical art history is currently available to teachers and undergraduate students, coupled with our own longtime passion for teaching, motivated us to set out to bridge the gap. Our goal is to present a textbook that may be of use to art historians, art conservationists, art or science students intending to engage in a career straddling Arts and Science. This book may also be of use to connoisseurs and curators with little to no scientific background.

The following two questions guided our endeavor:

1. *How can we provide an educational tool in* Technical Art History *that can capture the imagination of the reader and not solely rely on the recollection of a collection of facts?*
2. *How can we simultaneously develop critical thinking, provide content knowledge, and engage readers?*

Through our experience teaching the interdisciplinary course *Chemistry, Art and Archaeology* at the American University in Cairo, we were very satisfied by the results brought about by using both *fictional* and *real case studies* to challenge undergraduate students to think creatively and critically.[1] As we set out to design our textbook, the effectiveness of the *Case Study* approach we had employed in the course led us to believe that the same pedagogical strategy would most effectively deliver our intended educational message.

As a sample of comments on the course *Chemistry, Art and Archaeology* suggests, the approach draws students to the material and successfully engages them in active learning:

> *In my experience, I think what made the class so effective was the use of many interesting case studies and preparing presentations.*

> *The material was not only new and interesting, but it was presented in an inventive and passionate way that drew us into the lively classroom discussions.*

> *[The] blend of theory and practice brought variety to the classwork.*

*Technical Art History: A Journey Through Active Learning* brings together nine very diverse fictional *case studies* in which there is a buildup of investigating techniques introduced on *a need-to-know basis* from the simplest to the more intricate, while always in keeping with the introductory spirit of the book.

We define objectives for each chapter, followed by a narrative that intends to bridge the divide between Art and Science. This is followed by two types of questions: *Revision questions*, which can be answered through a close study of the text, and *Exploratory questions*, which require extra reading and research. We also provide *Classroom activities*, *Homework*, *Explanatory endnotes* as well as an online *Teacher Guide* (https://www.worldscientific.com/worldscibooks/10.1142/q0276-sm).

---

[1] We were particularly inspired by the case **As Light Meets Matter: Art Under Scrutiny** by Eleonora Del Federico, Steven T. Diver, Monika I. Konaklieva, Richard Ludescher, published online by the **The National Center for Case Study Teaching in Science (NCCSTS)**, sciencecases.lib.buffalo.edu.

We hope that this cross-disciplinary narrative will aid the reader in developing better critical thinking skills and allow them to emerge with:

- A better understanding of the main concepts underlying the various technological approaches used in art authentication endeavors.
- An increased appreciation of the value of an integrated approach in the evaluation of an artwork.
- An ability to discern the most appropriate technique(s) in a particular authentication process.
- A better means of understanding and evaluating stories about fakes conveyed through the media.

We wish students, teachers, and other stakeholders the best of luck. As you join the growing battle against art forgery, may this book help you become effective warriors.

Jehane Ragai
Tamer Shoeib

# About the Authors

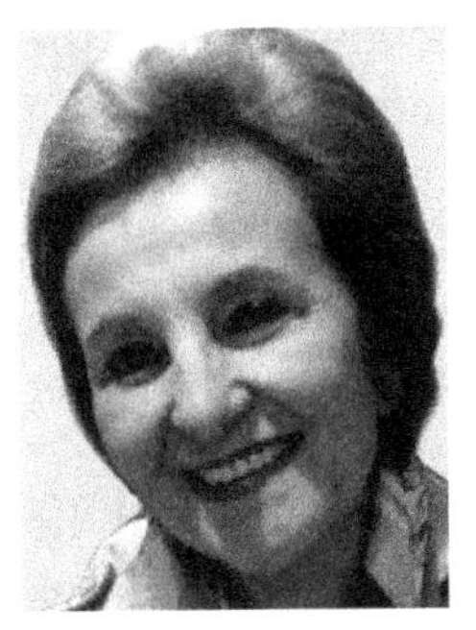

**Jehane Ragai** is an Emeritus Professor of Chemistry at the American University in Cairo.

She has lectured extensively in the US, Europe, and the Middle East to university and museum audiences on the scientific detection of forgery in paintings and on topics related to Ancient Egyptian Science.

Owing to her additional interest in archaeological chemistry, she became a consultant to the American Research Center in Egypt (ARCE) Sphinx project. She has served on the National Committee for the Study of the Sphinx, and from 2001–2008 was a member of the Board of Governors of the ARCE.

Since 2008 to date, Dr. Ragai has been a jury member for the l'Oreal-UNESCO For Women in Science Awards, founded by the Nobel Laureates Christian de Duve and Pierre-Gilles de Gennes.

As a faculty member in the Department of Chemistry of the American University in Cairo, she has chaired its Senate, its Department of Chemistry, and was the Director of its Chemistry Graduate program. The recipient of several AUC Trustees Merit Awards, Dr. Ragai also received the School of Sciences and Engineering Award for her role as chair of the Department of Chemistry and in 2013 she was awarded the university-wide Best Teacher Award.

Dr. Ragai is a foreign member of the Royal Swedish Academy of Arts and Sciences in Gothenburg (established in 1778).

She is the author of the two editions of *The Scientist and the Forger* published in 2015 and 2018. The first edition was translated into Korean and the second into Chinese.

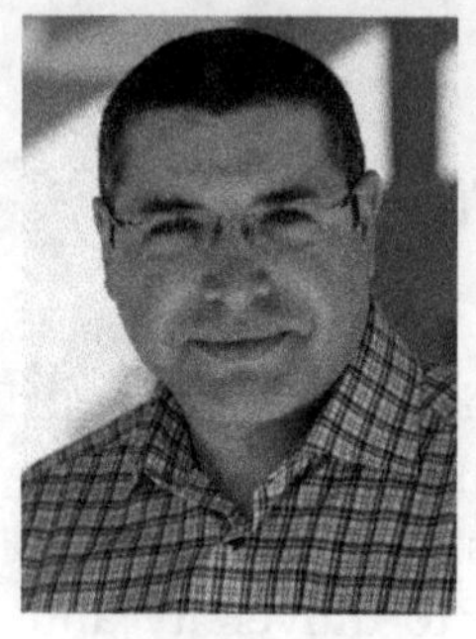

**Tamer Shoeib** received his Bachelor's degree with honors in chemistry from York University in Canada where he was awarded the top-rank for his doctorate thesis in mass spectrometry and computational chemistry.

Following a prestigious fellowship at the Institute for National Measurement Standards in Canada's National Research Council, he decided to pursue a career in academia, receiving an honorary fellowship at the Centre for Analytical Science at Loughborough University in England, where he worked collaboratively with other scientists to conduct promising cancer research.

Having joined the American University in Cairo (AUC) in 2011, he continued to work on personalized cancer treatment as an innovative alternative to standard chemotherapy, increasing the efficacy of the drugs while decreasing side effects and lowering cost. The promising results of this research efforts were featured on the covers of several issues of leading Royal Society of Chemistry journals with one of his publications being recognized by Nature Index for its quality and impact. Dr. Shoeib received several awards including the Provost Excellence in Research and Creative Endeavors Award from AUC. His broader research interests lie in the areas of analytical chemistry, biophysical chemistry, and molecular structure with the goal of understanding the structure, reactivity, and function of metal-containing bio-molecules, the complexes formed by these interactions, and their uses in medicinal and pharmaceutical chemistry. Dr. Shoeib is an active member of the AUC Department of Chemistry having served as Senate representative, Acting Graduate Program Director, Graduate Program Director, and as Department Chair.

# Acknowledgments

We are greatly indebted to the many people who shared their time and insight with us. In particular, we would like to thank profoundly three persons for their very close assistance and guidance. Prof. Roger Lewis (Physicist and Associate Dean (Research) Faculty of Engineering and Information Sciences, Wollongong University, Australia), who has critically scrutinized all the chapters of our book and made many valuable suggestions as well as improvements to our original text. His generosity of spirit has touched us deeply. Prof. Maurizio Seracini (renowned diagnostician of Italian art, and founder of the Center for Interdisciplinary Science for Art, Architecture, and Archaeology at the University of California, San Diego) who has meticulously gone through several of our chapters and generously given us the benefit of his invaluable expertise in Technical Art History. Finally, Nazli (Jehane's daughter), who patiently went through the whole manuscript contributing many emendations and bringing focus and clarity to the text.

We are especially thankful to the editorial team of World Scientific Publishing Europe, to Laurent Chaminade for his support, and to Michael Beale and Aanand Jayaraman for their excellent work.

We would also like to express our deepest gratitude to a long list of experts and scholars who have read sections (and often entire chapters), in our book and generously gave us the benefit of their expertise: Prof. René De La Rie (Conservator, former Head of Scientific Research 1984–2012, National Gallery of Art, Washington DC, Guest Researcher 2012–present, University of Amsterdam); Prof. Francis Gadala-Maria

(Chemical Engineer, University of South Carolina); Dr. Richard Henderson (Medical Research Council Laboratory of Molecular Biology (LMB), Cambridge, Chemistry Nobel Laureate 2017); Prof. Dudley Herschbach (Harvard University, Chemistry Nobel Laureate 1986); Vivien Perutz (Art Historian and Lecturer, University of Cambridge); Prof. Sir John Meurig Thomas (Materials Scientist and Chemist, University of Cambridge); Dr. Anna Tummers (University Lecturer Early Modern Art and Theory, Leiden University Centre for the Art in Society); Dr. Nigel Unwin (LMB, Cambridge).

We are especially thankful to the following people as well: Ming Aguilar (Collection Information Specialist at The Huntington Library Art Museum, LA); Aleksander Balos (Artroster Mt Shasta, California); Dr. Danilo Bersani (Physicist, University of Parma); Dr. Spike Bucklow (Conservation Scientist, Cambridge Hamilton Kerr Institute); Dr. Antonino Cosentino (Physicist, Director of Cultural Science Open Source CHOS); Dr. Giuseppino Fortunato (Chemist, Swiss Federal Laboratories for Material Science and Technology); and The XOS company (New York), for their generosity in allowing us to use *pro bono* their images in our book.

We are extremely grateful to Gaby Bocchetti (University Chemical Laboratories, Cambridge) for her selfless and highly professional work in producing most of the pictures in this textbook. We also owe a special debt to Nathan Pitt (Gaby's mentor), for his valuable advice and assistance in creating some of the images. We also thank Fadia Badrawi for cleverly producing some of the figures. We also wish to thank Gehan Ghali for her help with the references.

We are indebted to Bianca Carpeneti (former Gates Cambridge Scholar) for allowing us to use part of her case study as an inspiration for our own work. Grateful thanks also goes to Milko Den Leeuw (Painting Restorer and Researcher ARRS, The Hague) for his laudable efforts as Congress Organiser, *Authentication in Art Foundation*, and for all his support.

We are very appreciative to the many people who have helped in the production of this book; the responsibility is entirely ours if some omissions or mistakes may still be present.

Closer to home, Jehane would like to express her most profound love and gratitude to her late husband John Meurig Thomas, who was her greatest support and source of inspiration. She also thanks her sister Aziza and daughters Nazli and Heddy for all their invaluable encouragement. Tamer is grateful to his wife Rim for her endless patience, support, and encouragement. He also thanks his greatest sources of motivation, his parents Mahiba and Abdel Moneim, and his sons Karim and Selim.

# Contents

# Acronyms

| | | |
|---|---|---|
| AMS | — | Accelerator mass spectrometry |
| CCD | — | Charge coupled device |
| CSI | — | Crime scene investigation (*refers to a famous TV series*) |
| EDX/EDXRF | — | Energy dispersive X-ray fluorescence |
| FTIR | — | Fourier transform infrared spectroscopy |
| GC | — | Gas chromatography |
| GC/MS | — | Gas chromatography-mass spectrometry |
| IR | — | Infrared spectroscopy |
| IRCCD | — | Infrared charge coupled device |
| IRFC | — | Infrared false color |
| IRR | — | Infrared reflectography |
| IRT (imaging) | — | Infrared transmission (imaging) |
| LA-ICP-MS | — | Laser ablation-inductively coupled plasma-mass spectrometry |
| LA-MC-ICP-MS | — | Laser ablation multiple collector inductively coupled plasma-mass spectrometry |
| MS | — | Mass spectrometry |
| $\mu$FTIR | — | Micro-Fourier transform infrared spectroscopy |
| $\mu$XRD | — | Micro X-ray diffraction |
| PIXE | — | Proton-induced or Particle-induced X-ray emission |
| PLM | — | Polarized light microscope |
| Py-GC-MS | — | Pyrolysis-gas chromatography-mass spectrometry |

| | | |
|---|---|---|
| SEM | — | Scanning electron microscopy |
| SXR | — | Synchrotron X-ray |
| SXRR | — | Synchrotron X-ray radiography |
| UV | — | Ultraviolet spectroscopy |
| UVF | — | Ultraviolet fluorescence |
| UVR | — | Ultraviolet reflected |
| XRD | — | X-ray diffraction |
| XRF | — | X-ray fluorescence |
| XRPD | — | X-ray powder diffraction |
| XRR | — | X-ray radiography |

# Case I

# A Clever Manipulator

## Learning Objectives

To introduce — *on a need-to-know basis*:

1. Different layers in a painting.
2. The structure of the atom.
3. The element.
4. The different ranges of electromagnetic radiation.
5. The meaning of natural craquelure.
6. The optical microscope.
7. The stereomicroscope.
8. Fluorescence — Ultraviolet fluorescence (UVF) and X-ray fluorescence (XRF and EDXRF) and their role in the authentication process.
9. The principle of infrared reflectography (IRR), and the kind of information it can provide with regard to the process of authentication.

The French art world was rocked by the news that for decades it had been duped by Lise de Nablé, an intelligent, charismatic woman in her 60s. Lise was sought for her valued expertise as an art connoisseur and awarded The Order of Arts and Letters by the Ministry of Culture. The shrewd swindler had mercilessly sold forgeries of renowned paintings to unsuspecting victims, relying on her strong reputation and aristocratic background to protect her from public scrutiny.

The scheme had been carried out with the help of a gifted Jamaican accomplice, the artist Abigail Akeem, whom Lise had manipulated and ended up subjugating. She had recruited Abigail from the more impoverished Parisian 18th district and would proudly claim, "I taught her opera, classical music, how to dress elegantly, and how to live the good life." Abigail remained profoundly grateful and loyal to her alleged protectress.

Lise, who quickly became aware of Abigail's uncanny ability to copy the styles of renowned painters, made her create new artworks and put them up for sale together with some of her authentic pieces. For almost twenty years, forgeries painted by Abigail, and attributed to a plethora of famous artists, circulated in the French art market.

Lise's reputation as an art connoisseur who belonged to the Parisian high society lent credibility to her claim that she had inherited all her paintings from her grandfather the late Viscount Gerard de Nablé. The ploy worked surprisingly well. The Viscount had indeed bequeathed her an impressive collection of artworks. Countless pieces attributed to Matisse, Modigliani, Cézanne, Manet, and those of Old Masters adorned the walls of her elegant Parisian home in the 6th Arrondissement, Saint-Germain-des-Prés — and there was no reason to doubt the authenticity of what she was selling.

Lise made Abigail copy genuine paintings of both Old Masters and impressionists she possessed. She would go on to hide the authentic paintings in a secure place for possible future speculation. Every time the young woman set out to forge a painting of Lise's choosing, the mastermind would scrupulously determine the palette of pigments corresponding to the lifespan of the artist in question. She would instruct Abigail not only to use just those pigments but also to avoid anachronistic ones. In this manner, the two avoided common pitfalls.

Collectors paid large sums of money for many of Lise's made-to-order paintings. One such avid collector, Pierre Moulin, son of the successful and wealthy businessman Charles Moulin, bought several paintings for which he paid a hefty price. These included two Dalís, a Courbet, and a Monet, which he proudly displayed in his home on the exclusive Rue Faubourg Saint-Honoré.

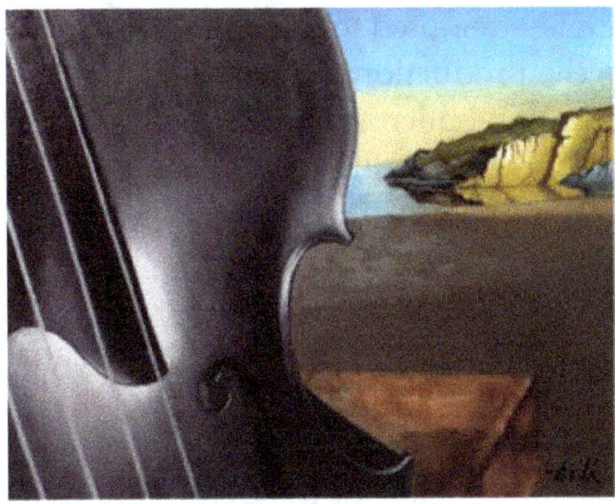

**Fig. 1.1** *View from the Sea* attributed to Salvador Dalí.

A few years after his expensive art spree, Moulin fell on hard times after engaging in a doomed business transaction. He concluded that the only sure exit from his financial crisis would come from selling his Dalí painting *View from the Sea* (Fig. 1.1). He had initially been attracted to Dalí's surrealistic style and his tendency to place recognizable images in an unfamiliar context but had inexplicably grown less attached to the work and thus, thankfully, this was one painting he did not feel too sad to part with. Moulin contacted the reputable Duras & Associés Gallery, put up *View from the Sea* for sale, and ardently hoped for a few million euros from the sale.

Aware of the growing problem of forgeries flooding the art market, the gallery owner carefully exercised due diligence and requested its expert connoisseur Jean Ricard and its technical art historian, Jean-Pierre Valois, to examine the painting.

Ricard, a specialist in modern, surrealistic paintings, set out to analyze the artwork.

The overall style seemed to be in keeping with Dalí's surrealistic approach, characterized by his unexpected placement of commonplace objects. Here the very large violin juxtaposed with a landscape and the painting was executed with delicate brushwork and technical precision, aptly reflecting Dalí's dream world.

Wanting to ensure that he was looking at an original and not a copy, using a powerful magnifying glass Ricard looked more in-depth at the craquelure and attempted to identify features of both spontaneity and inhibition in the production of the work.

He then used a stereomicroscope (Endnotes page 100) to examine the pattern of fine cracks resulting from the aging paint layers and their shrinkage over time. Natural cracks were clearly discernible; they exhibited a maze of tortuous lines. This puzzled Ricard as in an authentic painting the crevices are supposed to be in line with one another. He was nonetheless aware of the suggestion made by some researchers that the stretching and slackening of the canvas, the different environmental conditions, and the relative concentrations of pigments and binder could result in the deformation of the canvas and influence the extent of craquelure (Endnotes page 99).

The painting had a characteristic Dalí signature on the lower right corner. Ricard consulted Dalí's catalogue raisonné, which included a complete list of the many different forms of his signature, and he identified one, which was quite similar to the one in the painting. The position on the lower right corner was also in keeping with some of Dalí's paintings: *The Accommodation of Desire* (1929), *Burning Giraffes and Telephones* (1937), and *Rhapsodie Moderne* (1957). This, however, was not a regular practice by Dalí as in some of his other works — *Catalan Bread* (1932) and *The Man with the Head of Blue Hortensias* (1936) — the signature occupied the lower left position. In yet another set of paintings, the signature was not discernible at all.

Rumor also had it that Dalí sometimes secretly allowed a pupil to produce works in his name, which he later signed.

Ricard was noncommittal in his verdict on authenticity and further investigated the work with his colleague Jean-Pierre Valois, a Technical Art Historian.

Valois stepped in using a spectrum of different techniques. He proceeded to inspect the painting by using a longwave UV light source (Endnotes pages 98 and 101). Such an examination might reveal a natural resin varnish which should fluoresce and appear greenish-yellow, or maybe a linseed oil varnish fluorescing with a bluish tint. A mixture of natural resin and linseed oil would fluoresce at a longer wavelength and would appear more yellow than in the case of natural resin. Dalí was known to use either natural resin or a mixture of linseed and natural resin.

He also looked for areas that had undergone recent restorations; these would appear darker under UV light, as compared to the rest of the painting materials (Endnotes pages 101–103).

The painting emitted a blue fluorescence in particular from the violin (suggestive of linseed oil varnish), and a yellowish fluorescence in the background of the painting. A somewhat darker patch could be observed in that yellow region which fluoresced much less brightly (Fig. 1.2). He speculated that this might be due to some retouch (Endnotes page 103) or possibly resulting from superficial dirt and grime.

Valois hoped that some more definitive results could be obtained by looking at the underdrawing by infrared reflectography (IRR) (Endnotes page 105).

It would undoubtedly be helpful if one could observe some pentimenti (i.e., alteration in a painting identified through the reappearance of earlier images or details that have been modified and painted over by the artist), which would make it *less likely* for the painting to be a forgery (Endnotes page 105).

Using his recently acquired state-of-the-art portable infrared reflectography camera, with its InGaAs sensor, Valois obtained a high-resolution reflectogram (Fig. 1.3). The underdrawing was characteristic of Dalí's technical precision and clarity and suggested that a carbon-based sketching material such as graphite or charcoal may

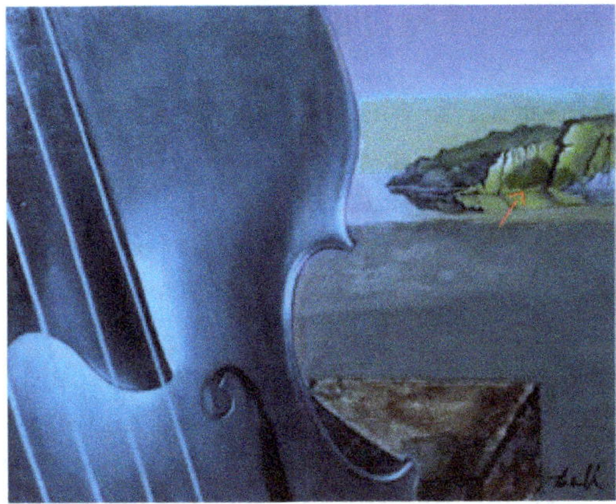

**Fig. 1.2** *View from the Sea* under UV light.

*Note*: Arrow indicates observed fluorescence (darker area).

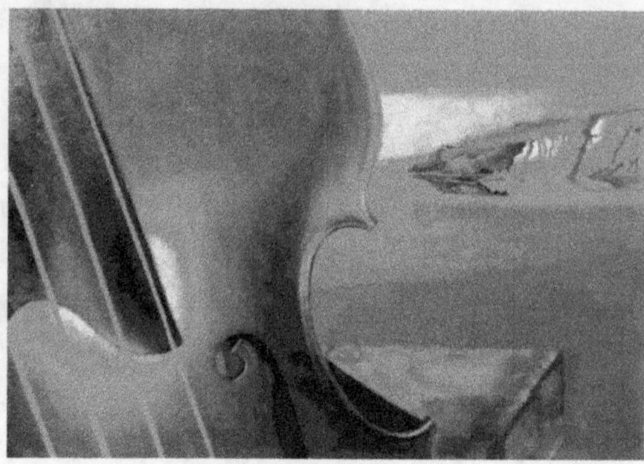

**Fig. 1.3**   Infrared reflectogram of *View from the Sea.*

have been used. These absorb infrared light very well and are particularly suited for detection by infrared reflectography.

Alas, no pentimenti could be detected!

Valois then resorted to the nondestructive technique of analysis, X-ray fluorescence using his portable XRF instrument (Endnotes pages 103 and 104).

Such a technique would allow him to determine, *in situ*, the entire elemental composition of the painting and possibly reveal some anachronistic pigments suggesting inauthenticity. Valois had consulted Dalí's book *50 Secrets of Magic Craftsmanship* published in 1948, where the exact nature of the entirety of the artist's palette was revealed.

When the experiment was carried out, most of the identified elements appeared to belong to Dalí's palette. Valois was however somewhat puzzled by the detection of titanium. He knew that titanium dioxide had indeed been discovered as a white pigment during Dalí's lifetime, but hadn't the artist always used lead carbonate or zinc oxide instead?

Valois speculated that the detected titanium could have been the result of a retouch (Endnotes page 103). Had he not observed under UV light a darker area in the yellow region of the painting? Testing his hypothesis, he carefully determined the XRF spectrum of the dark area in the yellow region (Fig. 1.4) as well as that of another yellow area that had not darkened under UV light (Fig. 1.5).

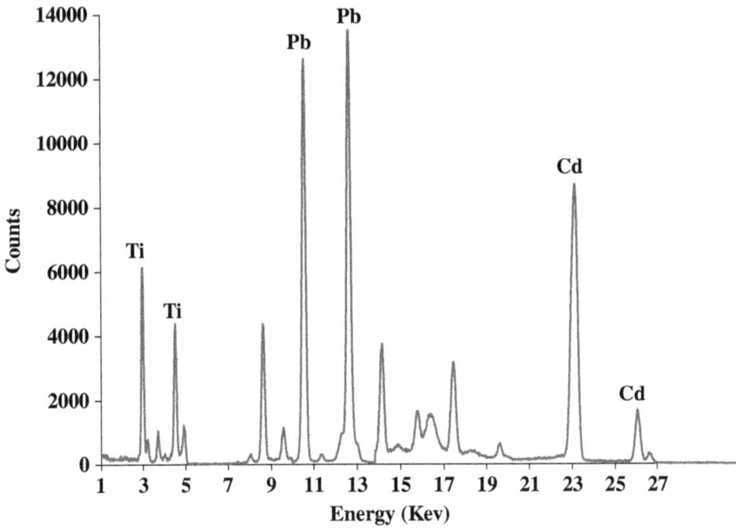

Fig. 1.4   XRF obtained from the darkened under UV light of the yellow area.

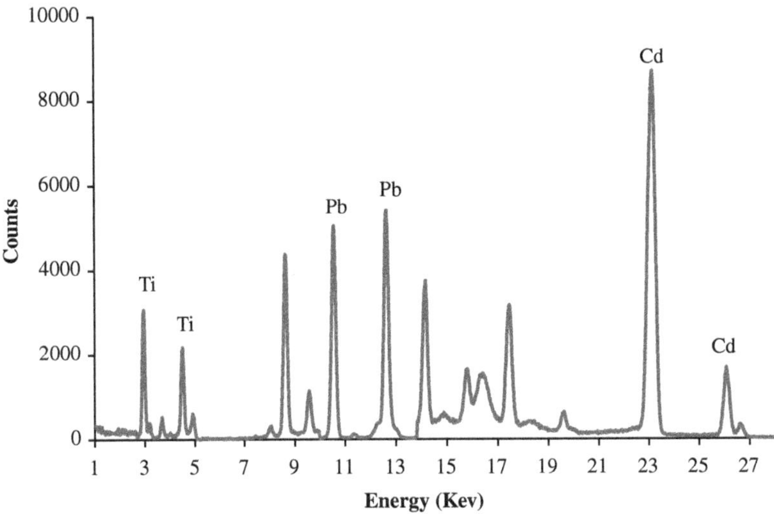

Fig. 1.5   XRF obtained for the yellow area with no restoration.

XRF revealed cadmium and lead in both yellow regions, suggesting the use of cadmium yellow together with white lead carbonate in keeping with Dalí's palette. Furthermore, the peaks characteristic of titanium appeared in the analysis of both the darkened area and the area with no restoration.

Valois checked Dalí's palette, called Ricard, and as both specialists discussed their findings, a conclusion was reached on the work.

## Questions and Classroom Activity[1]

**Revision questions:**
1. What are the indications that the painting purported to have been created by Dalí may be forged?
2. What are the indications that it is authentic?
3. What is meant by an electromagnetic spectrum?
4. What is fluorescence and UV fluorescence? Does the observed color of the fluorescence in *View from the Sea* point to a case of forgery? What is the UV fluorescence color of a natural resin? Explain.
5. Describe the technique of infrared reflectography (IRR) and indicate instances where it can detect a forgery and instances where it can point towards authenticity.
6. Which of the IRRs of the painting below suggests authenticity Fig. 1.6 (b) or 1.6 (c)?
7. Describe the technique of X-ray fluorescence. (a) What are its limitations? (b) Dalí never used $TiO_2$ as a white pigment. What needs to be done if, in a cross-section analysis, the anachronistic Ti element is detected only in the darkened area?

**Exploratory questions:**
1. Explain the difference between infrared, visible, and ultraviolet radiation.
2. Comment on the following two pictures (Figs. 1.7 (a) and 1.7 (b)). Check on Picasso's styles during different periods.
3. Search on the internet the case of the *Prado Mona Lisa* and write a small paragraph commenting on the observed pentimenti.

---

[1]Endnotes have to be read first.

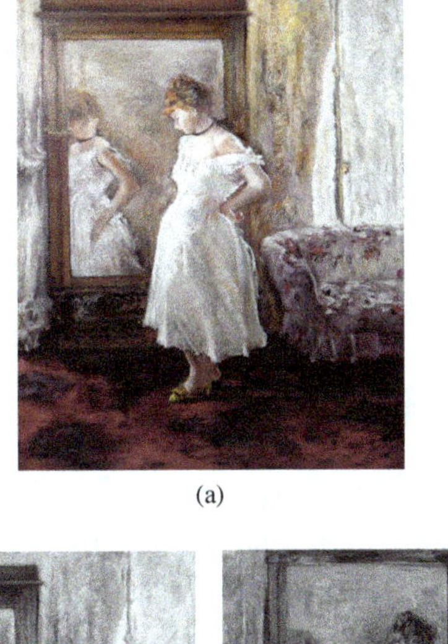

(a)

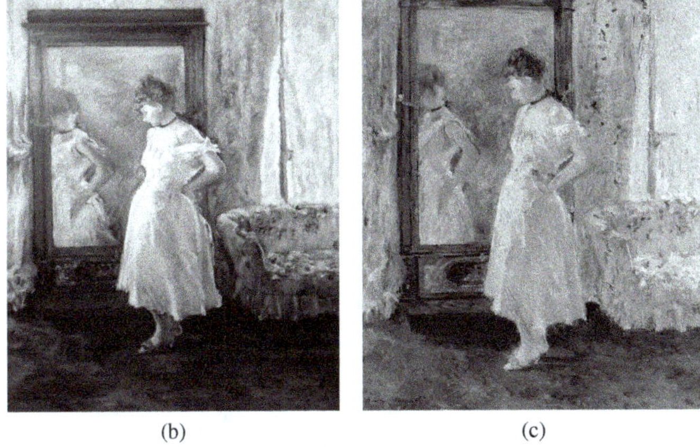

(b)                                    (c)

**Fig. 1.6** (a) Berthe Morisot, *The Psyche Mirror* (1876). (b) and (c) Two possible infrared reflectographs.

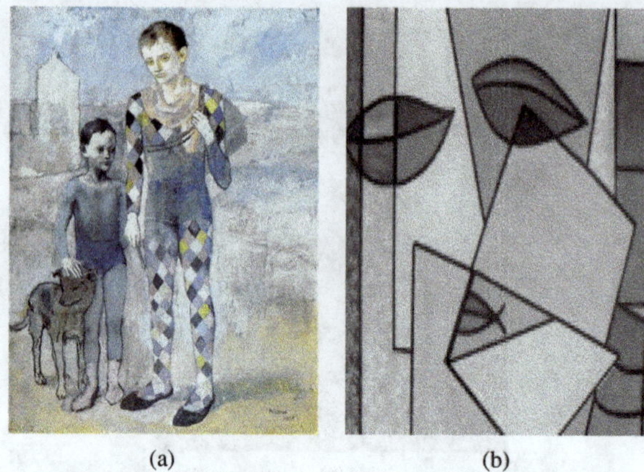
(a)          (b)

**Fig. 1.7**   (a) *Two Acrobats with a Dog,* painting attributed to Pablo Picasso's pink period (1904–1905). (b) Image obtained by infrared reflectography.

**Classroom activity:**

Search on the internet the case of the National Gallery painting *The Virgin and Child with an Angel* attributed to Francisco Francia, which was found to be a forgery. Identify the techniques described in this case and describe how they were used to prove its inauthenticity.

# Case II

# A Visit to Argenteuil

## Learning Objectives

To introduce — *on a need-to-know basis*:

1. The method of cross-section analysis
    i. Preparation of the sample.
    ii. Differentiating between wet on wet and wet on dry painting.
    iii. The staining technique for the identification of organic media.
2. Scanning electron microscopy (SEM) and how it is used in conjunction with energy dispersive X-ray fluorescence (EDXRF) to identify pigments in a painting.

Elena Laurent was a student traveling in Europe in the fall of 2007. She had graduated the previous spring from a small school in Northern California where, among other things, she had been a creative artist. Elena painted and sewed extensively and was especially fond of using old materials in her work, which required foraging through antique shops and second-hand clothing stores. In the process, she developed an eye for beautiful works.

During her time abroad, she spent two months backpacking through the French countryside, painting landscapes and soaking up the culture along with the wine. As a devotee of the French Impressionist movement, she was especially enthusiastic about the chance to visit some of the areas in which the masters had painted *en plein air*. Among her pilgrimage sites was Argenteuil — that small French town located

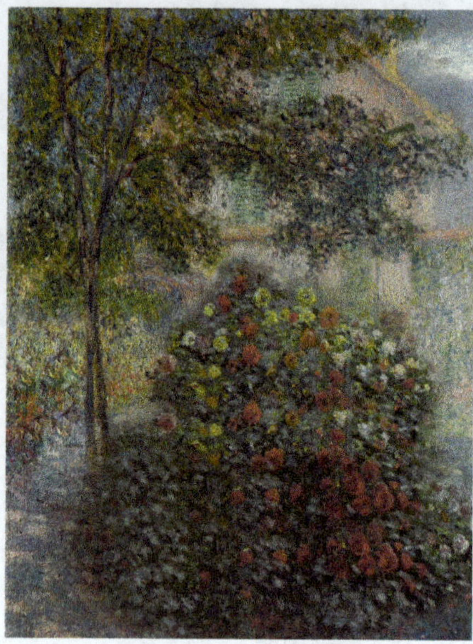

**Fig. 2.1**   Is it a Monet?

in the northwestern suburb of Paris, which in the 1870s provided an essential source of inspiration for impressionist artists. Had they not immortalized its gardens, rivers, and streets with their revolutionary paintings?

While wandering through a dusty second-hand store outside the town, Elena came across a canvas tucked behind a bookshelf that caught her eye (Fig. 2.1). The shop was run by an older man who quietly read his newspaper and turned its pages with his frail fingers. He appeared to be oblivious to her presence, so it was with some shyness that she interrupted his reading and asked if she could purchase the painting. He looked at her, and like one who was done with this world, readily sold it for an insignificant price.

Elena left the shop in a state of agitation. As a dedicated lover of the arts, she thought she might have stumbled upon a Monet. Familiar with much of his work, she noted the canvas's similarity to his painting *Garden in Argenteuil* produced in 1873.

Elena's acquisition had been predominantly executed in greens, with a loosely painted blue sky and scumble of white clouds, the total achieving the effect of daylight. Although it revealed compositional elements that were similar to *Garden in Argenteuil*, the lighting and palette of the latter were suggestive of late afternoon. This did not surprise her; in fact, it reinforced her hunch that the piece was authentic since Monet was known to paint scenes under different lighting conditions.

She noted the short thick strokes of paint, the complementary colors used for their vibrant contrasts, and paid attention to the impasto application (thickly applied paint layers). She also noticed the absence of sharp edges and felt the artist's endeavor to capture a fleeting moment in the ever-changing face of nature.

Having heard about the widespread occurrence of forgeries in the art world, however, Elena decided to subject her piece to scientific examination by a reputable firm in Paris. Elena knew that if the tests were to reveal she had discovered a missing Monet, the amount of money generated from its sale would not only put her through school but would also allow her to set up an art and antique gallery.

While tests were being conducted on the piece, Elena spent her time in Paris reading up on the scientific techniques used to probe into the nature and authenticity of a piece. As she discovered the information that testing could yield, she recognized the importance of a historical and artistic framework in which to situate this scientific information. She also quickly realized she would need to take into account the techniques Monet used and the resources available to him. She spent her mornings in art galleries familiarizing herself with Monet's work, and her afternoons in cafés consulting books and articles on the artist and on the types of painting materials he had access to.

She learned how Monet always painted on canvas, which was of a light color, such as white or very bright yellow, how he mixed complementary greens in his depiction of landscapes, and how he used thin broken layers of paint that allowed the lower layers of color to radiate through. She also learned that Monet used commercially produced oil paint sold in tubes and that he did not mix his colors on the palette but applied them straight from the tube on the canvas.

All these new facts fitted extremely well with her newly discovered little treasure, and, to her great delight, she found out that Monet, very much in keeping with her painting, thickly applied the paint layers with variously sized brushes.

When she sat down with M. Bray, the firm's director, Elena was excited to discuss the test results and develop an informed decision of her own.

"Well, Miss Laurent, we have some interesting finds to discuss today! Let me begin with the first look we took at your piece. We started by using a stereomicroscope to examine the surface of the painting for craquelure and other indications visible under 6X-50X magnification. As a piece ages, the paints shrink, causing a matrix of cracks that run from the surface through the layers of paint to the canvas. The craquelure in this piece appears to be natural and seems to go deeply through the paint layers."

"Next, we ran infrared reflectography tests —"

At this point, Elena broke in, "Wait, wouldn't that test be impractical, given the heavy brushstroke and thick palette-knife application we observe in this piece, and which is, in fact, a characteristic of Monet?"

"Excellent, I see you've come prepared," M. Bray replied. "Yes, indeed, the test did not yield as much as we would have hoped for. The thickness of the paint prevented us from seeing any underdrawings or sketching. However, the fact that we confirmed the thickness of the paint is important."[1]

"What about further surface examinations?" Elena asked. "I understand that you can examine the painting using UV light under which older material fluoresces more while newer material fluoresces less and synthetic materials not at all."

"Of course, we performed just such a test using longwave UV light and found that the level of fluorescence was fairly appropriate for such a painting. As you said, the amount that a painting fluoresces increases as the painting ages. Our numbers are close to, but not perfect for, a painting purported to be 140 years old. There are slight

---

[1]Notice: In this particular case, M. Bray should have used IR reflectography in *transmitted* light. This technique, which is described in a later case, can yield better results.

inconsistencies though: some areas fluoresce more than others. Additionally, we found that an area in the upper left-hand corner fluoresced very little."

"Oh, dear," began Elena.

"No need to worry, yet," M. Bray assured her. "There are rational explanations for these inconsistencies: first, pollutants could have contaminated the piece, causing some areas to fluoresce less or not at all, also a later retouch could explain such variability, especially if synthetic resins were used. A retouch might have been necessary if the piece sustained damage."

Elena nodded, "Yes, it was in a less than desirable storage setting. Though, for a retouch to have taken place, someone must have deemed it worth maintaining. I wonder when the piece's identity was 'lost' from the records."

"Let us address the concern of fluorescence — or lack thereof — next because we can examine the pigments, which can tell us more about why they did or did not fluoresce. It could be that we have a legitimate explanation. And as to the provenance of the piece, perhaps Monet left it in Argenteuil to some art-lover who maintained it while alive, and afterward, the piece lost its record."

"Okay," began Elena, "but I have strong reservations about any destructive processes, so I hope this is possible without any damage being done to the piece."

"Certainly, Miss Laurent; though it is our job to test the authenticity of the piece, we are also concerned with respecting its integrity. It was, however, necessary for us to use the stereomicroscope once again to look at a cross-section of the artwork under visible and ultraviolet light and to carefully study the internal layers of the painting (Endnotes page 107). I am fully aware that you are concerned about the integrity of the work, but rest assured that our sampling was performed extremely carefully and that we chose only very restricted areas of the painting that are needed for the purpose of our investigation. We carefully removed a minute core sample, mounted it in a block of clear resin, cut it, and polished it with a fine micromesh until we obtained a perfectly flat and smooth surface with the edges of the sample clearly displayed" (Fig. 2.1E, Endnotes page 108).

Elena forgave M. Bray for not having sought her permission to remove minute samples, and turned her full attention to M. Bray's explanation; she fully realized how important it was for her to get a proper evaluation of her painting.

M. Bray continued, "As you probably are aware, any artwork can be considered as a layered structure" (Fig. 2.2) (Endnotes page 109).

"In this case, the visual examination of the cross-section under normal light indicated a layering technique of paint application very much in keeping with Monet's approach. From the bottom layer, six different material layers were discerned: the canvas, a primer, a second primer, a paint layer, a glaze layer, and a varnish layer."

"Also, in the painting of the foliage, it appears that subsequent layers of paint were applied before those underneath had dried. This is a method referred to as wet on wet" (Fig. 2.2E (a), Endnotes page 109).

Excited by the results obtained so far, Elena asked:

"Is there a way of identifying the components of each layer?"

"Yes, the observation of a cross-section is also particularly helpful (a) for the identification of organic materials and (b) as a support for any further analytical technique. Let me elaborate a bit! We used a staining technique (Endnotes page 109) to identify the binding media and opted to use the non-destructive technique of scanning electron microscopy in conjunction with energy dispersive X-ray fluorescence (SEM/EDX) (Endnotes page 110) to determine the inorganic pigments in the ground and paint layers.

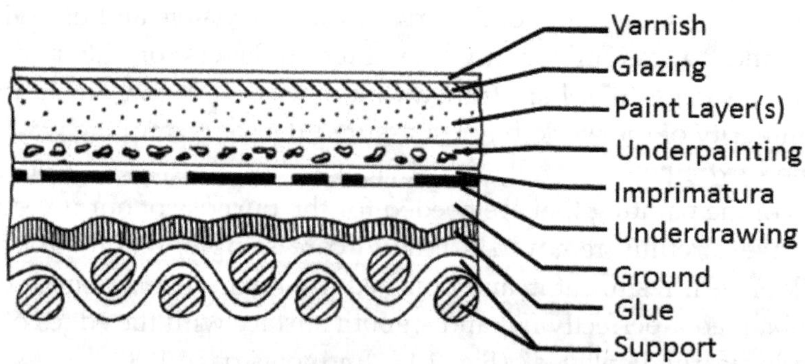


**Fig. 2.2**  Layered structure of a painting.

The staining technique detected 'glue' on the canvas as well as on the priming layer. The glue was most probably applied by the commercial colormen. By the 1840s, it made sense in France, from an economic standpoint, for artists to buy commercially prepared canvases on which to paint. The same tests carried out on the second priming as well as on the paint layers tested positive for oil, which also agrees with the fact that Monet used oils (linseed or poppy) as binding agents."

Elena was trying to absorb all this new information while M. Bray continued reporting the findings of his study.

"We also found that the older part of the painting contained pigments appropriate to the late 19th century, including French ultramarine, veridian green, cadmium yellow, cobalt blue, vermilion, and lead white for the second priming layer. The pigments became available in the 19th century before Monet was painting. Therefore, they certainly would have been accessible to him and are in keeping with Monet's own palette. When we examined the sample from the weakly fluorescing section however, we found manganese blue. This pigment wasn't available in 1907, which makes it an anachronism in a possible Monet."

At this point, Elena was feeling overwhelmed by all the information. Stylistically and historically, the piece seemed to fit; observation of the craquelure under surface magnification also gave encouraging results. The infrared reflectography testing had been inconclusive, and the UV fluorescence had been somewhat problematic but not without explanation: a retouch and pollutants from the environment were not improbable culprits. The SEM/EDX test had been helpful, because — despite the pigment anachronism — the analysis had indicated that this anomaly was confined to the area with incorrect fluorescence in keeping with the theory that there might have been a later repair of the piece. On the whole, it seemed to her that the test results supported a positive identification of the piece.

So far, so good until M. Bray added:

"In all of this, Miss Laurent, something is puzzling me! You see, the size of canvasses available at the time of Monet measured 670 x 540 mm, and it is known that he regularly used this size as it was easily transportable for painting outdoors. The canvas you found measures 800 x 600 mm, and I cannot find an explanation for that!"

Unperturbed, Elena retorted, "Yes, of course, Mr. Bray, that is a matter of concern, but remember that the recent Van Gogh *Still Life with Meadow Flowers and Roses* was authenticated at the Kröller-Müller Museum in spite of the unusual size of the canvas (100 x 80 cm). This size was not common practice for a Van Gogh painting. So, you see exceptions can and do happen..."

In giving his final verdict to Elena, the expert was non-committal:

"All these results are very encouraging, Miss Laurent, but to provide a final decision on authentication, I need to find *one definitive test* which would allow me to declare it as authentic. In your painting, many observations point towards authenticity, but we cannot be sure as there is the troubling presence of the detected manganese blue... Could the significant decrease in fluorescence in that area be due to irreversible damage caused by some pollutants or could it be due to a restoration or a retouch? And had it been the case, could all our observations lead to the verdict of *'authentic'*?

"Thank you," replied Elena feeling slightly disappointed, "It's been a pleasure working with you."

"Likewise, Miss Laurent. I have no doubt that should you wish to pursue a career in the field of art analysis, you would go far!"

Elena left still feeling hopeful that her piece may be a Monet and in quest of a lab capable of performing more sophisticated tests.


## Questions, Classroom Activity, and Homework

**Revision questions:**
1. What are the indications that the painting thought to have been painted by Monet is a forgery?
2. What are the indications that it is authentic?
3. Provide at least three characteristics of Monet's style of painting.
4. Name one technical feature of Monet's style that eliminated an important technique of analysis. Identify the technique and explain why it was done away with and deemed to be non-useful.

5. Why is the layered structure in this painting assumed to be by Monet?
6. Explain how a cross-section is prepared for the analysis of a painting.
7. How can you differentiate between wet on wet paint and wet on dry paint?
8. Describe the technique of scanning electron microscopy and show how the cross-section analysis can be useful for the SEM/EDX technique.
9. What needs to be done to better assess the significance of the detection of the manganese element by EDX, i.e., what test may rule it as a forgery?
10. What is the sequence of events in a typical SEM/EDX analysis?

**Exploratory questions:**
1. What is polyester resin? What is it used for in pertaining to paintings?
2. What are the possible reasons for a decrease in fluorescence under ultraviolet light?
3. What is the difference between a glaze layer and a varnish layer?
4. Elaborate more on the staining technique in cross-section analysis.
5. In the painting subject of this case, the following different material layers were discerned: a primer, a second primer, a glaze layer, and a varnish layer. Please discuss the utility of each of these layers.

**Classroom activity:**
Students are to search the Internet with a colleague for a case or two where any of the techniques described in this chapter have been used to identify a forged painting or to authenticate it.

**Homework:**
Prepare a short report to describe the above classroom activity, together with a PowerPoint presentation.

# Case III

# One More Bedroom?

## Learning Objectives

To introduce — *on a need-to-know basis*:

1. The techniques of X-ray and synchrotron X-ray radiography (SXRR).
2. The principle of Raman spectroscopy (RS).

It was a lovely warm evening in May 2016, and Tim Johnson, a recent graduate in Art History from Young Harris College — a stone's throw away from his native town Madison, Georgia — was bubbling with excitement. A week to the day, Tim had won a local radio station contest and was now flying to Chicago for the first time. He had also won tickets to a special exhibit by the Art Institute of Chicago. What a lucky break, Tim thought to himself, "I shall be combining both my love of travel and my passion for the arts!"

He was very eager, as he knew the exhibition would be unique. Indeed, for the first time in North America, all three known versions of *The Bedroom* by Vincent Van Gogh would be displayed side by side. Tim was familiar with the master Dutch Post-Impressionist painter from his studies in college. He knew that Van Gogh was a prolific painter who favored vibrant colors and used bold, dramatic brushstrokes to express emotions. He also knew that Van Gogh, who committed suicide in 1890, was not successful during his lifetime and was plagued with episodes of depression and mental illness. It was not until well after his death that the world started to recognize his genius. His paintings are now displayed in the most famed galleries across the

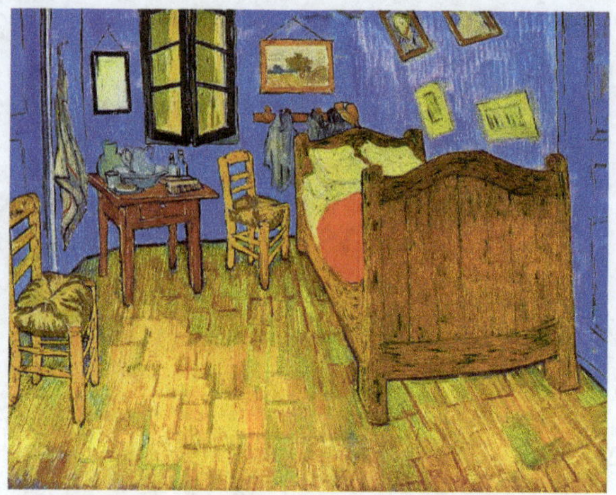

**Fig. 3.1**   Fourth version of *The Bedroom.*

globe; his legacy is even honored by a museum in his namesake in Amsterdam. The very few paintings by Van Gogh that ever came up for public auction were among the most expensive ever sold.

Once at the Art Institute, Tim stood mesmerized in front of the paintings, all three were nearly identical with minimal compositional differences. They were depictions of the artist's bedroom at 2 Place Lamartine — a lodging which would come to be known as the Yellow House — in Arles, France. Tim listened intently to one of the exhibit curators as she explained how through his use of contrasting colors, Vincent expressed the warmth of his simple bedroom and let the colors do the talking.

She mentioned that the first version of the painting, which was on loan from the Van Gogh Museum, had been painted in October 1888 but slightly damaged during a flood. Nearly a year later, in September 1889, Van Gogh executed a second version in the original scale — now owned by the Art Institute of Chicago. In the summer of the same year, Van Gogh decided to redo some of his best paintings and produced the third version in a reduced scale for his family in Holland.

Almost one year later, as Tim was going through the morning paper, he came across an article about a newly discovered and controversial fourth version of *The Bedroom* (Fig. 3.1). From the article, he learned that two eminent technical art historians were contesting the authenticity of this version in court.

Tim, wanting to find out more, identified the courtroom where the two experts sparred before a US District Court Judge and made sure he was part of the audience.

The owner of the painting wished to sell it and had recruited Ms. Lisa Kemp, a renowned expert, to convince the court that the artwork is genuine. Mr. Steven Richards, another expert of good repute, represented Van Gogh's estate and argued that the painting was inferior to an authentic Van Gogh and was undoubtedly a forgery.

Concentrating on the technical investigation of the work, Ms. Kemp started by presenting the optical microscopy results of the analysis carried out on the painting surface, which indicated heavy brushstrokes and thick palette-knife application (impasto) characteristic of Van Gogh's style. She then presented data obtained using a stereomicroscope (Endnotes page 100), which showed a craquelure pattern that appeared to be naturally produced. More importantly, she argued, there was no evidence detected of artificial aging or previous intervention on the painting.

Steven Richards argued that costly experiments carried out at a synchrotron research facility in Maryland using synchrotron X-ray analysis — deemed appropriate in view of the importance of the artist (Endnotes page 113) — revealed no underdrawing. The use of synchrotron X-ray analysis as opposed to the conventional X-ray radiography (XRR) (Endnotes page 113) and infrared reflectography modes of analysis was justified given the heavy brushstroke and thick palette-knife application, so characteristic of Van Gogh's style, but which would make identifying the presence or confirming the absence of any underdrawings by IRR and XRR very difficult (Endnotes pages 105 and 113).

Mr. Richards pointed out that it was only by synchrotron X-ray analysis that he could definitely confirm that there was no underdrawing — a fact strongly suggesting that the painting was a forgery since in all the other three Van Gogh paintings entitled *The Bedroom* underdrawings could be observed.

However, Ms. Kemp suggested to the court that in producing this fourth version of *The Bedroom*, there was no need for an underdrawing since having created three other versions and several pencil sketches in his letters to his brother Theo and friend Gauguin, Van Gogh had probably become intimately familiar with the scene.

Mr. Richards then proceeded to present data obtained on a yellowish-orange area of the painting using X-ray fluorescence (Fig. 3.2), indicating the presence of cadmium which he said was evidence for cadmium yellow was a pigment not in Van Gogh's palette.

This argument was immediately challenged by Ms. Kemp who showed the court data obtained by UV-induced infrared fluorescence (Endnotes page 101) from the same area of the painting that does not support the presence of cadmium yellow which should show maximum fluorescence at 750 nm, a signal which was not observed.

Mr. Richards offered a different interpretation of the UV-induced infrared fluorescence result, attributing the absence of the expected signal for cadmium yellow to degradation. He continued saying that degradation products such as cadmium carbonates, cadmium sulfates, or oxalates may have formed, which would lead to a layer of

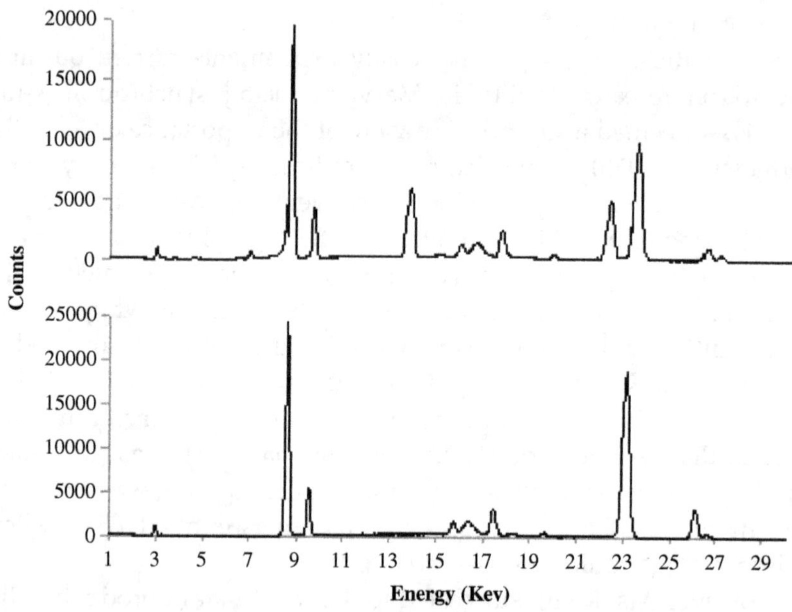

**Fig. 3.2** Top panel X-ray fluorescence (XRF) spectrum from the yellowish orange area of the painting. Bottom panel XRF spectrum of a cadmium salt.

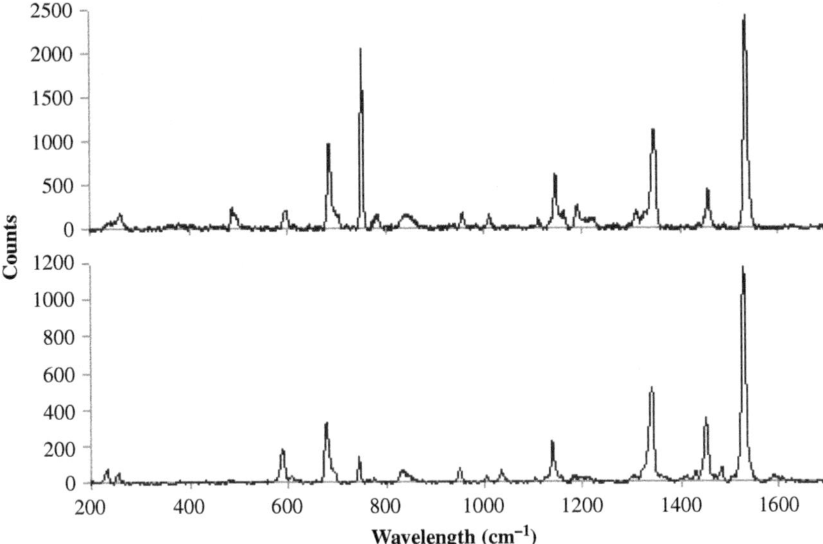

**Fig. 3.3** Top panel Raman spectrum obtained from the blue area of the painting. Bottom panel is a reference Raman spectrum of copper phthalocyanine.

crust covering the original yellow pigment, preventing the detection of the signal associated with cadmium yellow by UV-induced fluorescence.

He subsequently explained to the court that in the present case, X-ray fluorescence is more reliable than the UV-induced infrared fluorescence technique as it can identify cadmium with or without a layer of degradation products.

Mr. Richards also pointed to the fact that X-ray fluorescence showed no signal for mercury, which would be indicative of vermillion (mercury sulfide) being a pigment that was commonly used by Van Gogh in his vibrant reds.

Ms. Kemp answered that the absence of vermillion was irrelevant since Van Gogh also used red organic pigments that do not contain mercury such as cochineal lake or carmine red!

Tim felt somewhat overwhelmed by this flood of information and was relieved when the judge adjourned the session to the following day. He was keen, however, to witness the unfolding of the whole case and canceled his next day appointments to join the audience in the courtroom once more.

As the session started, he felt that both experts had a self-satisfied expression on their face, could it just be his imagination?

Decisively Ms. Kemp stated, "Mr. Richards asserts that this painting is a forgery given the detected cadmium! Well, a very recent study at the Kröller-Müller Museum, of the *Flowers in a Blue Vase* painted in 1887 by Van Gogh, has indicated that he had indeed used cadmium sulfide as a yellow colorant. So even if Mr. Richards has convincingly argued that cadmium was present in this new version of *The Bedroom*, his evidence does not support his assertion that it is a forgery!"

Unperturbed, Mr. Richards retorted, "We have just received the results of the micro-Raman spectroscopy tests (Endnotes page 116) carried out on both the red and blue pigments in the painting (Fig. 3.3). We had contracted a lab to carry out such an investigation using this *in situ* highly sensitive and non-destructive technique. This test is capable of indicating the presence of some organic pigments that could not otherwise be detected by X-ray fluorescence. The red dye, in keeping with Van Gogh's palette, was indeed identified as a cochineal lake; however, copper phthalocyanine was the main colorant used in the blue part of the painting. Such a pigment is anachronistic with Van Gogh's palette as it was only discovered in 1927 and produced commercially in 1935, more than four decades after Van Gogh's death!"

So with what appeared to be a little dramatic gesture, turning towards the US District Court Judge Mr. Richards declared: "Your Honor, Honorable Members of the Jury, I rest my case!"


## Questions

**Revision questions:**

1. What are the indications that the fourth version of *The Bedroom* may be a forgery?
2. What are the indications that it is authentic?
3. IR reflectography and X-ray radiography are techniques of immense importance for painting restorations and in the field of Technical Art History. Detail the similarities and differences between these

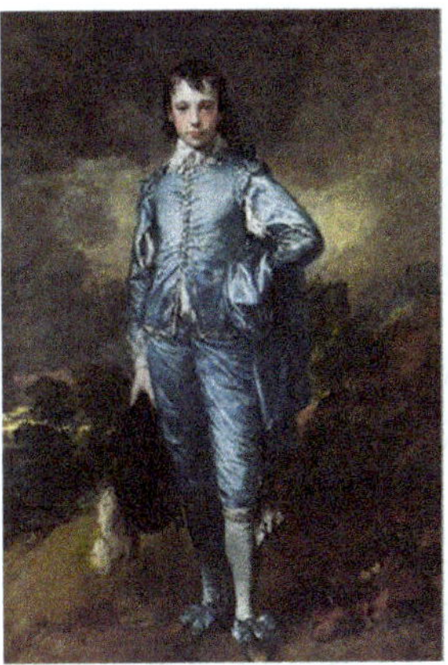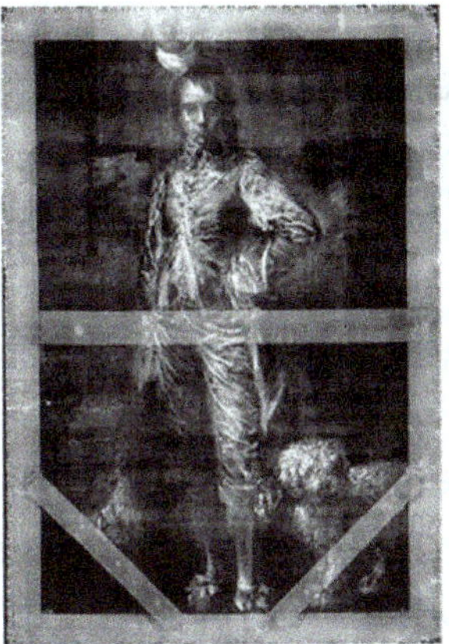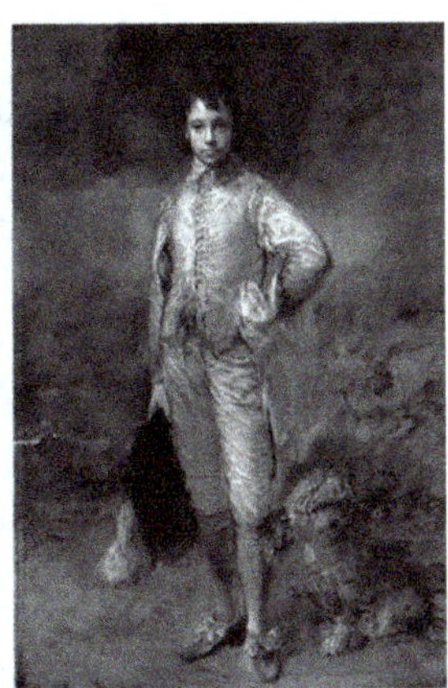

**Fig. 3.4** *The Blue Boy* (ca. 1770) by Thomas Gainsborough (1727–1788) shown in normal light photography (left), digital X-ray radiography (center, including a dog previously revealed in a 1994 X-ray), and infrared reflectography (right). Images courtesy of The Huntington Museum of Art, San Marino, California.

techniques and highlight scenarios where one should be employed over the other see (Fig. 3.4).

4. Under what circumstances could UV-induced infrared spectroscopy detect cadmium? If it had indicated the presence of cadmium, would this have suggested that the painting is a forgery?

5. What was the alternative technique to X-ray radiography and infrared reflectography used to test for the underdrawing? Describe it.

6. Relying on the X-ray fluorescence data obtained on a yellowish-orange area of the painting indicated the presence of cadmium, Mr. Richards concluded that this is evidence for cadmium yellow. Is this conclusion supported by the data? Why or why not?

7. Why was the X-ray fluorescence more reliable than the UV-induced infrared fluorescence technique in this particular case? Why is UV-induced infrared fluorescence more useful in some cases than UV–Vis-induced fluorescence?

8. Explain, why in some cases, Raman spectroscopy is more useful than X-ray fluorescence for the identification of certain pigments.

**Exploratory questions:**

1. What are anti-Stokes Raman bands and what are Stokes Raman bands?
2. When is infrared reflectography more useful than X-ray radiography?
3. How are X-rays produced?
4. Find out, by searching the internet or by consulting relevant references, the case of Van Gogh's *Still Life with Meadow Flowers and Roses* (1886) where X-ray radiography and infrared reflectography revealed a very unclear underdrawing, whereas synchrotron X-ray radiography gave an extremely clear picture, allowing the authentication of the painting. Write a summary of the case.
5. Was Mr. Richards justified in resorting to Synchrotron X-ray radiography to ensure that there was no underdrawing in *The Bedroom* purported to be by Van Gogh?
6. Compare and contrast Raman spectroscopy and X-ray fluorescence, highlighting their strengths and limitations.
7. What is the Raman scattering effect? What kind of information is contained in a Raman spectrum?
8. Find out, by searching on the internet or by consulting proper references, the case of *Nude* (1913) purported to be by Marc Chagall. Could X-ray fluorescence have been used to clarify the case?
9. What other yellow pigment did Van Gogh use apart from cadmium yellow; find out by consulting either the internet, or alternative sources, the main pigments used by Van Gogh?

# Case IV

# An Unusual Find

## Learning Objectives

To introduce — *on a need-to-know basis*:

1.  The classification of the different types of craquelure.
2.  Fast-scanning X-ray fluorescence mapping.
3.  The principle of gas chromatography.
4.  The principle of mass spectrometry (introducing: atomic number, isotopes, mass number, atomic mass, ion).
5.  The use of gas chromatography in conjunction with mass spectrometry (GC/MS).

I, Giovanni Romano, left Florence for the United States of America at the tender age of eighteen. My father, Carlo Romano, was a cobbler who lived and worked in the working-class Oltrarno district in Florence. He toiled away daily in his modest shop and, despite the meager returns of his profession, felt a deep-seated sense of pride when he examined the beautiful shoes he made.

I lived with my father, my mother Carla, my elder sister Martina, and my uncle Roberto in a small house located in the Santo Spirito suburb of Oltrarno. My mother was devoted to my father and took care of the household chores. She had heavy responsibilities, as my poor sister Martina had been afflicted with cystic fibrosis since she was ten. She had frequent lung infections with a persistent cough, often accompanied by wheezing. Uncle Roberto, who had never married, considered my sister and me his children. He was a bookbinder

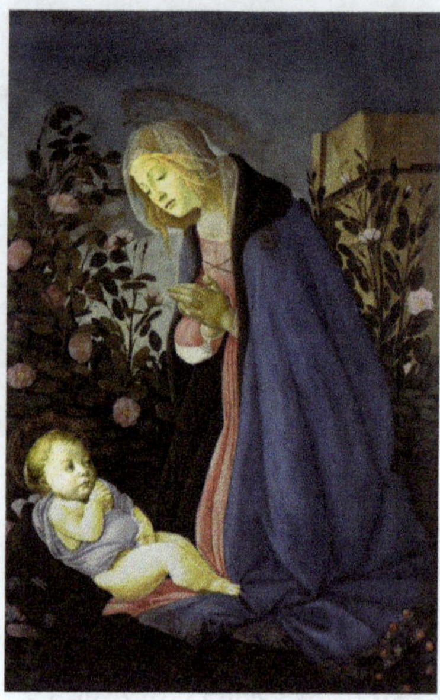

**Fig. 4.1**   *Discovered painting.*

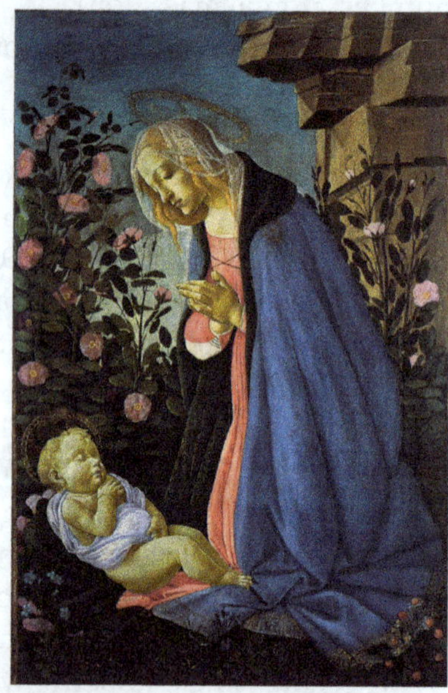

**Fig. 4.2**   *The Virgin Adoring the Sleeping Christ Child* by Botticelli.

and had a small shop in the nearby Via Luigi Michelazzi. I remember him buried in rows of bookshelves; his head bowed as he worked at his desk. I would spend all my free time in his shop, with Uncle Roberto giving me lessons in bookbinding. He would often exclaim, "Young man, you just wait and see how much you will love this absorbing and addictive craft!"

Indeed, I did; but I had my plans.

Ever since I was fourteen, I ardently desired to go to the United States to pursue the American Dream, an admirable set of values (rights, opportunities, and equality) that allowed upward social mobility for everyone, irrespective of background. I wanted a greater opportunity for prosperity and success. I could then help my family by providing enough money to treat my sister, and I would alleviate their poverty. When I reached the age of eighteen, it was with a heavy heart that my father and my family let me go. I had been a good student at school and had also excelled in the craft of book-binding. I managed to secure a cheap plane ticket to the US, paid partly from my savings, with the rest covered by my father and uncle's meager ones.

In the US, life was good to me. I started a small business, which prospered, as people were delighted to rediscover the age-old art of Italian bookbinding craftsmanship. I married a young American designer, and together our business grew and thrived. I regularly sent money back home and — whenever possible — I visited my family although unfortunately I could do so only rarely.

As the years went by, my parents were distressed to lose Martina, and then my mother died most suddenly. Life for my father was more than he could bear, and he passed on a few months later. Poor Uncle Roberto was left all alone, with little money and the pain of losing all his loved ones. He moved to an ancient building that needed extensive restoration and lived a reclusive life.

I used to write to him regularly, but he seldom answered. One day I received the dreaded telegram announcing Uncle Roberto's death. The old neighbor who had sent it also wrote that I needed to travel to Florence to dispose of his belongings and make arrangements for his funeral.

Saddened by such a sudden disappearance, I left for Florence. In my old city, I was struck by the simplicity of Uncle Roberto's dwelling. A few books were carelessly thrown over the chair next to an old bed; a dilapidated bookshelf held others he had probably bought from street vendors and rebound himself.

I proceeded to empty the house as fast as I could. I gave away most of his books to my parents' surviving neighbors, and once the bookshelves had also been removed, they revealed an odd-looking crack in the wall. I saw what looked like a hidden door, barely perceptible to the naked eye.

My heart fluttering, I gently tapped the wall all around the crack. When a door was flung open before me, I almost fainted. What was this tiny space behind it? What is that painting (Fig. 4.1) I was bewildered to find myself standing in front of? It represented a Madonna and Child very much in Botticelli's style; the robe slightly damaged on the lower right side. How could this painting have ended here? Was Uncle Roberto aware of its existence? What should I do next? If this painting turns out to have been created by a true Master, how my life would change! I was overwhelmed by my mixed emotions: my grief for Uncle Roberto but also a growing feeling of excitement about my find.

Straight after Uncle Roberto's funeral, I decided to contact the Giuliano Laboratorio Autenticazione Artistico in Rome, a laboratory with an excellent reputation that mostly dealt with the authentication of paintings.

I was told that the laboratory had a broad range of sophisticated equipment. One person who knew its work well said that the laboratory had recently acquired an X-ray fluorescence spectrometer that uses synchrotron radiation (Endnotes pages 103 and 113). It allows advanced analyses to be carried out and even allows for the identification of other artworks underneath the painting. Not being a scientist, I did not understand much of this technical language but was sure that some explanations and clarifications would come in due course.

I traveled to Rome and entrusted the painting to Mr. Bruno Barbieri, who promised to get back to me once the work had been carried out. Two weeks later, he contacted me. As I made my way to the laboratory, I remember feeling my legs almost paralyzed with anxiety; luckily, I had thought of taking along a tape-recorder.

Mr. Barbieri introduced the resident art historian, Mr. Angelo Bianchi, and connoisseur, Mr. Alberto Russo, and said, "It is an exciting and somewhat puzzling find that you made Mr. Romano. Let me share with you our findings. We were quite impressed by certain similarities as well as differences between this artwork and another 1485 painting by Botticelli entitled *The Virgin Adoring the Sleeping Christ Child* (Fig. 4.2) present in the National Galleries of Scotland. I shall let Mr. Russo describe some of his observations."

"Well," said Mr. Russo, "It is interesting that this work, in a manner akin to *The Virgin Adoring the Sleeping Christ Child*, is also carried out on canvas, which was quite an unusual feature during the time of Botticelli. Interestingly in the Scotland painting, The Christ Child is shown sleeping, which is a rare occurrence in Botticelli's artworks in contrast with your painting where he is being shown awake."

"Is there hope then that my painting is authentic?" I said.

"Not so fast," Mr. Russo laughed and then continued, "What is encouraging is that Madonna's face has all the hallmarks of Botticelli: pale, porcelain-like, with faintly pink blushes in the areas of the cheeks. However, in contrast with the child in your painting, Botticelli's infants and children are generally more intensely colored with ruddier complexions. We should not worry too much, though, as in the Scotland painting the face of the Madonna is also somewhat dark, which indicates that there may be exceptions to Botticelli's rules concerning complexion. I feel that the face of the Madonna may be overly tender and romantic compared to a genuine Botticelli, but I do not doubt that a very skilled draughtsman created the work."

Listening to Mr. Russo, I went from excitement to disappointment and back again.

Mr. Russo went on, "This painting is distinguished by the fine quality of line and shape, and the hair of the Madonna is shaded with light and slightly darker cadenced lines to reflect the appearance of her flowing locks very much in keeping with Botticelli's style."

His words gave me a growing feeling of hope. I looked at Mr. Barbieri, who took over, "Now, I would like to share the results of our scientific investigation. Under a stereomicroscope, the craquelure seems to be the result of a natural aging process. Upon close examination, we found that it was indeed a natural *Italian* craquelure (Endnotes page 119). We were, however, puzzled by the fact that the pigments, as revealed by optical microscopy, were fine-grained and not of the coarser kind as would be expected in the case of 15th century hand-ground pigments. We then checked the UV-visible fluorescence images of the painting to see if there were small areas that were retouched or covered with pollutants or grime, and we identified a small-darkened area on the upper right side of Madonna's blue robe. Newer varnish does not fluoresce under UV, and retouchings, if done in recent times, appear as dark patches on the varnished surface."

Mr. Barbieri then added a note of caution, "We must bear many factors in mind Mr. Romano; there are quite a few synthetic resins today that have a strong light blue or grey fluorescence that are used by restorers to hide their retouches when seen under UV light. Furthermore, the kind of varnish and pigment binder, as well as the nature of the fluorescent materials present in the artwork, might affect the observed fluorescence. The latter can also be greatly affected by the presence of possible multiple layers (or leftover) of varnishes spread on the surface of the painting through the centuries, as well as by old repaintings."

By this point, I was already lost, and even now, I have to play back my tape-recorder to recount my story.

Barbieri went on to say, "We decided, nevertheless, to measure the UV–Vis-induced fluorescence, resulting from absorption by the darkened part as well as by other areas in the painting. We thought that this might be helpful, through a comparison of the results with other Botticelli artworks. In the past, we had measured and kept a record of the UV–Vis-induced fluorescence emitted by a few authentic Botticellis."

Mr. Barbieri was speaking with authority and continued his explanation, "The observed fluorescence spectrum displayed a maximum around 440 nm, (as shown in Fig. 4.3 (a)) and indicated a sharp decrease in fluorescence in the case of the dark area as compared to that from the rest of Madonna's gown. The latter observation is encouraging Mr. Romano, as lazurite, the main component of lapis lazuli, generally shows a maximum of 440 nm in the case of a tempera painting (Endnotes page 120). As I shall shortly indicate, we identified lazurite when we analyzed the pigments. Furthermore, the amount of

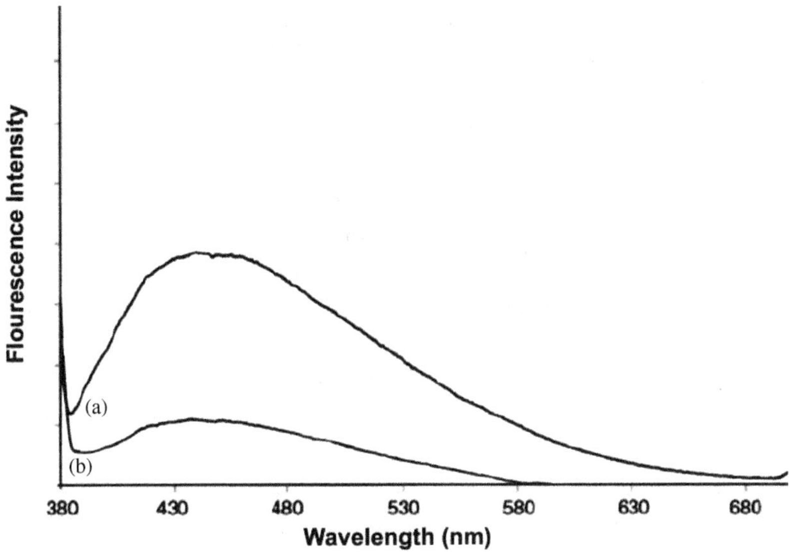


**Fig. 4.3** (a) Fluorescence from darker area. (b) Fluorescence from Madonna's blue gown.

fluorescence observed in the rest of the painting did not deviate significantly from measurements carried out on an authenticated Botticelli. We must, however, bear in mind that the fluorescence intensity of the surface of this painting could have been affected by variations of environmental conditions in the locality where the painting was kept or by cleaning with strong solvents."

My confusion only deepened as Mr. Barbieri went on, "It was also important for us to look at the underdrawing to discern any pentimenti (Endnotes page 105). Unfortunately, our attempts to use the conventional techniques of infrared reflectography as well as X-ray radiography (Endnotes page 113) failed as both methods gave a very unclear black and white underdrawing.

"We, therefore, resorted to applying a non-invasive, fast, high-definition synchrotron X-ray fluorescence (XRF) elemental mapping technique, which allows the complete identification of the pigments in the painting as well as in the underdrawing and can reveal previously unknown underpaintings." (Endnotes page 120).

All I could understand from this jargon was that he was looking for an underdrawing below the painting. "Did you get any interesting results?" I said.

"Yes, we got several important ones, Mr. Romano. The elemental test indicated one anachronistic element, cobalt, while all the rest of the detected pigments, including lazurite, were in keeping with those used in Botticelli's time. You see, in any painting, one crucial test is identifying its elemental composition to look for any pigment anachronisms or anomaly (pigments not discovered in the lifetime of the artist or never used by him). In the case of Botticelli, we cannot identify which pigments he never used as too few paintings by Botticelli were examined scientifically. Still, it is possible to detect pigments that were not discovered during his lifetime.

As we speculated that the cobalt might arise from a later retouch, we compared the pigments in the blue darkened area with those in that part of the robe that had not darkened. So, we carried out a cross-section analysis of microscopic samples taken from both the darkened area as well as from another close area in the column, intending to study the elemental composition of both the upper and lower paint layers. Synchrotron X-ray beams were shot into these samples, and we analyzed the emitted fluorescent X-rays."

"We identified cobalt (most definitely due to cobalt blue, a 19th century pigment) in the upper paint layer of the darkened region." continued Mr. Barbieri. "This element was not identified in the other blue area of the robe, which indicated that the detected cobalt was most definitely the result of a later retouch."

"But," continued Mr. Barbieri, "we also carried out a test on a sample taken from the brown foliage, and we were surprised to identify iron and manganese suggesting that umber was used as a brown pigment. Since the original color of the leaves must have been green and since Botticelli is known to have used either verdigris or malachite as green pigments, we had expected to find copper instead. With time, these copper compounds become darker due to the darkening of the oil, causing the leaves to acquire a brownish hue. I am therefore wondering if the depiction in your painting of the foliage in a brown color as opposed to green was intentional to suggest discoloration due to the passage of time."

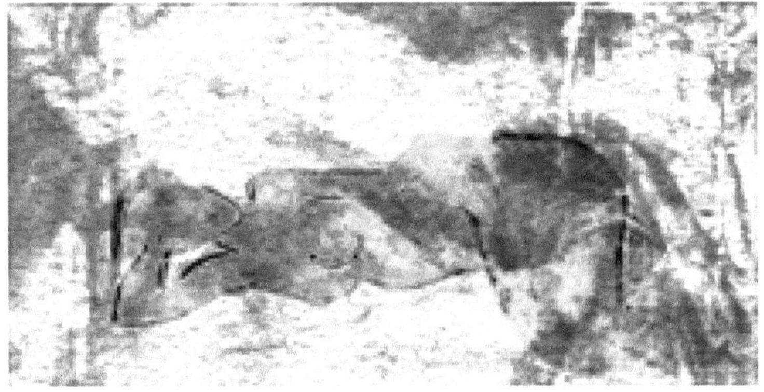

**Fig. 4.4** Underpainting.

As Mr. Barbieri proceeded with his explanations, mixed feelings of relief and disappointment sat heavy on my chest.

Mr. Barbieri continued, "We also used synchrotron X-rays in conjunction with an advanced fast and precise X-ray detector, and identified an underpainting of a naked woman (Fig. 4.4 and Endnotes page 113). I shall let our art historian, Mr. Angelo Bianchi, elaborate on this interesting matter and explain the importance of such an observation."

Mr. Bianchi, who had all along been silently listening to our conversation, joined in and said, "This discovery has a historical significance because, as we know, Botticelli had embraced the ideas of Girolamo Savonarola, a puritan and fanatic monk who became the moral dictator of the city of Florence. Savonarola had commanded that artists who paint nude figures should either destroy them or paint over them. In an act of extreme loyalty to the Dominican friar, Botticelli had destroyed some of his work and in some cases painted over some of the nude scenes, he deemed unacceptable. So the fact that we observe a nude figure as an underpainting is very, very interesting."

Mr. Russo, however, intervened with a somewhat skeptical look on his face, "This underpainting does not seem to be in keeping with the depiction of a Renaissance female nude. I am not sure that Botticelli would draw a nude body in that style!"

Mr. Bianchi seemed half-convinced but did not comment and concentrated on Mr. Barbieri's description of the rest of his technical analysis. The latter, with a half-smile on his face, said, "We are grateful Mr. Bianchi that you have granted us permission to test the binding media using the technique of gas chromatography-mass spectrometry (GC-MS) (Endnotes page 126). The latter is a very sensitive and specific method for determining organic substances and is very appropriate to test this picture which is painted in tempera." And, as if he felt the need to reassure me he added, "As I explained to you, Mr. Romano, very few micrograms were extracted from a small corner of the painting, and we have therefore minimized any possible damage to the artwork. The analysis showed evidence of proteinaceous materials confirming that animal glue was used as a binding material in keeping with some of Botticelli's practices." (See Fig. 4.5).

I could understand these last findings, which seemed very encouraging to me. I, therefore, felt deeply disappointed when Mr. Barbieri finally turned towards me and with a regretful tone concluded, "As I mentioned earlier, Mr. Romano, you have made an exciting find, and although I am unable to give you a final verdict on authentication, these results are very encouraging indeed!"

I felt a bit in a daze and left the lab somewhat discouraged but still hopeful that I would find an expert or a lab willing to authenticate my painting.

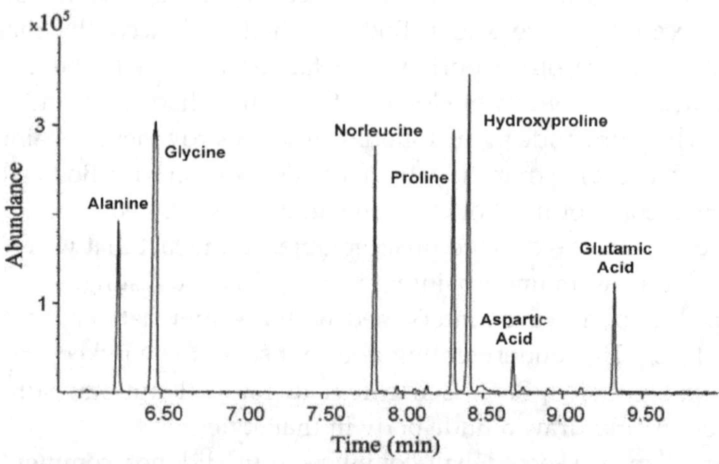


**Fig. 4.5**   Detection of proteinaceous materials by GC-MS.

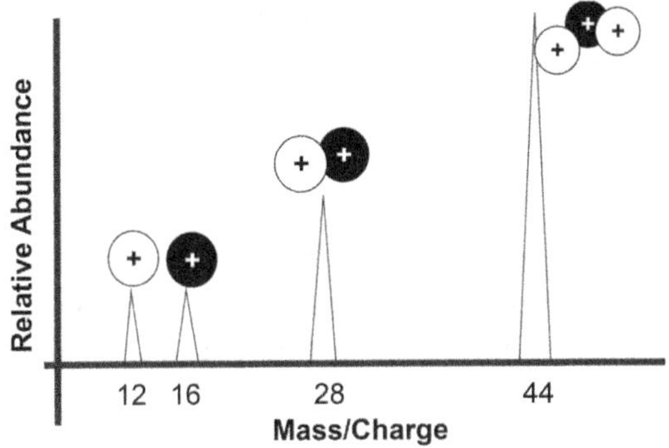

**Fig. 4.6** Mass spectrum of carbon dioxide.

# Questions and Classroom Activity

**Revision questions:**
1. What are the indications that the painting is forged?
2. What are the indications that the painting is authentic?
3. What is the role of art history in this authentication process?
4. What is the principle of gas chromatography? On what basis is the separation of the components carried out?
5. What is the principle of mass spectrometry?
6. What are isotopes?
7. If the atomic mass of carbon (C) is 12 and that of oxygen (O) is 16, what can you conclude from the diagram shown in Fig. 4.6?
8. How is an underpainting determined by synchrotron X-ray fluorescence?

**Exploratory questions:**
1. In a mass spectrum, why is the vertical axis labeled 'relative abundance'?
2. Explain why if iron (Fe) and manganese (Mn) are both located in the hair of a painted figure, umber was probably used as a pigment?
3. What is the difference between tempera, watercolor, and oil paintings?
4. What is animal glue used for and what is its composition? Explain why the result of the gas chromatography test indicates that Botticelli used animal glue.

5. What is the difference between gas chromatography and liquid chromatography?

**Classroom activity:**
Students are to find out individually on the internet, a case where synchrotron X-ray fluorescence mapping was used to reveal a 'hidden' Van Gogh painting. Students are then asked if one is voluntarily willing to describe the case to the rest of the class.

# Case V

# Woman

## Learning Objectives

To introduce — *on a need-to-know basis*:

1. Polarized light microscopy and its application.
2. Infrared spectroscopy and micro-Fourier transform infrared spectroscopy ($\mu$FTIR) as a suitable technique for the analysis of inorganic as well as organic pigments.
3. Pyrolysis-gas chromatography-mass spectrometry (Py-GC-MS) as a complement to GC-MS.

Mark Allister showed up at the reputable ArtNov Gallery in Manhattan, sporting a red bow tie and meticulously parted hair. An observer watching the middle-aged man walk up to the information desk just beyond the portico entrance may have been intrigued by the roll he hugged under his arm and kept close to his chest. He asked the staff member at the desk to meet the gallery's curator, "I have an important matter to discuss," he explained.

The staff member — tall, well built, and an imposing figure in his own right — eyed Mark suspiciously from behind his black-rimmed eyeglasses.

"It is a busy day today, sir, and no curator is available at present at the gallery. Can you tell us about the purpose of your visit?"

Mark, who was more comfortable gazing at the posters hanging on the wall behind the information desk than at the unaccommodating face before him, hesitated for a moment before reluctantly

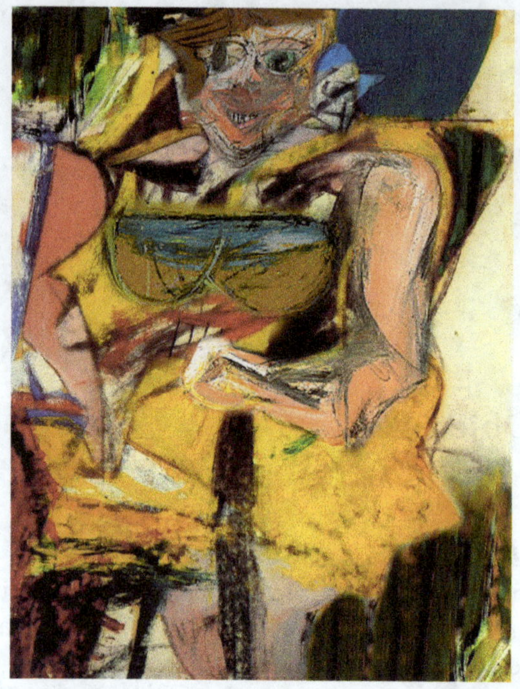

**Fig. 5.1**   Painting purported to be by Willem de Kooning.

providing his explanation, "I am here to present a painting that might be of some value…"

"Well," said the attendant, "I shall inform our administrators and try to find someone who might help you, come back in a day or two."

Disappointed but not discouraged, Mark muttered, "I shall be back tomorrow," and left the gallery at an unhurried pace.

At the gallery's opening hour the next day, Mark was disappointed to find the same man at the desk. At the sight of Mark, however, he exclaimed, "Oh, I remember you! I have not as yet contacted anyone, but will do so now, can you give me your name?" He made a quick phone call and asked for Jack Caladine.

"Sir, there is a Mr. Allister who would like to meet you. He claims he has a painting which might be of some value and is seeking an informed opinion." He seemed to be listening to a reply at the other end of the line before hanging up. He then turned to Mark and asked him to go to the first floor and ask for Mr. Caladine.

Feeling more confident, Mark went up the stairs to the first floor and moved towards a desk where a plump young lady seemed to be expecting him. She promptly directed him to a small waiting room. "Mr. Caladine will meet you here in a few minutes," she told him with a half-smile. As Mark was about to sit down, an impeccably dressed, relatively younger gentleman appeared at the door and greeted him matter-of-factly.

"Good afternoon Mr. Allister, I believe you have a piece of artwork that might be of interest to us, and you are seeking our candid opinion." He then sat down in a nearby chair and invited Mark to do the same.

"Tell me more about it. Is it this picture rolled under your arm?"

Slightly surprised by the suddenness of the encounter, Mark carefully unrolled the painting (Fig. 5.1), spread it out the meeting room table, and said, "Yes, I received it from an old friend, Marion Rosalind, who gave it to me as an expression of gratitude for the care I took of her in the last months of her life."

"What makes you think that it is a painting of value?" Mr. Caladine asked.

To this Mark replied, "I think it might be Willem de Kooning as it looks like one of his famous paintings depicting the personage of a woman. There also seems to be some circumstantial evidence as Marion Rosalind was a close friend of Marjorie Luyckx, the younger sister of Elaine de Kooning, Willem's wife."

Jack Caladine was listening carefully and asked, "Have you ever met Marjorie?"

"No, I have not. Marjorie died in 1998 about fourteen years ago; that was before I moved to the same apartment building as Marion and became her neighbor and friend. You see, Marion was a very lonely person and had no family. Before dying, she called me one day and gave me this picture and said she had received it years ago from Marjorie," Mark explained.

Jack took out a large magnifying glass from a nearby drawer and examined the artwork. It did look like one of Willem's Women, but it might be a fake. "Forgers today can emulate the style of any artist," he thought. He was no expert on abstract expressionism and would call upon the in-house connoisseur, Tim Bartlett, who happened to be an authority on de Kooning to examine the painting. If the provenance proved to be convincing, there would be much work to test the artwork.

"We shall have to look at the painting carefully, Mr. Allister, and examine first the style and brushwork. You must, therefore, leave it with us for some time. If the results are convincing, we shall then take it to the Artechni Laboratory. It is a lab of good repute, and we have collaborated with it for many years. The tests will cost you some money; I wonder if you are ready to put up with such an expense? However, it would certainly be worthwhile if it happened to be an authentic de Kooning. Furthermore, you must allow us to extract minute amounts of samples for the purpose of analysis if need be."

Mark thought about the proposition for a minute and said, "Fine, I shall leave it with you to examine, and I am ready to put up with the analysis expenses."

"Great, please leave your address and phone number at the reception, Mr. Allister, in order for us to contact you. Goodbye, Sir!" Jack quickly uttered while his hand extended towards the door.

Once more, taken aback by the sudden end of his encounter with Jack, Mark provided the receptionist with his contact information and quickly left the gallery.

Jack's first action was to call Martin Livingstone, a young staff member at the gallery, "I want you to go to the following address in Downtown Brooklyn and check if a Marion Rosalind lived there and had a neighbor named Mark Allister. Also, if you can find any evidence of a friendship that existed between this Marion and a Marjorie Luyckx, it would be helpful."

On this matter, Jack was determined to exercise due diligence. He recalled Shaun Greenhalgh, the British forger who, with the collaboration of his elderly parents and brother, cleverly concocted schemes and convinced auction houses, museums, and galleries of the provenance of his forgeries. He also remembered Glafira Rosales, who paid a few thousand dollars to a talented Queens artist to create forgeries. She then attributed these to titans of modernism such as Rothko and Pollock and sold them to renowned Manhattan galleries. However, the excitement he felt, he could not explain. He went back to his office and called Tim Bartlett, saying, "Tim, I want you to come and have a look at a painting which is purported to be by Willem de Kooning and give me your opinion. I have a feeling it might be authentic. A man named Mark Allister presented it to the gallery and claims to have received it from a neighbor named Marion Rosalind. According to him, she was a good friend of Marjorie Luyckx, de Kooning's sister in law. Just imagine what discovering a new de Kooning would do to the reputation of the gallery!"

A few minutes later, Tim, a bookish middle-aged man with spectacles, appeared at the door saying, "Hello Jack, good thing you found me today, let me examine the artwork you seem so enthusiastic about."

"Yes, I guess I am a little excited by this challenge, but do have a look and let me know your first impression," Jack replied.

Bending forward towards the table with the painting spread on it, Tim examined the work carefully, and exclaimed, "It does look like one of de Kooning's figurative abstractions, Jack. From early on — in the late 1940s — he was painting women, including the significant rendition *Woman* (1948). In the 1950s, he started *Woman* (1953), which was the most important piece of a new series. This artwork went through many revisions before completion. We also understand that while working on it, he produced some other paintings depicting women. Can this painting also be one of them?

"Look at the vampish-like appearance, Jack, the anatomical distortions, those globe-like eyes, and huge pillow-like breasts they indeed fit the de Kooning style.

"Such details reflect his notorious negative view of women. You see, it is generally believed that his depiction of females subconsciously or consciously mirrored the bullying ones in his own life — his ruthless mother and his bossy wife, Elaine."

Using a medium-sized magnifying glass, Tim took a closer look at the painting and carefully articulated, "At first sight, the craquelure (Endnotes page 119) seems natural, but it still needs to be examined with a stereomicroscope (Endnotes page 100). It is also interesting that this painting was produced on a sheet of rag paper of size 65 × 50 cm, in a manner akin to *Woman* (1953). Note also that the background composed of broad paint strokes integrates this female figure, again a de Kooning characteristic. What is interesting is that there seems to be in the position of the figure's eyes and breasts some early but still visible revisions made in charcoal. We know that de Kooning, by a conscious decision, retained evidence of his earlier revisions in a number of his works.

"We have to be very careful, however, in our assessment, Jack, as forgers today are so ingenious that they can emulate all the characteristic features of a given artist. Also remember that in 2010 The Getty Conservation Institute published a book by Susan Lake describing de Kooning's materials and techniques, a Holy Grail for any forger!"

Jack listened intently and asked, "What is your advice, Tim?"

"I do think it might be worthwhile taking this work to the Artechni Laboratory for further investigations," Tim answered.

To that, Jack immediately replied, "You are right. I shall send the work for analysis to this lab, and will specifically ask for James Johnson. I have dealt with him before; he is very thorough in his work and generally gives me detailed comments once he has done the analysis. I shall, nevertheless, wait for Martin Livingstone, who is checking the address of this Allister guy and his purported neighbor Marion Rosalind. It would also be great if we could trace a link with Marjorie Luyckx."

Two days later, Livingstone confirmed that the two addresses were indeed correct. He found no proof, however, that Marjorie Luyckx visited Rosalind. By now barely able to manage his mounting expectations, Jack sent the painting for examination at the Artechni Lab and was contacted three weeks later by James who told him that they have completed their analysis and would like to share the results with him.

Jack was visibly excited, saying, "Great, James let us meet tomorrow in my office; I shall also tell Tim Bartlett, our in-house connoisseur on de Kooning, to be present."

The next day, James, with his report in hand, appeared at the ArtNov Gallery, and familiar with the drill, went directly to Jack's office on the first floor. He found both Jack and Tim waiting for him, and after greeting them, he started unemotionally to report his results, "Both of you may be familiar with some of the techniques we used; however, I shall describe some of the tests we carried out, as well as our interpretation of the results."

"Great! But before you continue James, can I get you something to drink?" Jack interrupted.

"Yes, thank you, Jack, I'd like a cup of coffee." James said and, without losing a beat, he continued, "Using Infrared reflectography (IRR) (Endnotes page 105), an underdrawing in charcoal was observed. It was not a very clear sketch, as the paint layers were rather thick. Some of the lines around the body, the eyes, and the breasts resembled the end product, but other parts exhibited some pentimenti. The latter, may in general, suggest authenticity.

"Paint cross-sections (Endnotes page 107) taken from different locations in the painting and observed with a stereomicroscope indicated that the artist who created it built up his paints in successive Wet on Wet layers. Look at the four layers in the picture of the cross-section (Fig. 5.2) and observe the relatively soft layer boundaries. Observe how the contact surface between some of the paint layers is wavy and irregular and how the last underlayer blends with the upper layer next to it. This suggests that the gap time or time elapsed between painting each layer was not big."

At this point, Tim interjected, "I am reassured by the wet on wet paint (Endnotes page 108) observed in the cross-sections. Indeed if de Kooning painted this picture after 1950, we would expect such an approach. During such a period, he used his paint lavishly and with high speed, and this did not allow the lower

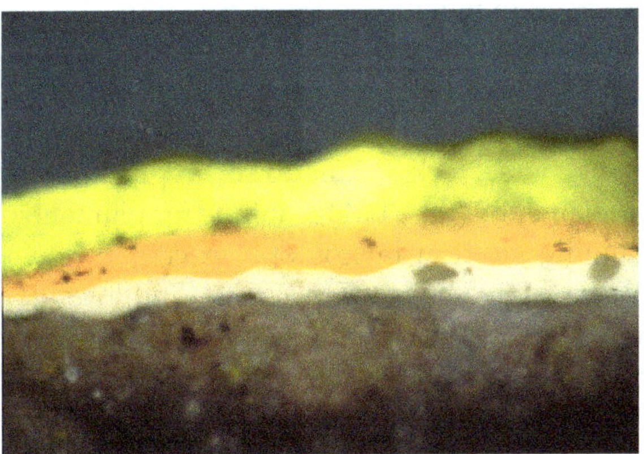

**Fig. 5.2** Paint cross-section taken from one location.

layers to dry before adding an extra layer. Furthermore, your infra-red reflectography result is quite encouraging, Mr. Johnson. It is in keeping with the fact that de Kooning drew many sketches while he composed and designed his paintings. In some cases, he even arranged in advance several preparatory drawings and moved some to the support of the artwork. His approach was contrary to that of most abstract impressionists. We must be cautious, however, as forgers are talented enough to fool experts by pretending in an underdrawing that the artist had second thoughts during the process of painting.

"In addition, I find it interesting that our painting is on a sheet of rag paper, the same support used for *Woman* (1953). In contrast, *Woman* (1948) is reported by Lake to have been painted on the rough side of a fiberboard panel."

With a nod of the head, James proceeded, "Thank you. These are indeed interesting remarks, Mr. Bartlett. The results I shall shortly report might further help us in our evaluation. We used polarized light microscopy (PLM) (Endnotes page 129) to look more closely at the cross-sections and to study the pigments the artist used. To this end, we identified a small area of the painting using an optical micro-scope and removed a sectional fragment using the point of a scalpel blade. We cut slowly down through the layers along a line of crackle, and the fragment was loosened at the bottom with a thin tungsten needle. We also removed with the same needle small samples, which were crushed to aid in identifying the pigments."

"James, please just name for us the techniques you used and the observed results without having to go into so much detail!" exclaimed a visibly anxious Jack.

"Yes, yes, of course, Jack, I shall do so," replied James and contin-ued, "We complemented the PLM technique for pigment identification by using scanning electron microscopy in conjunction with energy dispersive X-ray fluorescence (SEM/EDX) (Endnotes page 110). The binding media were identified using micro-Fourier transform infrared spectroscopy ($\mu$FTIR) (Endnotes page 132) and pyrolysis-gas chroma-tography-mass spectrometry (Py-GC-MS) (Endnotes page 134). We also had to use $\mu$FTIR for the identification of a blue pigment.

Analysis of the cross-sections by PLM astonishingly indicated that the artist incorporated quartz particles in some of the underlayers."

Tim interrupted with a certain degree of excitement, "How interesting; in the late 1940s, de Kooning added grainy foreign materials to his paints. Can it be that he also made such additions after 1950, and would a forger be so clever as to emulate one of de Kooning's characteristics, namely experimenting with non-art materials?"

"Yes, this is undoubtedly an encouraging result, Mr. Bartlett," replied James, and continued, "The pigments identified using PLM and SEM/EDX were lead white, zinc oxide, cadmium yellow, cadmium red, and carbon black, with no detected anachronisms. The blue color was thought to be organic as it had an amorphous appearance (Endnotes page 132), and was identified by $\mu$FTIR as copper phthalocyanine (Fig. 5.3), which was produced commercially starting from 1935 and was therefore available when de Kooning produced his work."

Jack felt increasingly excited, "All these results seemed to point towards authenticity!" he said.

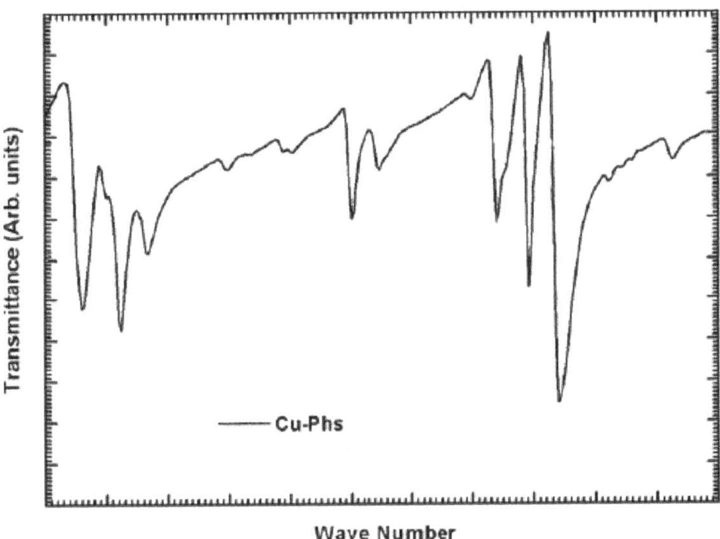



**Fig. 5.3** $\mu$FTIR of copper phthalocyanine.

"Not so fast, it is true that copper phthalocyanine was available when de Kooning produced his work. However, I have not encountered any reference that he used it as a blue pigment in any of his paintings," replied Tim.

"The following might help you shed some light on this anomaly," said James. "When we examined the binding medium by $\mu$FTIR, we found it to be linseed oil in keeping with de Kooning's practice in the late 1940s (Fig. 5.4). However, surprisingly, in the case of the blue copper phthalocyanine, we encountered a nonvolatile binding agent of very low solubility. We resorted to pyrolysis-gas chromatography-mass spectrometry (Endnote page 134) for its analysis and found that it was a terpolymer (composed of polystyrene, polyacrylonitrile, and polymethyl methacrylate) available since 1970. Would this have any significance, Tim?"

"This binding material was indeed, as you say, available during the artist's lifetime, but 1970 is well beyond the date at which de Kooning drew his *Woman* series," answered Tim. He then queried, "Since there is an anachronism concerning both the phthalocyanine and the binding agent, is there a test that would indicate if it is a later retouch?"

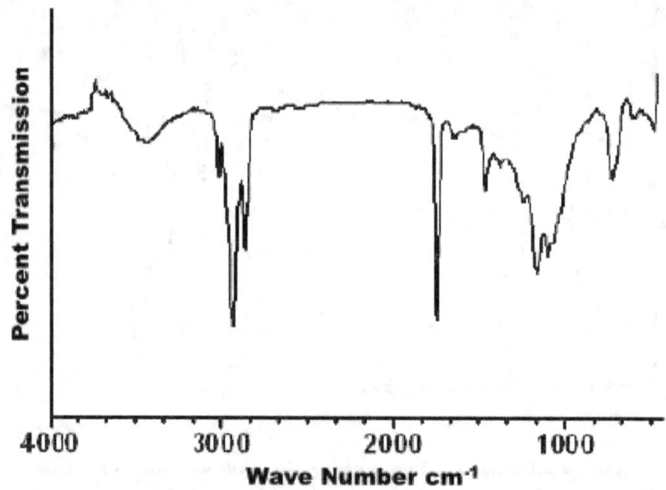


Fig. 5.4   $\mu$FTIR of linseed oil (see Endnotes page 132).

"We have done precisely that and examined the surface using UV light. The latter induces visible fluorescence and can reveal the presence of natural varnish layers (Endnotes page 101). If the painting has been treated, the areas of recent retouching usually fluoresce less brightly than the original oil paint and varnish or may not fluoresce at all. We found that the copper phthalocyanine area fluoresced only slightly less under UV light than the rest of the painting, indicating that it might possibly be a retouch (Endnotes page 103).

To further confirm this observation, we used PLM to look at a cross-section from the same blue area. Some traces of dirt could be detected between the upper paint layer and the lower one, suggesting a later addition to the painting," answered James.

Jack listened intently to the comments of both James and Tim and, leaning forward, asked, "If this painting is a forgery, why would the forger restore it? And if it is authentic and owned by Elaine de Kooning as claimed, being a painter she could in her own right have added the blue color. Also, why would this Allister guy offer to pay for a scientific investigation if he was not convinced that it was authentic? What is your take on it, Tim?"

"These are indeed interesting questions; they suggest that this painting is not a forgery," replied Tim.

James, who had been listening quietly, spoke up, "I do not believe that a forger could have created this painting; however clever he or she may be. The scientific results emanating from our laboratory are compelling and do not indicate any anachronisms. Furthermore, your art history and connoisseurship comments do not cast doubt in my mind on the authenticity of this work."

Positively bursting with excitement, Jack exclaimed, "Gentlemen, I think we have an authentic painting!"

## Questions and Homework

**Revision questions:**
1. What are the indications that the painting thought to have been painted by de Kooning is a forgery?

2. What are the indications that it is authentic?
3. Provide at least three different characteristics of de Kooning's style of painting. What are the ones that can be cleverly emulated by a forger?
4. Is there a difference between the polarizer and analyzer in a polarized light microscope? What is wave interference? From what does image contrast arise in a polarized light microscope?
5. Name two experimental approaches that indicated that the blue area identified in the painting as the anachronistic copper phthalocyanine pigment and terpolymer binding agent belonged to a retouch.
6. What is the basic principle of infrared spectroscopy? Why is this technique more useful in some cases than X-ray fluorescence for the identification of pigments?
7. What are the main advantages of Fourier transform infrared spectroscopy? Also, when testing a painting, why is it best to use such a technique in conjunction with a microscope?
8. Explain why there is a need sometimes to include a pyrolyzer in a GC-MS instrument?

**Exploratory questions:**
1. Among the challenges to the application of Py-GC-MS technique in the study of paintings are the low volatility of pyrolysis products arising from natural and some synthetic macromolecules that are typically used as binding materials and the large extent of fragmentation these macromolecules when pyrolyzed, providing data that are quite difficult to interpret. Please detail some properties of a good pigment binder and some means to overcome this extensive fragmentation due to pyrolysis.
2. Which part of the electromagnetic spectrum is known as the infrared region? Express your answer in terms of both frequency (wavenumbers) and wavelength (microns).
3. Indicate two important regions in an infrared spectrograph and explain what each region represents.
4. What is an interferometer?

**Homework:**
Students are to search for a case where polarized light microscopy was instrumental in the authentication of a painting by Manet. A short report is to be prepared and a short oral presentation on the case is to be made.

# Case VI

# The Missing Season

## Learning Objectives

To introduce — *on a need-to-know basis*:

1. Dendrochronology and the limits of its application.
2. Radiocarbon dating (RD) and the limits of its application.
3. Accelerator mass spectrometry (AMS)
   i.  Its advantages over conventional radiometric techniques.
   ii. Its application in radiocarbon dating.
4. Laser ablation-inductively coupled plasma-multiple collector-mass spectrometry (LA-ICP-MC-MS) and its application in identifying the geographic origin of a pigment.

Jean-Jack Régimbal was among the crowd that gathered in disbelief to what they were witnessing. The silence of the crowd was eerie as a colossal fire engulfed that most iconic of sites in the heart of Paris — the Notre Dame Cathedral — and only the crackling of wood could be heard a block away. As the spire of the Cathedral succumbed to the billowing flames and tumbled to the ground, the crowd reacted with a collective gasp of shock. Who would have guessed, thought Jean-Jack, that he would witness such a scene when he decided to have his lunch on-the-go, a short walk away from Hôpital Hôtel-Dieu de Paris, the oldest hospital in the city of Paris, and the place where he was doing his residency. Being mentally vigilant, Jean-Jack very quickly realized that he must hurry back to tend to the injured.

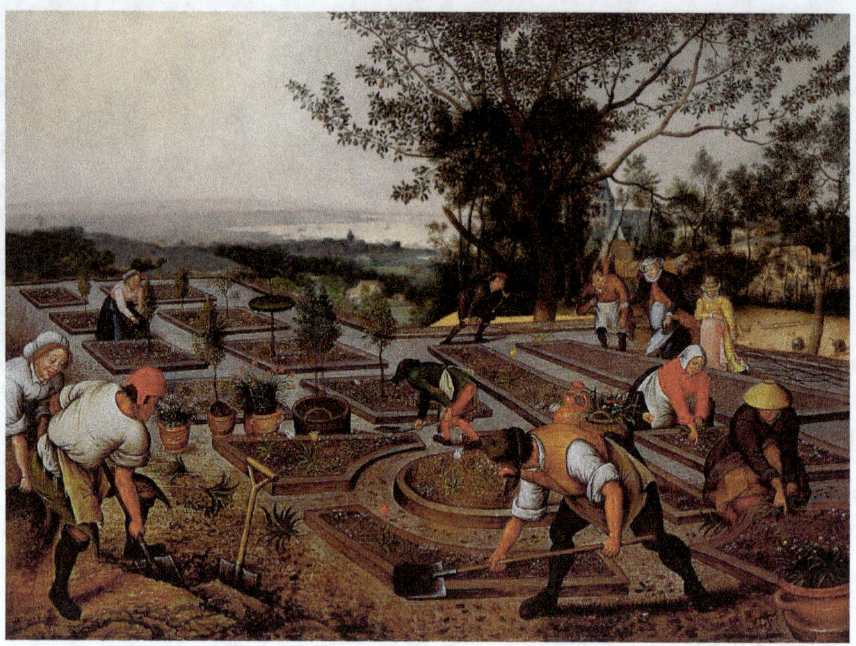

**Fig. 6.1** Painting suspected to be part of *The Months* (1565) by Pieter Bruegel the Elder.

Only after a long and grueling day did Jean-Jack learn the full fate of Notre Dame. He watched intently as newscasters described the damage to this jewel of Gothic architecture and the heroic efforts of firefighters and police officers to help salvage priceless artifacts. Officials used keys and codes to retrieve the Crown of Thorns, which some believe was placed on the head of Christ. Not surprisingly, it was considered the Cathedral's most precious religious relic. In the midst of the mayhem, one element provided some titillation. Among the many statues, paintings, and artifacts, rescuers came upon a previously unknown metal chest, which had apparently lain hidden in the roof joists of the Cathedral for hundreds of years until exposed by the fire, was now in the charge of the police.

The police made a detailed inventory of all artifacts before placing them in the custody of the Louvre for safeguarding during the renovation efforts. Officers responsible for the inventory did not open the chest, however, lest its contents suffer damage in the process.

Tasked with caring for Notre Dame's prized treasures, the Louvre's President-Director and Managing-Director formed several two-member teams, each given one of the recovered artifacts to care for. The hitherto unknown chest was given to the team of Dr. Gabriel Hugo, one of the museum's leading technical art experts, and Lèo Augustine, an internship student from the Paris College of Art. Once opened, the chest revealed a painting of a garden scene on a wooden panel signed and dated in roman numerals on the bottom right *BRVEGEL/MDLXV* which translates to *Bruegel/1565*. Aware that this inscription matched the style of Bruegel, Dr. Hugo showed visible signs of shock and excitement, surprising Lèo who knew his mentor as conservative and reserved.

Spurred by curiosity, Lèo listened intently as Dr. Hugo talked about *The Months* (also referred to as *The Series of the Months* or *The Seasons*), which he described to be amongst Pieter Bruegel the Elder's most famous works. *The Months*, he explained, is a series of six paintings depicting scenes of traditionally common Flemish and Northern activities that would take place during different months of the year. Dr. Hugo explained that the series, commissioned in 1565 by the Antwerp merchant Nicolaas Jongelinck, was used as collateral for tax arrears owed to the city magistrate and was in turn gifted by the city to the Archduke Ernst of Austria for his ceremonious entry into Antwerp. The paintings were passed down through generations of the Archduke's family in Prague and Vienna; however, in 1659, one of the pieces was lost. The five that survived remained in Vienna until the 19th century but subsequently ended up in different collections.

Three paintings, *The Gloomy Day* (1565), *The Return of the Herd* (1565), and *The Hunters in the Snow* (1565) which depict scenes of early spring (Feb/March), autumn (Oct/Nov), and winter (Dec/Jan), respectively, are still in Vienna as part of the large Bruegel collection at the Kunsthistorisches Museum; the *Haymaking* (1565) depicting early summer (June/July) is now in the Lobkowicz Palace in Prague and *The Harvesters* (1565) depicting late summer (Aug/Sept) is in the Metropolitan Museum of Art in New York. It was at this point that Lèo realized the reason for Dr. Hugo's excitement — could the newly dis-covered garden scene painting recently in possession of the Louvre

(Fig. 6.1) actually be the long-lost painting depicting a late spring scene (April/May) by Pieter Bruegel the Elder?

Dr. Hugo's initial inspection yielded no visible signs of deterioration. He then turned to Lèo and said, "You will observe that the painting is on wooden panels; this is important since only in the 16th century did canvas begin to gradually replace wooden panels as the commonly used support for paintings."

"The painting measures 115.4 × 158.2 cm, the exact same dimensions as the other five paintings in Bruegel the Elder's *The Months*." A closer examination of the back also reveals that the painting is supported by two adjoining panels held together by wooden dowels — called butterfly joints (Fig. 6.2).

"This is not unusual for paintings executed on wooden panels. In fact, I am aware of at least one other such example — *The Birdnester* (1568) — a smaller piece measuring only 59.5 × 68.3 cm made by Bruegel the Elder that contained dowels fastening two wooden panels together. Many paintings by Bruegel the Elder

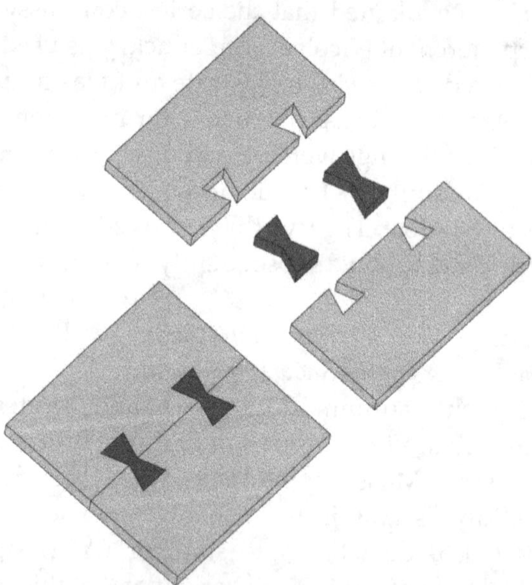

Fig. 6.2 Two wooden panel supports (light grey) held together with two wooden butterfly joints (dark grey).

utilizing multiple panels have been subjected to conservation measures, including sanding of the backs of the panels and adding salts and resins to glue them together, which is not observed in the painting at hand." Looking intently at the panels, Dr. Hugo pointed out to Lèo that while their appearance was very similar, including a visible and quite distinctive slightly angled saw mark on the back, no identifying maker's house marks were visible on the planks (Fig. 6.3).

Dr. Hugo explained that starting from 1617 to address quality control issues of oak panels for painters, the Antwerp panel maker's guild imposed on panel makers to issue each of their panels with the maker's personal house mark as a way to trace the panel's origin. Upon approval of the quality of the panels, the guild would then brand each of them with the Coat of Arms of Antwerp.

Showing Lèo the distinctive regularly spaced growth rings observable on the back of the panels, Dr. Hugo explained that while it is difficult to have a precise determination of the type of wood by visual inspection, it appears that the panels are oak, which would normally exhibit ring patterns similar to those observed.

Dr. Hugo went on to say, "These patterns are unlike the much more erratic growth ring patterns that would be exhibited by poplar wood," for example. This is another important clue since wooden supports other than oak were seldom used by early Netherlandish painters. In fact, Bruegel the Elder commonly used oak. This variety of wood, which is known to have been produced from Baltic oaks and grows slowly and relatively straight, was used mainly due to the high-quality panels it generated. The use of oak was also usually observed in other northern countries like France, England, and Germany, whereas Italian painters normally used poplar panels for their painting support.

"The observed match in the ring sequence in both panels most likely indicates that they were produced from the same tree," continued Dr. Hugo. "Et quelle chance! One of the two panels has retained some sapwood, which can help more accurately determine its age." Sapwood, he explained to Lèo, is the soft outer layer of recently formed wood that is found just underneath the bark of a tree.

Lèo recalled his lectures on dating techniques of artifacts and asked his mentor whether the use of radiocarbon dating (Endnotes

**Fig. 6.3** Example of a reverse side of a panel showing the Coat of Arms of Antwerp (two hands over a castle) and the panel makers house mark (the letter A shown here upside down, indicating Ambrosius Engelants as the maker).

page 139) could be appropriate in this case to get an age estimate for the panels in order to verify the inscribed date on the painting. Dr. Hugo concurred that the test was warranted and that it was appropriate since organic materials such as wood can be dated using this method.

Thrilled to be involved in such an important endeavor, Lèo mentioned to Dr. Hugo that he studied a new radiocarbon dating technique where an entire specimen was introduced in a chamber containing plasma, which slowly oxidized the surface of the object and produced carbon dioxide. The latter could, in turn, be analyzed to determine the date of the object. Impressed with Lèo's theoretical knowledge, Dr. Hugo, informed him that the available in-house facility was an accelerator mass spectrometer (AMS) (Endnotes page 140) which is not as sophisticated but is nevertheless still superior to the standard radiometric technique. "While it requires the consumption of a very small amount of sample to perform the analysis, a small sliver of wood from the back of the panel would hardly detract from the painting even if it proves authentic," he said.

Dr. Hugo then proceeded to the lab to extract the needed sample and provided it to a colleague for carbon dating. As he was feeling somewhat tired and the lab had promised that the carbon dating results would be related as soon as possible, he exclaimed, "It is time we draw this day to a close Lèo."

Lèo returned home and excitedly recounted all the day's activities to his roommate. The next morning, while reading the news on the internet, a muffled chime announced an email. The message reported the results of the carbon dating test, the panels were dated to 1549 ± 24 years. *Mais c'est génial!* Knowing that Bruegel the Elder died in 1569, Lèo immediately concluded that this result placed the wooden panel not only within the artist's lifetime but also in line with the date on the picture.

Lèo rushed to relate these results to his mentor. Dr. Hugo had already received the information, but was more cautiously optimistic, "It would be useful for us, Lèo, to confirm the results using dendrochronology. This is a method used to determine when the felling date of a tree occurred based on its growth rings. This, in turn, may provide an estimated production date for the panels. We may run into some impediments though. You see, for us to obtain a precise date, a full or at least half a cross-section of the width of the tree up to the edge of the bark is needed, something most trimmed timber, as in this case, will not provide. In addition, in most wooden panels, only a small part of the radius of the trunk is used so that dendrochronology would only, in some cases, be useful to provide a *terminus post quem* or 'the earliest possible date' for a panel's production."

The Louvre dendrochronology expert responded to Dr. Hugo's request and reported a sequence of 105 rings in one panel and 101 in the other. She then matched these to reference chronological growth sequences suggesting that the boards were obtained from a tree felled between 1539 and 1560. These results seemed to agree with those of carbon dating. Now, Dr. Hugo could not wait to examine the pigments on this mystery painting.

Using the conventional non-destructive X-ray fluorescence technique (Endnotes page 103), examination of minute cross-sections of several different colored areas on the painting was carried out. The following pigments were detected: red and yellow ochres, lead-tin-yellow, vermillion, and lead white, all of which were typical of the time of Bruegel, and no anachronisms were uncovered.

All results seemed to point towards authenticity. However, one last point was required, which was to confirm the painting's Dutch/Flemish origin.

Dr. Hugo had in mind a very sophisticated technique to determine isotopic ratios with sufficient precision to be able to detect natural minute differences in isotopic abundances of elements due to geographical origins, making it ideal for the determination of their sources. "The technique is laser ablation inductively coupled plasma multiple collector-mass spectrometry (LA-MC-ICP-MS)," he told Lèo, who was dumbstruck with the lengthy name and was determined to read up on it.

LA-MC-ICP-MS (Fig. 6.4), recently introduced into their laboratory, had been tested on several authentic paintings of Flemish/Dutch as well as Italian origin. It relied on the determination of the isotopic ratios of lead, $^{207}Pb/^{204}Pb$ and $^{206}Pb/^{204}Pb$ (Endnotes page 142).

With a great sense of anticipation, Dr. Hugo and Lèo submitted the panel for examination. Patience eluded both men as they waited for the results on a sample extracted from an area on the painting containing lead white. Alas, their hopes were soon to be crushed, as the results did not support a Dutch/Flemish origin for the material, suggesting rather, that the material had been sourced from Italy (Fig. 6.5).

Unable to reconcile the lead isotope ratio results with so many aspects of the painting consistent with Bruegel, Dr. Hugo was in a quandary. He looked at the hues, carefully graded to create the illusion of space and depth, a Bruegel trademark, the use of Baltic oak panels, the size of the painting — similar to the other five paintings of *The Months* — the dates obtained by carbon dating and dendrochronology — all these results could not be discounted.

He wondered whether it was possible that the lead white, so common to Bruegel's paintings, may have been obtained in this instance from Italy where the artist lived between 1551 and 1554. Is it plausible, he speculated, that Bruegel, who painted *The Months* after 1564, would have used white pigments he purchased in Italy more than ten years earlier?

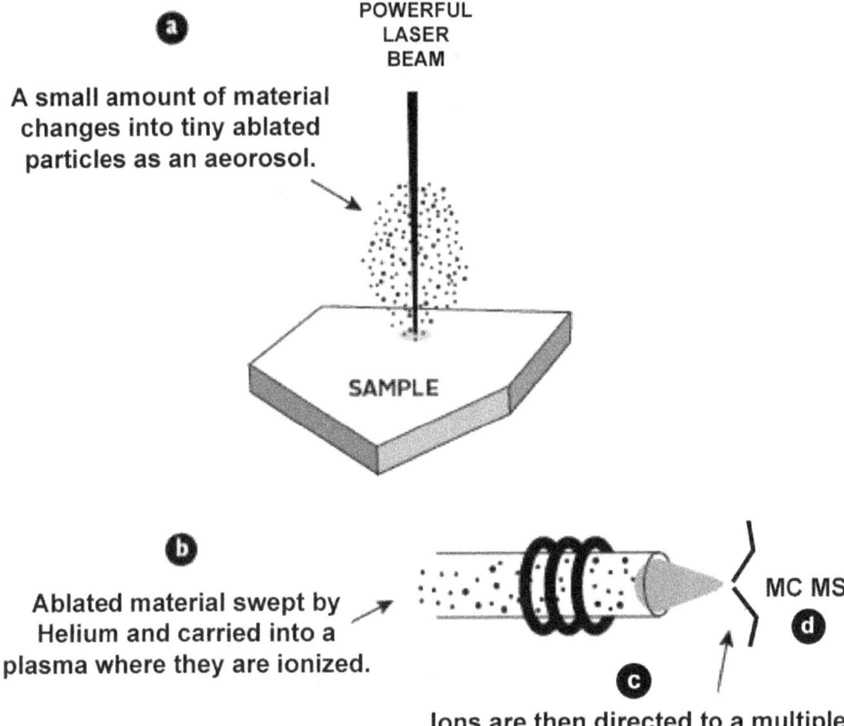



**Fig. 6.4** Principle of LA-MC-ICP-MS.

If only Jean-Jack Régimbal knew how electrifying the content of the mysterious metal chest on the evening news had turned out to be!

## Questions, Classroom Activity, and Homework

**Revision questions:**
1. What are the indications that the painting may be a forgery?
2. What are the indications that the painting is authentic?
3. The back of the panels showed no identifying maker's house marks or the Coat of Arms of Antwerp. Explain the significance of this observation and implications, if any, on authenticity.

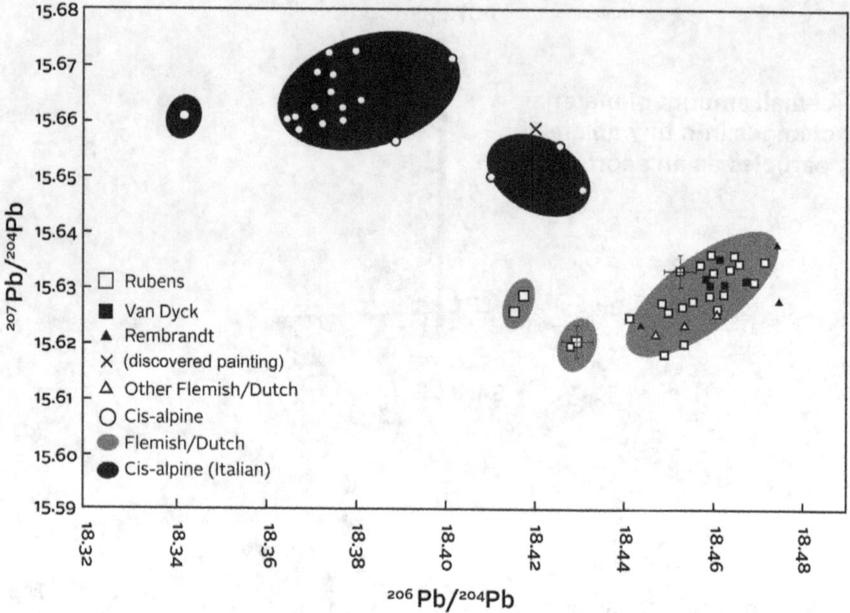



**Fig. 6.5** Origin of lead ores from which lead was extracted in case of authenticated Flemish and Italian artists and result (x) obtained on the discovered painting attributed to Bruegel indicating an Italian source (Endnotes page 142).

4. What is the principle of:
   (a) Dendrochronology?
   (b) Radiocarbon dating?
5. Why is the presence of sapwood in a wooden plank useful in obtaining a more precise date for the time of the felling of the tree from which the plank was produced?
6. Describe how lead isotope ratios can help identify the locality of the lead ore from which the lead in a pigment was extracted.
7. Describe how the measurement of the width of a ring in dendro-chronology can be made.

**Exploratory questions:**
1. Describe the significance and function of each part in Fig. 6.6.
2. Research and write about the use of X-ray radiography to uncover the evidence of forgery in panel paintings, such as artificial worm-

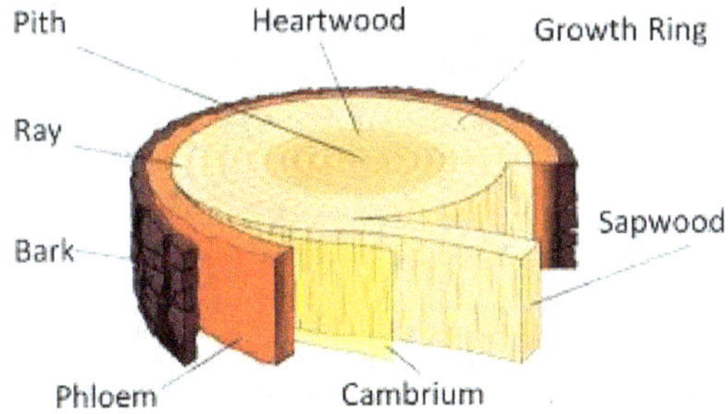



**Fig. 6.6** Cross-section of a tree.

holes or hidden metal-wires. *The Madonna of the Veil* (1920–29) bequeathed to the Courtauld Gallery, London in 1947 is a good place to start.[1]

3. Discuss factors that may affect tree ring formation and, subsequently, dendrochronological data.
4. Detail some limitations to both radiocarbon dating and dendrochronology dating.
5. Find on the internet three atomic isobars and three molecular isobars.
6. Give two characteristic techniques of Bruegel the Elder.
7. What is the half-life of a radioisotope in general, and what is the half-life of $^{14}C$? Explain why the upper limit for radiocarbon dating is 50,000–60,000 years.
8. What is the bomb peak effect in relation to radiocarbon dating?

**Classroom activity:**

Students are to work with a colleague to search out on the internet a case where the bomb peak effect was instrumental in uncovering a Fernand Léger forgery.

**Homework:**

Describe in a short report the Fernand Léger forgery case.

---

[1]See in Further Readings: Ref. [8] under *Additional readings combining a number of techniques* pp. 8–13 and Ref. [2] under *X-ray fluorescence and energy dispersive X-ray fluorescence* pp. 19–24.

# Case VII

# Looted by the Nazis?

## Learning Objectives

To introduce — *on a need-to-know basis*:

1. The technique of raking light (RL).
2. Canvas weave thread counting by conventional and digital techniques.
3. X-ray diffraction.
4. Micro-X ray diffraction and its limits of application.


Marilyn Littlewood lived with her retired husband Jack in South Kensington, the elegant West London district. They led a vibrant and happy life accentuated by visits to museums, art galleries, and concert halls. She loved the local architecture surrounding her home, with its mixture of terraced rows and detached houses, and enjoyed the neighborhood's wide range of chic bars and restaurants.

Despite her attachment to her life in London, Marilyn also looked forward to her annual trips to Buenos Aires, where Linda, her daughter, lived with her Argentine husband, Matias Romero. With its rich cultural life and impressive architecture, this vibrant city, long considered the Paris of South America, had instantly captured Marilyn's heart. She especially looked forward to visiting San Telmo's 'feria' a fair held every Sunday throughout the year. This enormous bazaar covering seemingly endless blocks of cobblestone streets was the perfect place not only to buy well-priced antiques but also to watch professional Tango couples dance to the accordion-like bandoneon in its famous Plaza Dorrego.

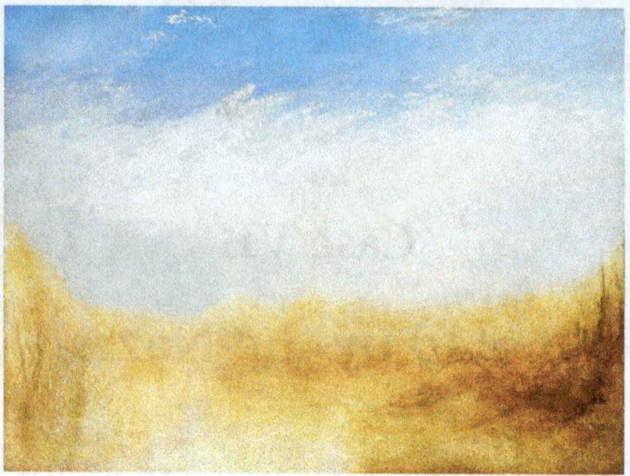

**Fig. 7.1**   Painting found at San Telmo.

On one of those visits to San Telmo, Marilyn entered a shop on the ground floor of an old colonial building. Its window displayed a beautifully decorated recipient for Maté, the traditional South American infused drink. Marilyn found the deeply etched silver floral designs extremely attractive, and as the quoted price was reasonable, she bought it without much thought.

On her way out, she fleetingly looked around the shop. A set of unframed paintings piled up on what seemed to be an old oak table aroused her curiosity. As an art lover, she asked the shopkeeper if she could go through the pile; he could not have responded to her request with more enthusiasm.

As she was inspecting one painting after the other, a beautiful landscape caught her eye. She felt that the painter had captured the effects of atmosphere and light and, to the shopkeeper's delight, also decided to purchase this painting.

Marilyn and Jack spent several months with Linda and Matias at their home in the exclusive Palermo Chico district of Buenos Aires, and after a wonderful stay traveled back to London where they slowly but steadily resumed their life in South Kensington.

While they were entertaining guests at home one evening, Marilyn mentioned her purchase of the beautiful landscape picture. She had not had time to have it cleaned and framed but intended to do so very soon. One of the guests, John Williamson, an art historian, connoisseur, and avid art lover, asked if he could have a look at it.

Delighted at his interest in her new purchase, Marilyn brought the picture out from their front room and spread it on a nearby table. The painting did look beautiful, she thought, and she loved its fluid composition and colorful abstractions.

John took one look at the picture and enthusiastically exclaimed, "You seem to have made an exciting find, Marilyn. If I am not mistaken, this looks like a Turner. Could it be one of the artworks smuggled by the Nazis to Argentina after World War II?"

Marilyn experienced a shiver as John continued, "We all know of the massive art looting that took place during the war. After Germany's defeat, Argentina received hundreds if not thousands of Nazis desperate for a new home far away from the Nuremberg Trials. Many prominent Argentines of German, Italian, and Spanish descent were supportive of the Axis cause because of close cultural ties with their root countries. They were even ready to pay the way for escaping Nazis, and Perón himself was sympathetic to the Axis powers."

"Can it be a Turner?" asked the visibly excited Marilyn.

"Yes, as I just mentioned to you, this painting might be one of the looted artworks. Smart Nazi officers and collaborators squirreled away paintings, money, and valuables to Argentina," answered John. "However, before jumping to conclusions, I need to have a closer look at the painting. I happen to have an absolute love for Turner's work, and maybe we can reach some preliminary conclusions."

Jack, now also pulled into the current, asked John, "Would it be too much trouble for you to come any time next week and inspect this painting more closely?"

A few days later, John arrived at the Littlewoods' home with a large magnifying glass and a handheld LED flashlight. Marilyn and Jack greeted him warmly, and they all proceeded to the dining room. The painting had been carefully laid out on a white sheet covering the table. John, who started to inspect it with his magnifying glass, said, "The craquelure does look natural to me. However, a more sophisticated stereomicroscope will be required for further confirmation; also, we must not rejoice too fast as Turner was one of the most copied artists, even during his own time."

"Why would they copy him?" asked Marilyn.

"He was extremely popular, and this encouraged many commercially minded forgers to do so. Even today, a few collectors have been devastated to find out that some of their paintings were not executed by Turner but by other 19th or 20th century impostors. However, let me have a closer look at your find."

This time, John examined it under raking light (Endnotes page 145) using his handheld LED lamp and, after a careful survey, mentioned, "I note that less attention is paid to the details of objects and landscape than to the effects of light and color, which is very much a Turner characteristic. It is common knowledge that at some point during his career, his paintings became more atmospheric and luminous. This work is very much in keeping with Turner's style in the 1830s.

"Although most of Turner's major works are very well documented and cataloged, some pieces do reappear from time to time. It is known that Mrs. Booth, Turner's landlady and lover when he stayed in the small Thameside cottage in Chelsea, had sold a cache of his paintings, some of which are unaccounted for today. Therefore, it might be worthwhile to have this work analyzed by a technical art historian to ensure that it has no anachronistic elements. I recommend Martin Baker's London lab. His services are quite expensive, but he has an excellent reputation, and his state-of-the-art lab has a broad spectrum of up-to-date instruments. I know him personally, and I can help you get an appointment."

Most relieved that John had not dismissed the work as an outright forgery, the Littlewoods decided to follow his advice and consult with Mr. Baker. Sensing she would be unable to contain her emotion on the day of the results, Marilyn asked John if he would accompany them, a request which John readily accepted. Marilyn and Jack delivered the painting soon after to Mr. Baker, a well-built man in his mid-forties who was very keen to investigate the artwork scientifically.

Mr. Baker completed his analysis a few weeks later and invited them all in. "Welcome, everyone," he announced with gusto, "I am pleased to meet you this morning. Allow me to start by describing to you our *modus operandi,* and then give you a blow-by-blow description of the tests we have undertaken." You know that the Tate Gallery has the most extensive collection of Turner's artworks in the world; it contains hundreds of his watercolors and oil paintings. It is therefore very fortunate for us that Dr. Joyce H. Townsend, the senior conservation scientist at the Tate Gallery, has carried out and published an impressive amount of research on Turner. Thanks to her work, we have at our disposal a sound basis for comparison in terms of this artist's techniques and the pigments he used.

"I will start by commenting on the size of your painting, which is 3ft 4in x 4ft 2in. These dimensions are close to some of the recorded canvases that Turner used. His father is known to have prepared some for him, but Turner also used a considerable amount of commercially prepared ones. This canvas is made of a closely woven plain weave, with 14-18 threads per centimeter, which is in keeping with some of the thread counts recorded by Townsend on authentic paintings by Turner."

"How promising!" exclaimed Marilyn.

"Yes, indeed, Mrs. Littlewood, these initial observations were very encouraging to us. I would, however, like you to listen to all the steps we undertook in our analysis for you to realize that we have worked diligently and to understand the reason for our conclusions," replied Mr. Baker. This disquieted Marilyn, of course, who fleetingly glanced at both Jack and John for reassurance and then continued to listen.

"We used a technique referred to as infrared reflectography (Endnotes page 105) to check if there were any underdrawings and found none. This, too, was encouraging as Turner seldom prepared an underdrawing, and his compositions in oil were generally blocked-in with thin washes of paint."

John, who was listening carefully, observed, "What is interesting in this painting is that rather than applying an even, fine brushwork, the artist seemed to use different brushes for distinct effects on different areas of the canvas. This again is very much a Turner characteristic!"

"John, I am pleased to see that you know a lot about Turner," replied Mr. Baker with a nod of approval. "I would like to add that using a special type of microscope called a polarized light microscope (Endnotes page 129), we observed that the pigments used in this picture were large-grained and coarse. That is also very much in keeping with Turner's practice, as he did not thoroughly grind his pigments, possibly to create a more luminous atmosphere. To ensure that there were no anachronistic pigments, we took very fine cross-sections (Endnotes page 107) from different parts of the painting. We examined them using energy dispersive X-ray fluorescence as well as micro-Raman spectroscopy (Endnotes pages 103 and 118), and we were pleased to find no anachronistic elements throughout the artwork."

Here Marilyn's face relaxed.

Marilyn and Jack were not familiar with the techniques referred to by Mr. Baker, but they avidly hung onto every part of this explanation that seemed to be leading them to exactly where they wanted to go.

"We found that the canvas was primed with a lean lead white/ linseed oil grounding. Examination of the yellow area indicated the presence of strontium, chromium, and lead, suggesting that the yellow pigment used was probably a mixture of strontium chromate and lead chromate. This result is in keeping with Turner's practice as he used a range of distinct yellow chromium compounds for his yellow colors. The white area also indicated the presence of lead, and we assumed that lead white was the pigment used," Mr. Baker continued.

Now growing impatient to hear Mr. Baker announce the final — positive — verdict, Jack interjected, "All your results seem to indicate that Marilyn did *discover* an unknown Turner."

"We were indeed of that opinion, Mr. Littlewood, until we decided to use micro X-ray diffraction (Endnotes page 150) to confirm and complete our analysis of the pigments. Although we did find that strontium chromate was, in fact, the yellow pigment, we were astonished that the diffraction patterns of lead chromate or lead carbonate (lead white) were not observed in spite of the detected lead in the yellow area.

"When we examined the white area in the sky, we found an X-ray diffraction pattern corresponding to lead oxychloride (referred to as Pattinson's white) instead of lead white. The same pigment was most probably also used in the yellow area of the painting as some overlap of its diffraction lines with those of strontium chromate could be observed. Lead oxychloride is a pigment patented in 1849 by the industrialist Hugh Lee Pattinson. It was rarely used in paintings and was never used by Turner, as indicated by Townsend's analysis of hundreds of his oil paintings and watercolors." Mr. Baker concluded with a slightly apologetic tone, "The circumstantial evidence, canvas size, choice, and coarseness of the pigments and the artistic process all pointed towards authenticity. However, I am so sorry to disappoint you all; in light of the micro X-ray diffraction results, the authenticity of this painting is questionable."

Jack and Marilyn reacted to Mr. Baker's conclusive remarks with stunned silence. Why did you give us so much hope then let us down, their faces seemed to say. It was John who interrupted the uncomfortable lull, saying with an upbeat tone, "From all this thorough analysis, I am inclined to believe that the painting was created during Turner's lifetime by someone trying to emulate his style and artistic process. Could it have been smuggled to Argentina by a Nazi convinced that he possessed a Turner? We shall never know. What we know Marilyn is that you have made an exciting find and that your beautiful painting is still worthy of hanging in a prominent place in your home."

## Questions and Homework

**Revision questions:**
1. What are the direct and circumstantial evidences that suggest that the painting is an authentic Turner?
2. What evidence suggests that it is a forgery?
3. Give two characteristics of Turner's style.
4. What is the most reliable technique in canvas weave counting? Explain.
5. Why is the manual counting of the number of threads in a canvas, using a ruler, an unreliable technique? What would be the most reliable technique?
6. Why is it not possible to obtain an X-ray diffraction pattern for an amorphous solid?
7. What is the advantage of micro X-ray diffraction in the analysis of a painting?
8. What kind of information is provided by X-ray diffraction that cannot be obtained by X-ray fluorescence?

**Exploratory questions:**
1. How are X-rays produced?
2. What is a crystallographic plane?
3. What do the horizontal and vertical axes in an XRD pattern represent?
4. During the Renaissance, canvas started to replace wood panels as the support medium for oil paintings. One of the earliest surviving oils on canvas paintings is a French Madonna with angels from around 1410 in the Gemäldegalerie, Berlin.
   (a) Research some reasons why canvas became a more popular support replacing wooden panels.
   (b) List some properties of the most common canvas materials used in paintings.

**Homework:**
Students are to find out on the internet a case where canvas weave analysis was instrumental in authenticating a Van Gogh and to write a short report to describe and comment on the case.

# Case VIII

# The Flight into Egypt

## Learning Objectives

To introduce — *on a need-to-know basis*:

1. Infrared transmission (IRT) imaging.
2. Proton-induced X-ray emission (PIXE).

The luxurious Manhattan penthouse he has just stepped into enraptured Christopher Givens. Its owner, the late Hachirou Katsu, was an eccentric Japanese tycoon and a passionate art collector. Givens, a world-renowned art historian and connoisseur, loves the art gallery feel to the place, its minimalist furniture, impressive number of paintings, and superb quality of displays.

Mr. Katsu recently passed away, leaving his four sons a vast empire to manage. The sons immediately set out to draw up an inventory of their late father's holdings with the help of Makoto Sora, Mr. Katsu's trusted personal lawyer of 37 years. That is how they learned, with enormous surprise, of their late father's ownership of the Flatiron District penthouse. They convened and decided to hire Berkshire Crossings Home Services — a leading luxury Manhattan-based real estate brokerage firm — to execute the sale and to entrust Mr. Sora with overseeing the process.

Mr. Sora soon received an email from the CEO of Berkshire Crossings Home Services informing him that the opulent apartment housed an immense art collection. The best thing to do, Mr. Sora

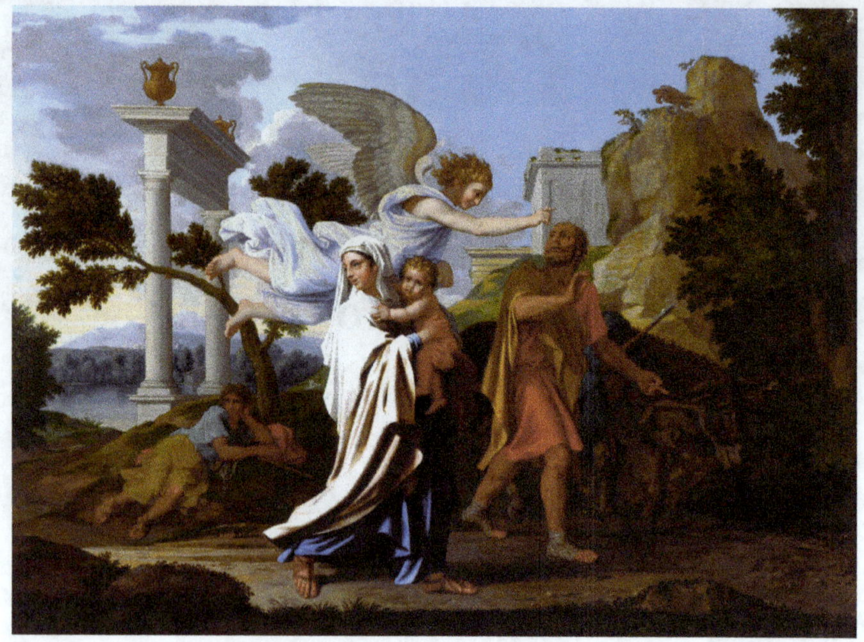

**Fig. 8.1.**  Suspected unknown version of Poussin's *The Flight into Egypt* (1657 or 1658).

decided, would be to fly to New York and draw on expert advice. That is how he got in touch with Christopher Givens.

Mr. Katsu's collection, some 30, mostly contemporary pieces, also holds some paintings from earlier periods. One particular oil painting attracts Mr. Givens' attention. In essence, it appears to be an unapologetic, stroke-for-stroke replica of *The Flight into Egypt* (1657–8) by Nicolas Poussin, the leading painter of the classical French Baroque period (Fig. 8.1).

Christopher Givens realizing Mr. Sora's puzzlement at the inordinate amount of time he is spending peering at the picture, decides to clue him in.

"This painting is very similar to one by Nicolas Poussin, who specialized in Biblical scenes, ancient history, and mythology and spent almost his entire working life in Rome while still being considered one of the great French classical painters; in this piece, he depicts the Holy Family on the path into exile from Herod's Massacre of the Innocents."

The less initiated Mr. Sora clearly appeared in need of a more extensive introduction, and Mr. Givens was happy to elaborate, "The Gospel of Matthew narrates that Herod the Great, King of Judea, afraid for his throne, orders the execution of all male children aged two years and under in the vicinity of Bethlehem.

"This picture depicts the flight of the Holy Family, guided by an angel directing them to safety. The event referred to as the 'Massacre of the Innocents' is the theme of several great paintings, including two versions by the Old Master Peter Paul Rubens. The first of these, dated 1611–1612, is housed in the Art Gallery of Ontario in Toronto. The second and later version, dated 1636–1638, is located in the Alte Pinakothek art museum in Munich."

Mr. Sora has caught on and immediately throws back in a posh unmistakable British accent, "You mean that this picture could be another version of the same painting by Poussin?"

Taken aback by Mr. Sora's perspicacity, Mr. Givens calmly replies, "If it turns out to be, it would make it the fourth version of the painting."

He enjoys walking Mr. Sora through the history and whereabouts of the three versions claimed to be original Poussins. "In 1986, British art historian Christopher Wright declared one owned by a local New York collector, Émile E. Wolf, as the original." Other experts unanimously dismissed it as an obvious copy, and it was eventually sold as such, in 2001, to an anonymous buyer.

"Barbara Johnson, the widow of John Seward Johnson, heir to the Johnson & Johnson pharmaceutical fortune, bought a second version of the work in 1989. Anthony Blunt[1], one of the world's foremost authorities on 17th century French paintings and on Poussin in particular, publicly authenticated this version."

---

[1] Formerly Sir Anthony Blunt, who had served the queen as surveyor of the royal collection, had also confessed to being a member of the Cambridge Five, a Soviet spy ring that had penetrated the heart of the British establishment during the Cold War. For many years, this was a closely held secret until its public revelation by Prime Minister Margaret Thatcher in 1979. Blunt was stripped of his knighthood immediately thereafter.

"The third version of the painting was included in the catalog of a major exhibition of Poussin's works at the Grand Palais in Paris in 1995, and now belongs to the Louvre but hangs in the Musée des Beaux-Arts in Lyon. Richard and Robert Pardo, the earlier owners, had bought the painting in 1986 from a family in whose ownership the painting had remained since the mid-1930s."

Perplexed by the existence of three versions of the same painting, Mr. Sora, who wanted a resolution to the issue, asked Mr. Givens for his opinion. Mr. Givens who loved the opportunity to showcase his knowledge commenced, "Let me first provide you with a very brief background on Poussin and on the picture. Nicolas Poussin spent virtually all of his working life in Rome except for a brief period in Paris where he served as First Painter to King Louis XIII and Cardinal Richelieu. Poussin focused on religious and, at times, mythological subjects; his earliest works are characterized by coloristic richness. He was influenced by Titian, who epitomized Venetian command of color as masterfully shown in his *Danaë* (1544–1546), where he used one single unifying color, duly earning his place as perhaps the greatest colorist of all time."

Mr. Sora had other commitments and, keenly aware of the time, interrupted Mr. Givens who was clearly in his element, "Can we please focus on Poussin and especially this painting?"

"Quite right!" said Mr. Givens, clearly irritated at the interjection. "In his later years, Poussin gave growing prominence to landscapes in his pictures, as you can see here. The influence of the Italian locale where Poussin spent nearly the entirety of his career is also visible through the ruins of classical architecture and distant countryside that form the backdrop of the painting.

"Stylistically, the art of line as exemplified in the physiognomy of the figures shows favor of draughtsmanship or *disegno*, which loosely translates to 'nobility of design', over *colorito*, which is the importance of color in painting as we can see here through the use of cooler colors consistent with his post-1630s palette. This painting, as many of his later works, owed much to his influence by the great Italian classicist painter Raphael. We can also see evidence of Poussin's handwriting in paint, if you will, in the long, graceful, barely noticeable brushstrokes in the cloudless blue sky of the upper right and hints of the shaking hand — with which Poussin was afflicted late in his life — in the cloud formation of the upper left of the painting, and most importantly in the emotional unity of this work, which are all good telltale signs."

Mr. Givens, who had not finished, paused for a few seconds then observed, "What is striking in this picture is how the artist creates the illusion of relief and space on the leveled surface by correctly depicting the relationship between light and shade. This is very much in keeping with Poussin, who was a meticulously deliberate painter."

By now, Mr. Sora was enthralled, "You mean to say this painting is authentic?!"

Mr. Givens continues to exhibit composure before the tantalizing possibility, "The painting is clearly very interesting and of high quality. My initial stylistic analysis does not indicate inconsistencies with Poussin's signature with a brush. However, one must be very careful. The painting *Jonah and the Whale* (1654) of the UK Royal Collection, long attributed to Nicolas Poussin, was recently credited to Gaspard Dughet, who is Poussin's brother-in-law and pupil."

"As we have no information related to provenance — Mr. Katsu is most unlikely to have left any of that — I cannot give you an answer until more scientific analysis is carried out. I can recommend a leading specialist lab, but I must warn you that such an investigation can be expensive."

To this, Mr. Sora curtly but very politely replied, "Mr. Givens, I assure you that expenses are not an issue; time, however, is a luxury I cannot afford. I wish to entrust this collection and especially this picture, which you have singled out, to your care for analysis — a service for which you shall be handsomely compensated." After the two agreed on the details of the arrangement, Mr. Sora flew back to Tokyo and awaited feedback.

Three weeks later, Mr. Givens arranges for a video conference between himself, Mr. Sora, and Mr. Jim Williams, the technical art historian from Scientific Art Services. Mr. Givens was first to speak, "Mr. Sora, I chose Scientific Art Services because it is the leading US-based art authentication lab. I knew that our painting would be in excellent hands."

Mr. Williams picked up his cue, "Our first concern was to ensure that the painting was indeed a 17th century creation. To this end, after its removal from the frame, a tiny but acceptable sample of the canvas was extracted from one of the wrapped edges for radiocarbon dating using accelerator mass spectrometry (AMS) (Endnotes page 140). This test yielded a dating of the canvas between 1600 and 1680 A.D., the period during which Poussin would have painted it. We are also very fortunate that a relatively recent online publication, curated by Helen Glanville and Claudio Seccarini on the occasion of the 350th anniversary of the death of Nicolas Poussin, gave us an in-depth technical analysis of a wide spectrum of his works. The published information provided us with a sound basis for comparison with your painting."

Mr. Sora said encouragingly, "Very interesting, Mr. Williams, go on!"

Mr. Williams did not heed the interruption and continues, "Our next test involved the use of raking light (Endnotes page 145), which revealed a very smooth painting surface suggestive of paint applied in rather thin layers. It also indicated a few distinctive surface brush-strokes. The craquelure patterns were quite clear and appeared to us as small rectangular blocks."

Here Mr. Givens stepped in, noting that a rectangular-shaped craquelure pointed towards an Italian origin (Endnotes page 119) consistent with Poussin's extended stay and work in Rome. He did comment, however, on the unfortunate observation of surface brushstrokes.

"Why is that unfortunate?" The question comes from Mr. Sora, of course, who is not keen on casting doubts, "one would think it natural to observe surface brushstrokes on a painting."

"You see, Mr. Sora, when oil painting was developed in Southern Europe; artists manipulated the properties of the oil paint to help model surface textures in the motif, leaving no overt evidence of the brush. Indeed, quite obvious brushstrokes are not in keeping with the classicism in French and Italian art of the 17th century, and certainly not with Poussin where typically, very little evidence of brushstrokes is observed in his work," replies Mr. Givens.

Mr. Williams, while silently listening to this exchange, but intent on relating the full findings of his lab continues, "Cross-section analysis (Endnotes page 107) confirmed that the paint is applied in rather thin layers varying in opacity. It also indicated a reddish ground overlaid with a second grey layer. X-ray radiography (XRR) and infrared reflectography (IRR) (Endnotes pages 113 and 105) studies revealed no pentimenti, which are alterations in a painting indicating a change of mind on the part of the artist. The latter observation is not in keeping with the investigative work by Glanville and Seccarini that points to the presence of alterations to the underdrawings in much of Poussin's work. We confirmed this result using infrared transmission (IRT) imaging (Endnotes page 153). This technique reveals the absorption of infrared by all the layers of the painting and generally provides useful additional information to that provided by the conventional infrared reflectographic technique —"

Here Mr. Givens once again interjects, "Your cross-section results are encouraging on two levels, Mr. Williams. First, the thin layers you observed are in keeping with Poussin's technique of using a multiplicity of thin layers of paint. Second, the red-grey double ground you observed is quite interesting. *The Flight into Egypt* was painted around 1657–58, and we know that after 1640 upon Poussin's return to Italy from France, he continued to use a reddish ground covered with a second grey layer and abandoned the common Italian mid-brown ground. I am, however, disappointed that the X-ray radiography and IRT imaging results revealed no pentimenti. We must remember that with a meticulous artist like Poussin, one would expect a careful rendering of the artwork, including several preparatory revisions."

"You are right," replied Mr. Williams, visibly interested in what Mr. Givens has to say, "As I mentioned earlier, most of the paintings analyzed in the Glanville, and Seccarini report *did* display some pentimenti. Assuming, notwithstanding, that Poussin made no alterations to the underdrawing of this particular picture, we proceeded to conduct further tests on the painting. We chose a state-of-the-art, non-invasive technique: proton-induced X-ray emission (PIXE) (Endnotes page 155) for the elementary analysis of the pigments. Their complete identification was carried out by the similarly non-invasive complementary technique of Raman microscopy (Endnotes page 116). We were pleased to find no anachronisms with the pigments of the period and noted the extensive use of the blue ultramarine pigment. The different shades of blue in the painting were obtained through modification of the ultramarine with charcoal and white lead carbonate. The green color also resulted from ultramarine mixed with lead-tin yellow. Such observations are in keeping with Poussin's techniques."

"Indeed, indeed!" Mr. Givens' composure is finally beginning to give, "blue ultramarine had symbolic importance for Poussin, incarnating the divine, and it is said that he mixed it with other pigments and often scattered it throughout many of his pictures. It seems to me, Mr. Williams, that the analysis of the pigments does not exclude the attribution of our painting to this Old Master of the 17th century."

"Well, that might have been so," retorted an almost apologetic Mr. Williams, "unfortunately, however, we were astonished to find out that the foliage on the left of the picture was slightly brownish and upon analysis revealed the use of the copper acetate pigment verdigris. The brownish color probably resulted from a reaction of the copper acetate with the varnish. Although painters most commonly used verdigris in the 15th and 17th centuries, the Glanville and Seccarini publication clearly does not detail a single instance of the use of this pigment by Poussin."

Unwilling to admit defeat, Mr. Sora offered, "Could it have been a later restoration?"

"The same thought crossed our mind, Mr. Sora, and we checked the painting using ultraviolet imaging (Endnotes page 101). That part did not appear darker under UV light, as compared to the rest of the painting. To confirm our result, we had a closer examination by cross-section analysis, which did not give evidence of any retouch."

"Discouraging," Mr. Sora acknowledges.

"Indeed," says Mr. Williams, "we made a final effort to identify a technical feature that would link this painting to any other of Poussin's works in the 1650s. The Glanville and Seccarini publication contains a comparative study of the canvas weave characteristics of a broad spectrum of Poussin's works, including the Lyon version of *The Flight into Egypt*. We came across significant variations in the reported weave types and thread. With so many alternatives, surely, we thought we would find a match for that used in Mr. Katsu's painting. Regrettably, however, our automatic canvas thread count and identification of weave type yielded no match to any of the other reported paintings, including the Lyon version. The original Lyon version was made out of tabby (plain weave), Mr. Katsu's, of twill."

Mr. Sora was impressed by the level of knowledge displayed and all the work carried out by these competent professionals with access to state-of-the-art tools. However, it had become clear to him that things had not gone the way he had hoped. Now thinking of his heavy agenda and the precious time he already devoted to this video conference call, he wanted to bring the matter to a close, "So, Mr. Williams, may I ask you if you have reached any firm conclusions?"

"I hope that Mr. Givens will agree with the verdict of our lab," Mr. Williams obliged, "We believe that this is a high-quality copy of Poussin's work, probably carried out by one of his assistants in his studio. Our dating of the canvas confirms that it is indeed a 17th century creation. The thin layers of applied paint, together with the red and grey double ground, suggest that the painting was executed by someone close to Poussin and familiar with some of his techniques. However, the detection of verdigris in the painting of the foliage, the lack of observed pentimenti, and the detection of some surface brushstrokes make it unlikely that we are before an original."

Mr. Givens regained his composure. Whereas another art historian faced with the possible discovery of a valuable original, only to find his hopes dashed may have revealed at least some dismay, Christopher Givens only allowed himself a measure of perplexity. "Your arguments are quite convincing," he remarked, "I remain mystified nevertheless that the transcription of detail and composition in this painting, together with the interplay of light and shadow is so remarkably close to the original Lyon version!"

## Questions

**Revision questions:**
1. What led to the conclusion that the painting was a copy of Poussin's *The Flight into Egypt*? What indications do we have that the copyist was closely familiar with Poussin's techniques?
2. Give three stylistic characteristics of Nicolas Poussin.

3. How does Poussin give the illusion of relief and space?
4. Were the scientific investigations carried out on this painting using totally non-invasive techniques? Elaborate.
5. What does the use of raking light reveal in a painting?
6. What did the cross-section analysis of the painting reveal? Why is cross-section analysis also needed to confirm or disprove the existence of a retouch?
7. Why did Poussin generally do underdrawings?
8. What is the difference of approach in the infrared transmission (IRT) imaging and the infrared reflectography (IRR) imaging techniques?
9. Why does IRT give us useful additional information as compared to IRR?
10. In Fig. 8.2E (Endnotes page 154), what additional information did the IRT give us that is not visible in the IRR image?
11. What is the principle of proton-induced X-ray emission (PIXE) and what are the advantages of such a method over the conventional X-ray fluorescence (XRF) technique?
12. What is the chemical name for verdigris? Why does it, with the passage of time, acquire a brown in a painting?
13. Why is verdigris considered in this case to be an anachronistic pigment even though it was extensively used in the 17th century?
14. What is the best kind of lamp to be used with IRT? Explain.
15. By what technique was PIXE complemented in the present case?
16. Why is this a particularly challenging case of authentication?

**Exploratory questions:**
1. It is not uncommon for art historians and curators to come to the conviction that pictures long thought to be by Old Masters were in fact the creations of one of the Master's advanced pupils. *The Adoration of the Shepherds*, which since the early 19th century was thought to be by Rembrandt and donated to the National Gallery in London by John Julius Angerstein, Lloyd's chairman between 1790 and 1796 and financial advisor to Prime Minister Pitt, is one

such example. Research this picture and detail why it is the current thought of the National Gallery curators that a pupil of Rembrandt executed it.

2. What is the difference between a twill and a tabby weave? Depict such a difference with relevant sketches.
3. What inconveniences or disadvantages does the PIXE technique have?
4. What is the composition of ultramarine?
5. What pigments do you suggest were used by Poussin to get the red and grey underlayers?
6. Find out on the internet if any of today's famous forgers had forged a Poussin painting.
7. The *Prado Mona Lisa* (1480–1524), a painting of the same subject as Leonardo da Vinci's Masterpiece *Mona Lisa* (1503–1506) held at the Louvre, has been in the permanent collection of the Museo del Prado in Madrid, Spain since 1819, cataloged as an anonymous copy of the *Mona Lisa* from the first quarter of the 16th century. After a 2012 restoration of the *Prado Mona Lisa*, in which the picture was scientifically analyzed, the attribution was changed. Through your research, list the evidence that convinced conservators and curators that the *Prado Mona Lisa* was most likely produced in Leonardo's workshop and at the same time as the *Mona Lisa*.

# Case IX

# One Man's Misery is Another Man's Fortune

## Learning Objectives

To introduce — *on a need-to-know basis*:

1. Multispectral imaging of a painting.
2. Infrared false color.
3. Terahertz imaging and spectroscopy.

An eternity of prodding, jabbing, and violent rattling of Riccardo Agostino's lifeless body and, finally, a whimper. Hunched over her boyfriend's body, Nicoletta Pietro was now eternally grateful and infinitely relieved. Yes, she was sure of it, he was emitting spurts of muffled breathing. She quickly collected herself, brushed away her tears, and checked his faint pulse, then turned her attention to his blue lips and fingers. As she fervently rubbed them back to life, she was talking to Riccardo, herself and thanking God all at the same time and with great ardor.

Nicoletta had walked in the tiny bedsit they shared in Rome's gritty Esquilino neighborhood only minutes earlier to the ghastly horrifying scene. Riccardo was unconscious, huddled in the corner, kneeling over to one side with a belt tied around his arm into a harrowing makeshift tourniquet — and a needle was still stuck into it! This was not the first time, but it was certainly the closest call.

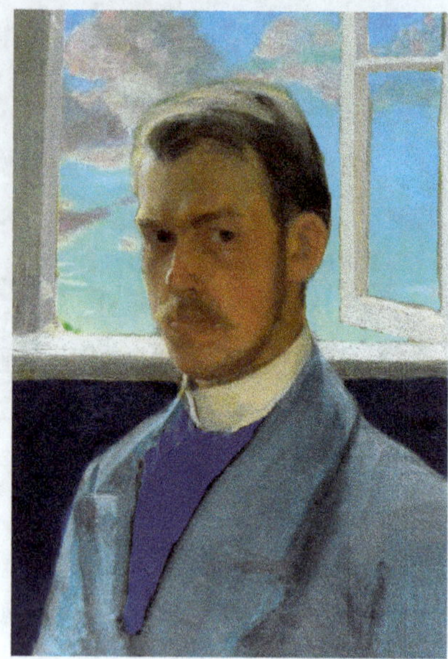

**Fig. 9.1**   Purported Kustodiev self-portrait.

Just as some color returned to Riccardo's face, his body was racked with violent retching, every inch of blood, skin and sinew intent on ridding itself of the deadly opioid. Nicoletta fetched a towel she had dampened in their small washbasin, only to be shoved aside by Riccardo. With the meager strength he could muster, he rose unsteadily and thrashed about, his throat releasing harsh rasps and the occasional scream. As his legs gave in, he sunk onto the floor mattress sulked over, sobbing while looking at the numerous self-harm marks all over his hands and legs. "Let me tell you, Nicoletta, I need to tell you," he said.

In unsteady fits of speech, Riccardo proceeded to tell her of his ordeal to get his latest heroin fix. He rummaged through his mother's flat just as he had done several times before, but no money or jewelry were to be found this time. "I had no choice but to sell the painting. I so needed the money, Nicoletta, I would have died if I hadn't sold it, I would have died." Was there no end to this horror? Nicoletta thought to herself. Riccardo had already told her about this painting (Fig. 9.1) — a signed self portrait of the now famous Russian painter and illustrator Boris Kustodiev — and how precious it had been, first to both of his parents and, after his father's passing, to his mother, who had it hanging in her living room.

Riccardo's father, Severino, and his grandfather Gaspare had both been talented painters. They had also both attended the Royal Academy of Arts, Britain's most prestigious art school and arguably one of the best in the world. After graduating from the Academy, Gaspare had moved to the medieval hilltop village of Anticoli Corrado, about forty kilometers northeast of Rome, which for centuries was home to painters and sculptures.

It was there that Gaspare had met the gifted 29-year-old Boris Mikhailovich Kustodiev. Boris was a recent graduate from the Imperial Academy of Arts in St. Petersburg who was traveling through Europe to widen his artistic horizons and cross-pollinate creative ideas. The year was 1907; the two young artists quickly got on and ended up exchanging self-portraits as a gesture of their hope for a long-lasting friendship. Severino would eventually inherit the self-portrait by Kustodiev along with letters from the Russian artist to his father.

The tears streamed down Riccardo's face as he described to Nicoletta how, painting and letters in hand, he had headed to Via dei Coronari, that historic road in the center of Rome skirted by 15th century Renaissance buildings and home to a plethora of antique dealers selling every kind of collectible. He made his way to Lorenzo Mattia's shop, Lorenzo was an art dealer who often dealt with his late father and, most importantly, knew of his grandfather's friendship with the famous Russian painter.

"You can't imagine how hard I was praying for Lorenzo to be there," Riccardo related to the incredulous Nicoletta. Riccardo was in luck. Lorenzo was in his shop and showed obvious curiosity at the large rectangular object covered in cloth. When Riccardo removed the cloth to reveal a figure that closely resembled Boris Kustodiev, he could have sworn Lorenzo had stopped breathing, but when he handed him the letters and told him of their content, Lorenzo bounced back from his stupor.

"I asked him for 50,000 euros for the painting," Riccardo told Nicoletta.

"What!! Did he actually give you that much money for it?!" Nicoletta immediately snapped back at him.

"You know this is nothing. In 2012 Kustodiev's *The Coachman* sold for 7 million dollars in an auction at Christie's London." Riccardo replied.

"You must be kidding!" said Nicoletta, utterly stupefied.

"No, really, it is true, but alas, I only got 2,000 euros," Riccardo whimpered in shame, then started bawling again. He regained his composure minutes later and went on.

"Lorenzo must have seen the needle marks in my arm and used my urgent need to his advantage. He ranted on about the risk he was taking by buying this painting and how he would have to pay for scientific analysis to authenticate it. He offered me all the money in his drawer, but being the shrewd dealer he is, only gave me the money after he had documented the sale and made me sign the receipt."

At Lorenzo's end, Riccardo had barely turned to leave from *Arte e Antiquariato*, when hopping with excitement, the dealer called to make an appointment at a local university-based lab. It was not the first time that Lorenzo had met with the lab's manager on similar business. Four days later, he entrusted Dr. Anna Marco with the painting, shared the possible attribution to Boris Kustodiev, and requested the lab's authentication services.

Dr. Marco was delighted. She disclosed that there might be a need to consult with an expert connoisseur from the university's Art History Department and that the whole process would probably take a few weeks. Dr. Marco's anxiously awaited call came at the end of that period, along with an invitation to her office. She met him warmly, "Mr. Lorenzo, I shall give you a detailed account of all the tests we have undertaken. There is no doubt that you have acquired a beautiful painting."

Lorenzo felt an apprehension he could not explain. Why should he worry, had he not already an iron-clad provenance back to the artist who created the painting? Could it be a hoax, after all, an invented story with forged documents? With fixed eyes and slightly raised eyebrows, he carefully listened to Dr. Marco's account.

"For a start," she said, "we applied multispectral imaging, the pioneering approach by Dr. Maurizio Seracini, which allows us to observe the painting using a selected range of wavelengths in the electromagnetic spectrum (Endnotes page 157). Our laboratory recently acquired a sophisticated multispectral imaging system (Fig. 9.2), which comprises a special digital camera containing several filters covering the visible to infrared spectral ranges. We were able to identify areas of interest, such as retouches, and made a tentative identification of pigments. A stereomicroscope coupled with that system provided us with additional information (Endnotes page 100), and we also carried out further analytical studies on the pigments and the painting as a whole."

Lorenzo did not expect this level of detail in Dr. Marco's account; maybe it all served to validate his prized acquisition.

"Under visible light and with the aid of the stereomicroscope, we confirmed that the craquelure is natural," explained Dr. Marco, unconcerned that Lorenzo might not understand all the jargon. She then elaborated her account, "Under raking light, the shape of the cracks suggested an Italian origin (Endnotes page 119). The ultraviolet fluorescence (UVF) image (Endnotes page 101) indicated a small dark patch on the collar resulting from what we interpret as a possible retouch in the blue area. To confirm the latter observation, we also used infrared false color (IRFC) photography (Endnotes page 158)."

Lorenzo only picked up on the word retouch, and familiar with its meaning felt some dismay. Why should there be a retouch on this painting? He tried to recall the historical trajectory of the artwork and remembered with a certain amount of relief that both Riccardo's father and grandfather were artists in their own right. Maybe for some reason, *they* were the ones who did the retouching.

Oblivious to Lorenzo's line of thought, Dr. Marco continued, "An important matter is that the IRFC indicated two different colors in the blue area of the collar, confirming the observation by UVF and suggesting the use of two different pigments. The latter's identification could not be carried out by IRFC but needed a more sophisticated technique of analysis as several factors influence the final false-color. To this end, we used commercial equipment for the generation of terahertz rays, and through a study by terahertz spectroscopy (Endnotes page 159), we obtained distinctive spectra that acted as fingerprints for these colorants (one of the spectra is shown in Fig. 9.3). The blue area was found to consist of ultramarine with indigo as a retouch. Both pigments were commercially available during Kustodiev's life, and he used them often. We also looked at the underdrawing by

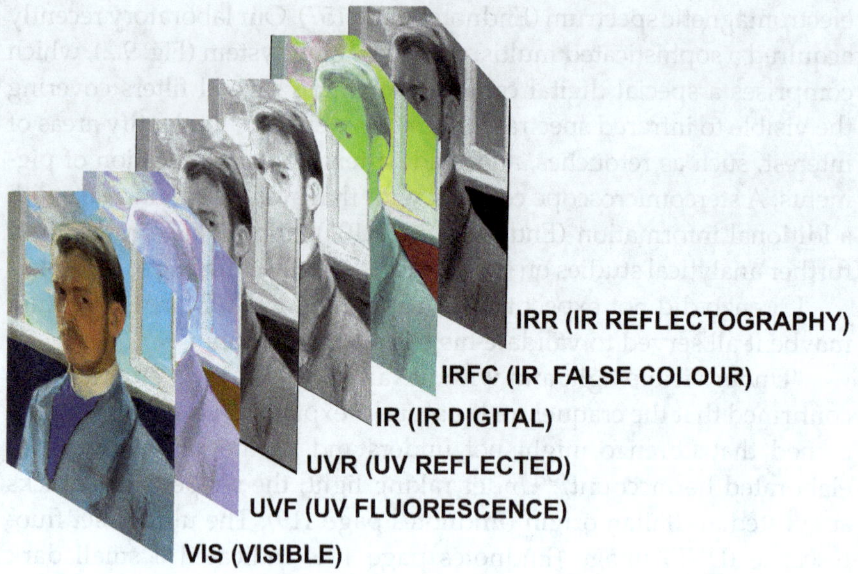


**Fig. 9.2** Multispectral analysis.

infrared reflectography, and identified some pentimenti (Endnotes page 105) in the background."

"That is very reassuring," said Lorenzo. At least to his untrained ears, many of the observations seemed to point towards authenticity. Joy!

"Yes indeed," replied Dr. Marco. She then leaned forward over folded hands and said, "At that point, we thought it wise to ask Dr. Barrow, our expert connoisseur, to inspect the painting. We were pleased to hear his observation that the diverse and carefully selected colors in this painting worked together to unify the image and were very much a Kustodiev characteristic. He observed that the work expressed sensitivity to emotion, mood, and atmosphere, also in keeping with the artist's approach; he referred in particular to Kustodiev's use of light in producing such effects. Most importantly, Dr. Barrow examined the underdrawing to discern features of both spontaneity or inhibition in the production of the work. He found no detectable hesitation suggesting that the painting was probably not a copy."

Now, all Lorenzo wanted to hear was the magical word *authentic*; when would they finally get to it? He tried to patiently listen as Dr. Marco carried on,

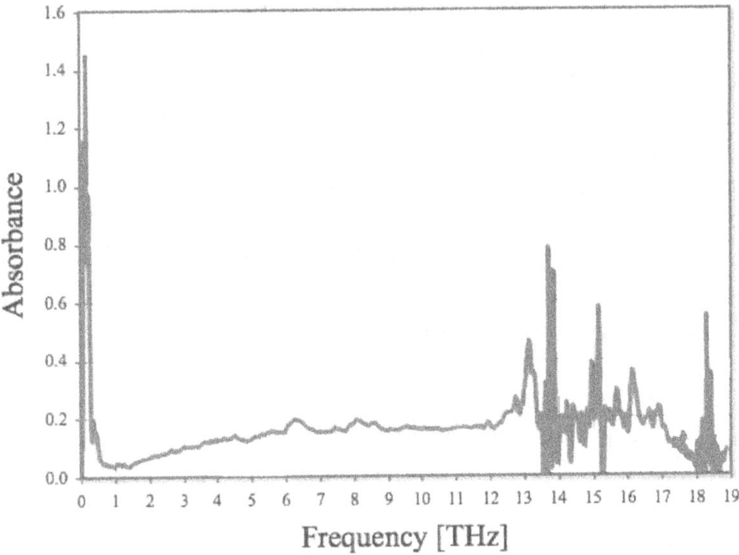



**Fig. 9.3** Terahertz spectrum of indigo.

"Using a technique known as Raman spectroscopy (Endnotes page 116), we identified a subset of pigments all, without exception, available in the 1900s. A cross-section (Endnotes page 107) examination of the signature was the only remaining aspect to complete our technical study. The signature, too, proved to be contemporaneous with the rest of the painting."

Dr. Marco threw her hands up in the air as though they were confetti, "Congratulations, Mr. Lorenzo, you may have hit the jackpot! As far as we can judge, the painting is authentic!"

Mr. Lorenzo could hardly contain a jubilant dance.

## Questions

**Revision questions:**

1. What were the different technical analyses that suggested that the painting was authentic?
2. What is multispectral imaging? What information can be gleaned from each spectral range?

3. Please list the differences and similarities between images produced through UV fluorescence vs. UV reflected techniques, as shown in Fig. 9.2.
4. What are the advantages of terahertz spectroscopy?
5. What is infrared false color (IRFC)? Why is it useful?
6. How can some 'same colored' pigments be separated by infrared false color?
7. Suggest one single observation that would have indicated that the painting was forged.
8. Why was the observation of a retouch in this self-portrait not a very alarming sign?
9. How can the cross-section analysis suggest that the signature is contemporaneous with the rest of the painting? When would it have indicated a later addition?

**Exploratory questions:**
1. Research on the internet six different pigments used by Kustodiev.
2. Why was Kustodiev's style different towards the end of his life.
3. Look at the terahertz database published on the internet and determine which one of the six Kustodiev pigments you found in the above question could have been identified by terahertz spectroscopy.
4. Find out a case where a Kustodiev was found to be a forgery.

# ENDNOTES

# Case I

## 1. Different Layers in a Painting[1]

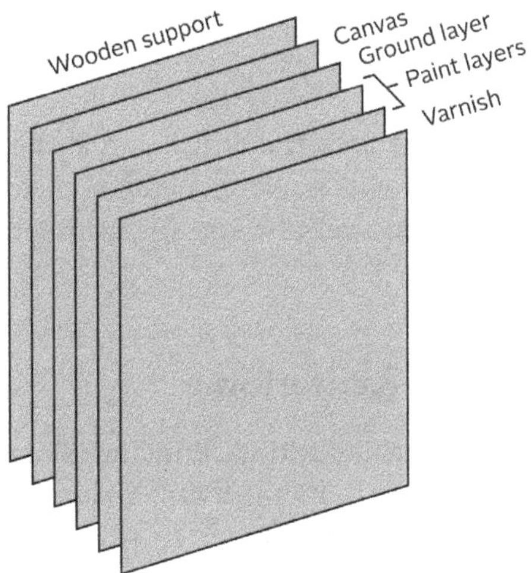



**Fig. 1.1E**  Different layers in a painting.

## 2. Structure of the Atom

An atom is the fundamental building block of all matter; it consists of a central nucleus composed of positively charged protons and neutrons with no charge, and it is surrounded by one or more negatively

---

[1]Paint layers may be more than two.

charged electrons. As the atom is electrically neutral, the number of protons equals the number of electrons.

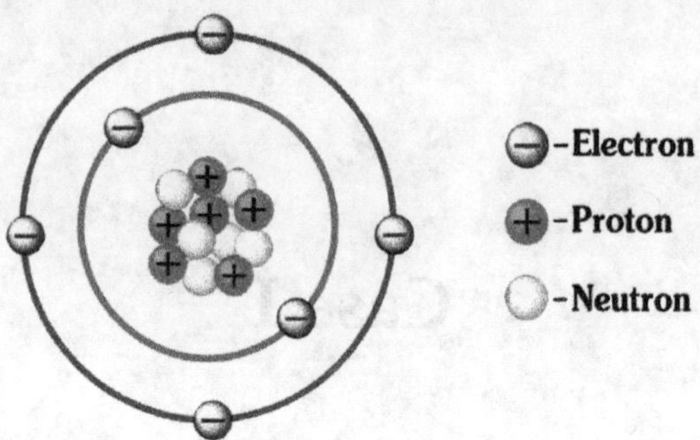



**Fig. 1.2E**   The atom.

## 3. The Element

An element is defined as a material which cannot be broken down or changed into another substance using chemical means. Each element is made up of atoms composed of a specific number of protons, neutrons and electrons.

## 4. Electromagnetic Radiation

It is a form of energy that is around us. It includes radio waves, microwaves, infrared rays, visible light, ultraviolet, X-rays and gamma rays. UV radiation has higher energy (shorter wavelength) than visible light. The most useful UV band in the examination of artworks is around a wavelength of 360 nm.

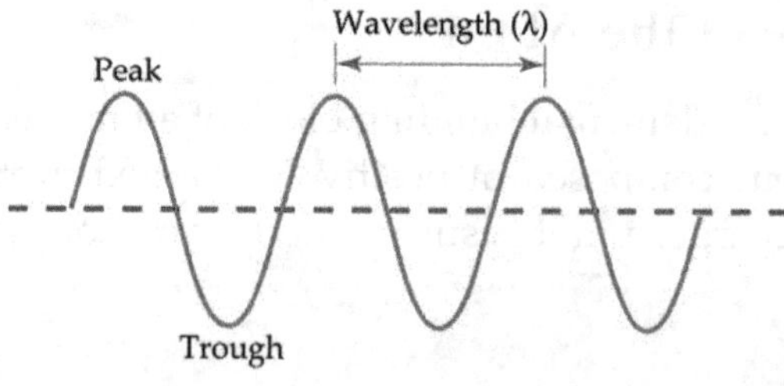



**Fig. 1.3E**   Electromagnetic wave.

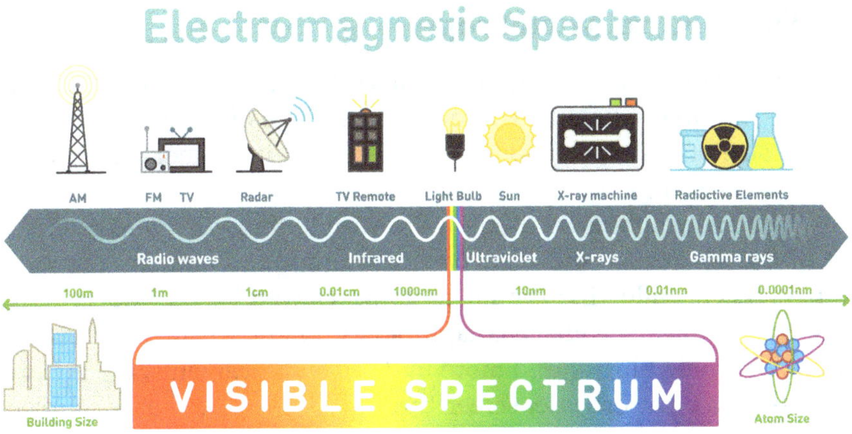

**Fig. 1.4E**   Electromagnetic spectrum.

## 5. Craquelure

Pigments in old paintings acquire, with time, two main properties: they become very hard and shrink slightly, causing the appearance over the paintings of a network of fine cracks, and it is these that are referred to as craquelure. If the pigment layer is reasonably thick, it may take a long time for a forgery in oils to dry to the hardness of old work. So to circumvent the hardness problem and speed up the drying process, the forger may add solvents to the paint or resort to heating to produce artificial cracks.

To produce a convincing craquelure, the forger must also bear in mind that cracks on old paintings become darker, almost black, because of dust and dirt. The forger, therefore, sometimes resorts to the difficult task of mimicking their effect by carefully painting fine black cracks[2] over the surface or by adding ink or dark matter into the produced cracks. However, this technique is generally detected by carefully looking at the surface. A description of craquelure as an authentication tool is given in detail in Endnotes page 119.

---

[2]It is not uncommon in a conservation treatment that restorers, to make their repainting job more realistic, would paint cracks in a retouched area.

## 6. The Optical Microscope

The optical microscope magnifies images of small samples and allows the observation of painted cracks on the surface of a painting as well as the size of the pigments. It is also the ideal instrument to observe tiny speckles of paint.

A beam of light is focused on the sample through a lens referred to as the condenser and then passes through an objective lens to a projector lens, allowing the image to be viewed by the observer. In case of paintings, the image is captured by a light-sensitive camera on a photographic film, and in more up-to-date instruments, the picture is displayed on a computer screen through the use of a charge coupled device (CCD).

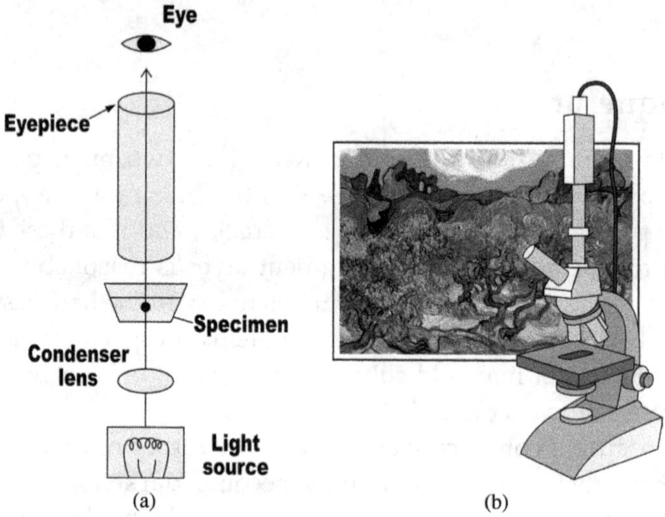


**Fig. 1.5E**   The optical microscope.

## 7. The Stereomicroscope

The stereomicroscope is the best tool to ascertain whether or not the craquelure in a painting is natural.

It makes use of light reflected as opposed to light transmitted from the surface of the painting. This instrument uses two independent

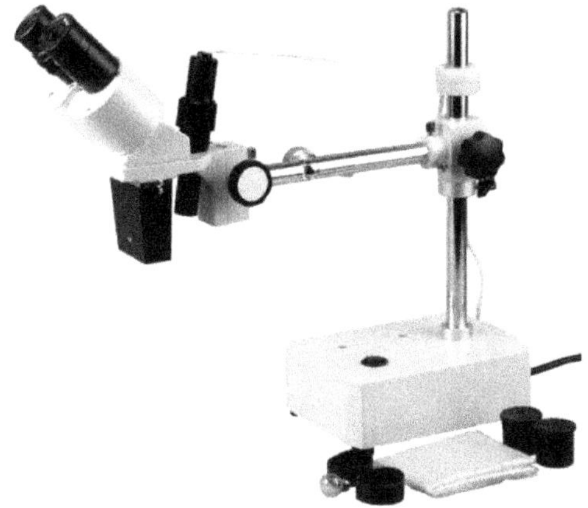

**Fig. 1.6E**   The stereomicroscope with an arm boom.

optical paths with two objectives and eyepieces to provide slightly different viewing angles for the right and left eyes. Fiber optics have also been used in this type of microscope to give high-quality flexible light allowing the examination of the surface of the artwork at a variety of angles.

## 8. Fluorescence

Property associated with the absorption of light of a certain energy and the subsequent emission of light of lower energy.

i.   **UV fluorescence** is quick and inexpensive
UV radiation causes painting materials (i.e., organic dyes, natural resin varnish, some pigments, and some binding materials) to fluoresce.

When UV radiation strikes the surface of the painting, it causes electrons to be promoted to higher energy levels. Their subsequent return to the ground electronic state leads to fluorescence, emitting radiation of lower energy.

UV fluorescence can be studied either by analyzing the visible fluorescent color emitted by the surface of the painting when

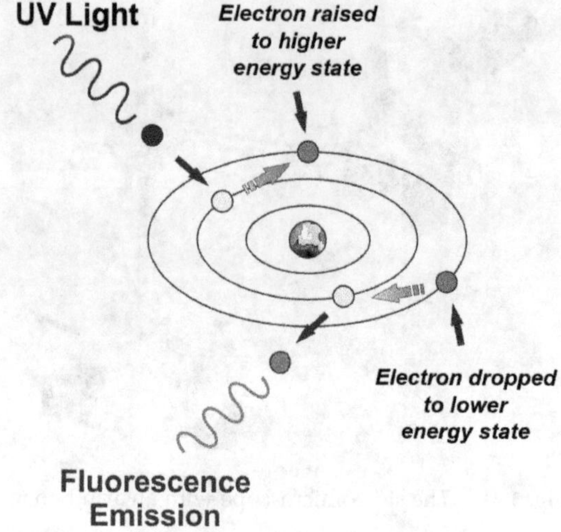


**Fig. 1.7E**    UV fluorescence.

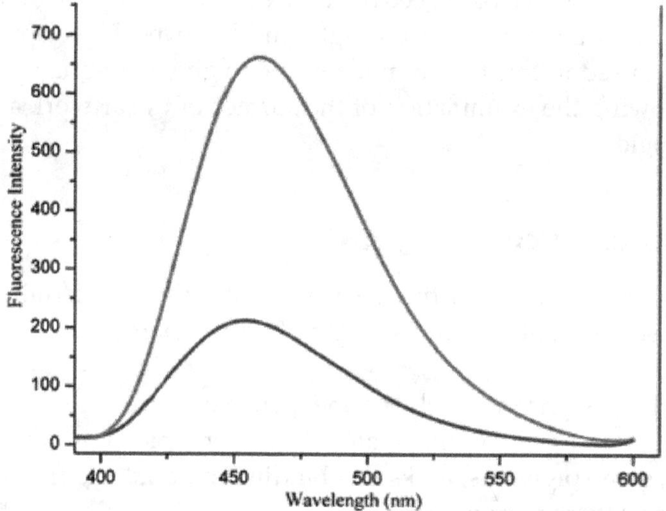


**Fig. 1.8E**    Characteristic spectra of UV-induced visible fluorescence.

subjected to ultraviolet light (Fig. 1.2) or by plotting a fluorescence spectrum due to the absorption of the UV light (Fig. 1.8E).

Traditional natural resin varnishes give off a characteristic greenish-yellow color, whereas a linseed oil varnish gives off mainly blue fluorescence. A natural resin/linseed oil varnish fluoresces at somewhat longer wavelengths and may appear more yellowish than varnishes that only contain resin.

Newer varnish does not fluoresce under ultraviolet light, which sometimes allows for the identification of retouches. The latter are expected to appear as dark patches on the surface of the painting (Fig. 1.2). However, it must be borne in mind that certain pigments fluoresce (e.g., zinc white) and other pigments stimulate fluorescence in the binder (e.g., lead white). Furthermore, other paints may show up dark, but only relative to the more strongly fluorescent areas. UV fluorescence alone is, therefore, sometimes insufficient to confirm the existence of a retouch.

UV-induced visible fluorescence is less selective as a technique as compared to UV-induced infrared fluorescence in the identification of certain pigments such as cadmium yellow and Egyptian blue (fluorescence maxima at ~750nm and ~900nm respectively). The latter can be obtained by using a visible light-blocking filter that halts the detection of any radiation below 715nm.

## ii. X-ray fluorescence

X-rays have much shorter wavelengths and a far greater penetrating power than visible light.

A primary X-ray striking a surface with sufficient energy can eject electrons from inner shells of the atoms and create vacancies there. When this happens, the atom becomes unstable, and electrons from outer shells will tend to fill these vacancies. In so doing, secondary X-rays are emitted at a unique set of lower energies and wavelengths that are characteristic of each element. This is referred to as X-ray fluorescence and allows the determination of the elemental composition of any given sample (Fig. 1.9E).

The results are depicted on a spectrum as a number of peaks, each occurring at a characteristic wavelength (energy) allowing the determination *in situ* and in a non-destructive manner, of the elemental composition of a given painting.

Another approach to X-ray fluorescence is energy dispersive X-ray fluorescence (EDXRF), in which all the elements present in a sample are concurrently detected. The spectrometer incorporates a

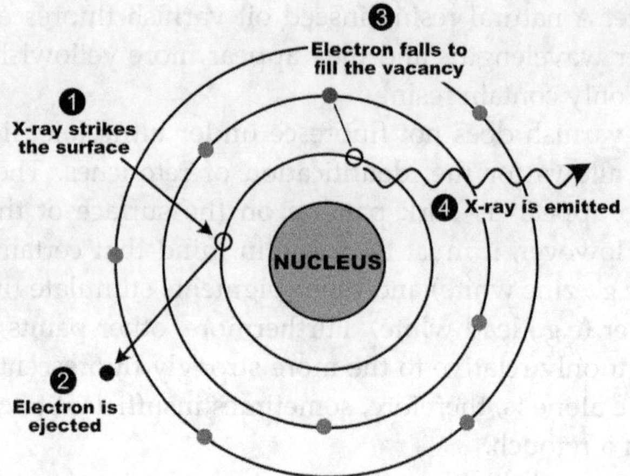


**Fig. 1.9E**   Principle of XRF — characteristic spectra are in Figs. 1.4 and 1.5.

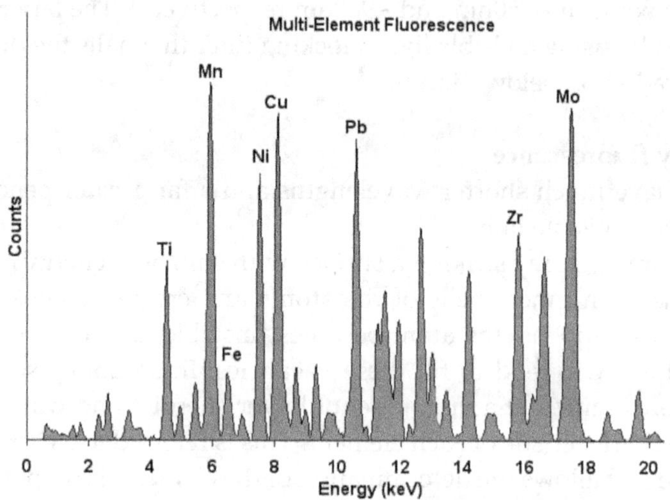


**Fig. 1.10E**   Energy dispersive X-ray fluorescence of a material containing a number of different elements.

particular type of detector that is connected to a multichannel analyzer allowing all the emitted fluorescent radiation to be simultaneously collected and the energies that characterize each element separated (Fig. 1.10E).

# 9. Infrared Reflectography (IRR)

The detection of underdrawings by IRR depends on the fact that infrared light penetrates many paint layers further than visible light, where it might be absorbed by elements in the background. The depth of penetration depends on the paint thickness and its composition. Light is then reflected back into a specially designed sensitive camera revealing details of the underdrawing. Graphite or charcoal, when used as sketching material, absorb infrared light very well and are particularly suited for detection by infrared reflectography (Fig. 1.11E).

An underdrawing may reveal a painting that belongs to a period after the purported painter's death or one that is anachronistic with the artist's stylistic development or may give indications on some of the materials used to prepare it.

Some artists may never use underdrawings in their artwork. Underdrawings can also indicate pentimenti (i.e., initial compositional ideas by the artist, which may subsequently be changed in the finished artwork); these may suggest authenticity.

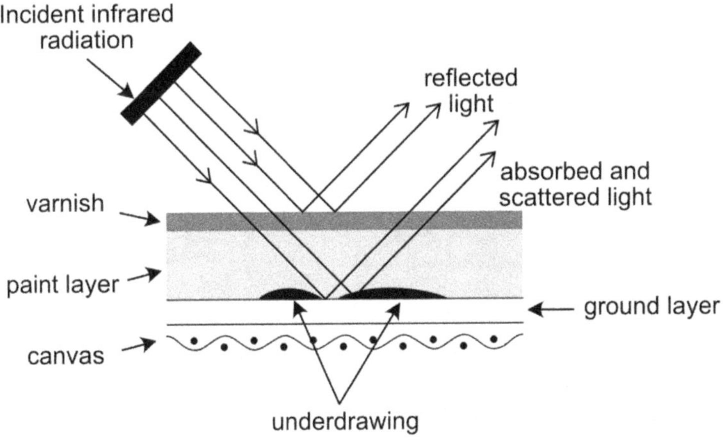


**Fig. 1.11E** Principle of IRR.

# Case II

## 1. Cross-Section Analysis

### i. Preparation of the sample

The study of a cross-section of a painting identifies and characterizes its layered structure. It can provide information about its composition and can be used as a support for other techniques to distinguish pigments and media. It also differentiates between *wet on wet* paint and *wet on dry* paint.

To prepare a cross-section, the following steps are taken:

(a)  A few micrograms of the sample are extracted using a scalpel and new blades, to get a smooth cut through a paint layer.

(b)  The sample is put in a block of polyester resin.[1] The orientation of the latter needs to be in such a manner to ensure that the cross-section is perpendicular to the original paint surface so that it could be adequately studied (Fig. 2.1E (a)).

(c)  Sandpaper is generally used to grind the side of the resin's surface to get a perfectly flat plane close to the sample. Grinding is followed by polishing using a fine micromesh although some analysts think that there is no need to polish after microtoming.

(d)  After grinding and polishing the sample should be visible in the transparent resin and ready for examination (Fig. 2.1E (b)).

---

[1] Polyester resins are a good option as they cut easily into thin slices with a microtome, they set rapidly without heat and polish readily.

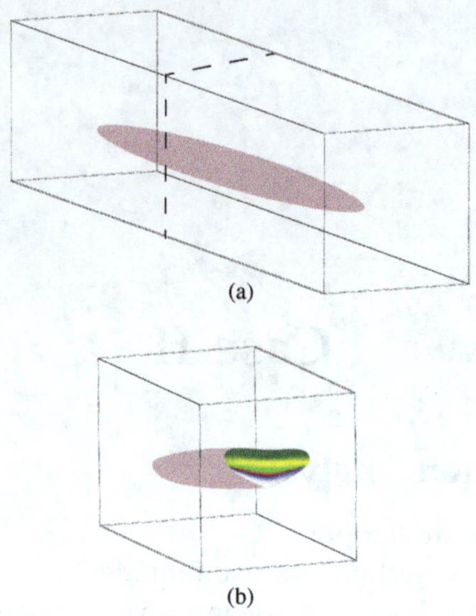

**Fig. 2.1E**   (a) Pigment embedded in a resin. (b) Cross-section.

A cross-section is photographed using a microscope, revealing the color and texture of the stratified layers of the painting.

This technique is also often used in conjunction with Scanning electron microscopy (SEM) and EDXRF. The latter complementary methods offer information on the morphology and composition of the pigments.

Embedded cross-sections can also be examined by a staining technique, through a study of the reaction of binding media on certain dyes.

### ii. Differentiation between wet on wet and wet on dry

In a cross-section, if no separation is observed between the layers and the underneath layer is blended with the upper layer, wet paint was added over wet paint (Fig. 2.2E (a)) obtained under visible light, wet on wet). Wet on wet can be easily recognized because the contact surface between the two paint layers is often wavy and hardly linear. If a clear separation is observed between some of the layers, wet paint was added over dry paint (Fig. 2.2E (b), the micrograph was obtained under visible light and (Fig. 2.2E (b′) under UV light, wet on dry).

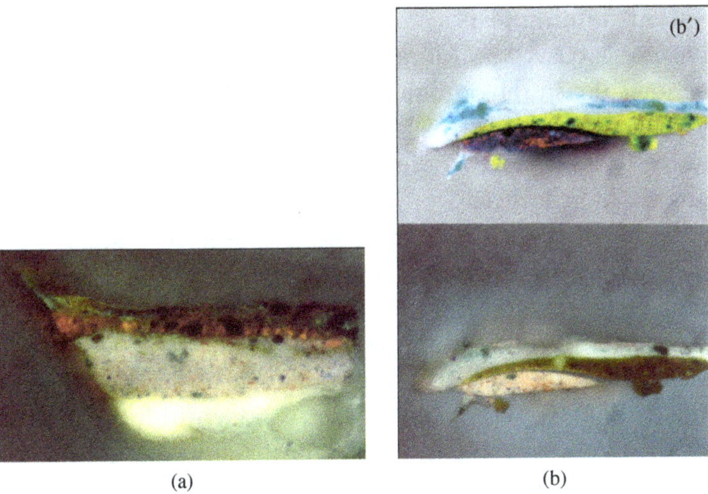

**Fig. 2.2E** Optical micrographs of chips removed from a painting by Claude Monet. (a) No separation and (b and b′) clear separation.

## iii. The staining technique

Some laboratories may not have the financial resources to carry out expensive analyses to identify binders and organic materials in paintings. The staining technique presents a useful alternative, albeit with certain limitations. In applying such an approach, the operator needs to be familiar with the artist's materials and techniques and must be wary of restoration interventions that add new materials.

### Traditional tests

This technique is based on the fact that some dyes form colored compounds with proteins, organic materials, resins, polysaccharides, and oils. A staining test is usually applied to cross-sections, and the accuracy of the method depends on the selectivity of the dye used in the test. For instance, the Amido Black (AB2) dye gives a dark blue color in the presence of aged proteins of animal glue, Oil Red (O) provides an intense red color in the presence of oils and waxes and Fuchsine (S) gives a light pink color with egg yolk.

**Fluorescent staining tests**

These tests are based on fluorescence i.e., the absorption of radiation by the molecules in the organic materials and its re-emission at a longer wavelength.

Fluorochromes refer to the chemicals that absorb such radiation resulting in fluorescence.

Examples of some fluorochrome dyes used for staining binding media in paints are Fluorescein isothiocyanate (FITC) [$\lambda_{exc}$(495nm) and $\lambda_{em}$(525nm)] for proteins, Rhodamine B (RHOB) [$\lambda_{exc}$(540nm) and $\lambda_{em}$(625nm)] for drying oils and fats, both in the visible range. Protein fluorescence is, however, generally obtained in the ultraviolet range by using SYPRO Ruby [$\lambda_{exc}$(250–350nm) and $\lambda_{em}$(610nm)] and SYPRO Orange [$\lambda_{exc}$(250–350nm) and $\lambda_{em}$(570nm)] staining dyes. Fluorescent stains are much more sensitive than visible stains and can detect materials at a lower concentration.

One shortcoming, however, is that such stains may be misleading due to the autofluorescence of the binding media interfering with that of the stain and also due to some fluorescence quenching by some pigments.

## 2. Scanning Electron Microscopy (SEM) and Energy Dispersive X-ray Fluorescence (EDXRF)

The composition of each layer in a cross-section of a painting can be determined using SEM.

In such a microscope, high-energy electrons emitted from a suitable source scan the surface of the sample in a raster scan pattern (see Fig. 2.3E). In such a process, the electrons interact in different ways with the atoms that constitute the sample and provide information on the sample's elemental composition and topography (i.e., the distribution of the particles on the surface).

Some of the incoming electrons will cause X-rays to be generated, and these will act as fingerprints of the elements from which they originated and can be assessed using EDX.

Other electrons in the original beam that bounce back almost in the direction they came are generally referred to as back-scattered

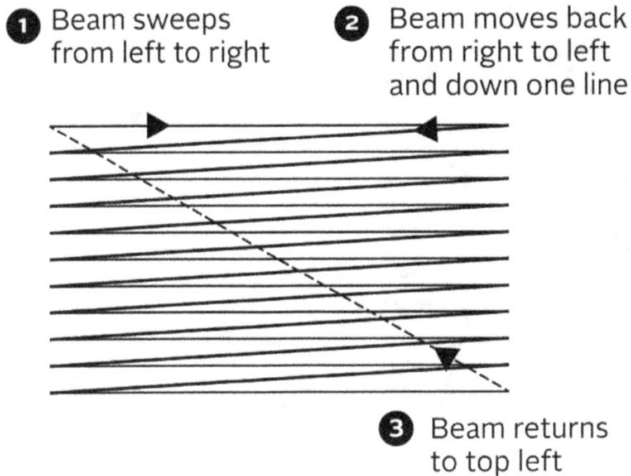


**Fig. 2.3E** A raster scan: The beam sweeps horizontally from left to right, then it is turned off and moves back to the left and down one line and when the beam reaches the bottom right corner it returns to the top left.

electrons. Regions of a different average atomic number are detected using back-scattered particles, which produce a contrast between various areas of varying chemical composition. In the images provided at very high magnification (up to 100,000 times), higher atomic number elements appear brighter than the lower atomic number ones.

In a typical SEM/EDX analysis of a painting, the following sequence of events generally takes place (Fig. 2.4E):

1. The cross-section of the sample is prepared (see Section 1) and observed using a visible light optical microscope to show the layers of paint (see top part of the Fig. 2.4E (b)).
2. The SEM helps in distinguishing between pigment particles and at mapping areas of different chemical composition (see Fig. 2.4E (d)) in preparation for EDX, which identifies elements within small agglomeration of particles; these are generally displayed in a typical spectrum (Fig. 2.4E (c)).

It is worth pointing out that both the back-scattered and EDX signals can be obtained at any point and that rastering builds up a survey over the painting.

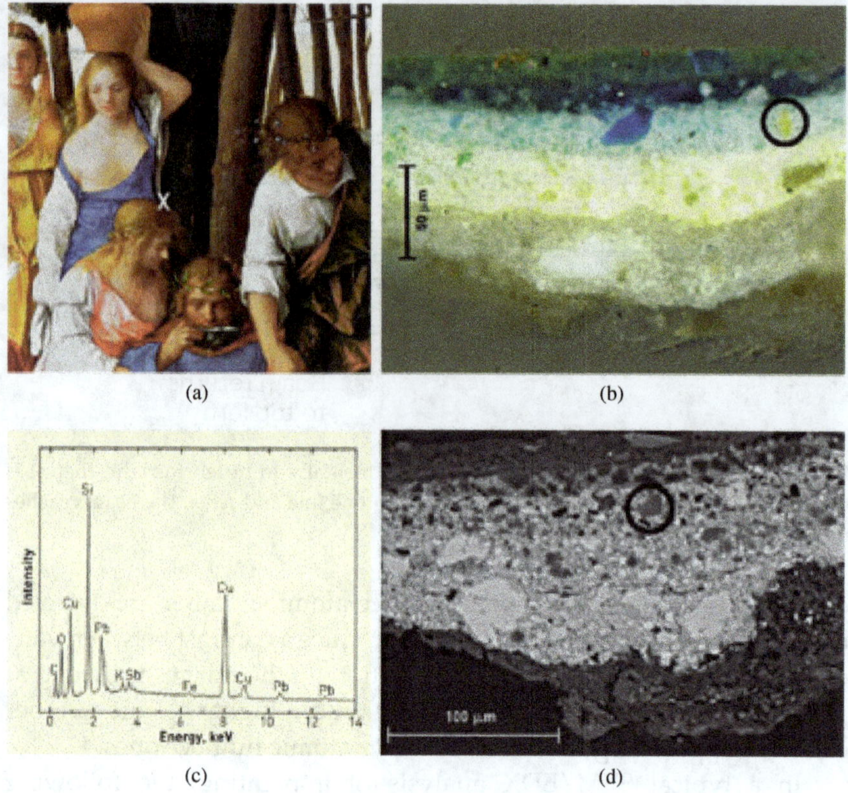

**Fig. 2.4E**    Bellini's *Feast of the Gods*.

This sequence of events can be observed in Fig. 2.4E, representing Bellini's *Feast of the Gods* together with the visible optical micrograph of a cross-section taken from the cross on the image ((b) top right), the back scatter SEM ((d) bottom right) and the elemental composition ((c) bottom left) of the yellow-orange obtained by EDX.

# Case III

## 1. X-ray Radiography (XRR)

X-rays are, in essence, electromagnetic radiation, much like visible light but with much higher energy and greater penetrating power.

They pass easily through the layers of paint, and the extent of penetration depends on the atomic weights of the elements constituting the pigments being X-rayed. Dense elements such as lead in the pigment lead white attenuate X-rays, resulting in bright areas on the radiographs.

Investigation of paintings using X-ray radiography entails the non-destructive imaging of underdrawings. A wealth of information can be obtained regarding the compositional changes made by the artist as well as the execution technique of the work of art.

In conventional radiographic analysis, the paintings are placed horizontally on a supporting table with the X-ray source beneath that table. An X-ray-sensitive film records and displays the images (Fig. 3.1E).

Today, advances in technology have led to a great versatility of approaches in the analysis of works of art.

## 2. X-ray Synchrotron Radiation

If inconclusive imaging results are obtained by means of the conventional X-ray radiography techniques as well as by infrared reflectography, it is sometimes necessary to use much more powerful X-rays for the radiographic analysis.

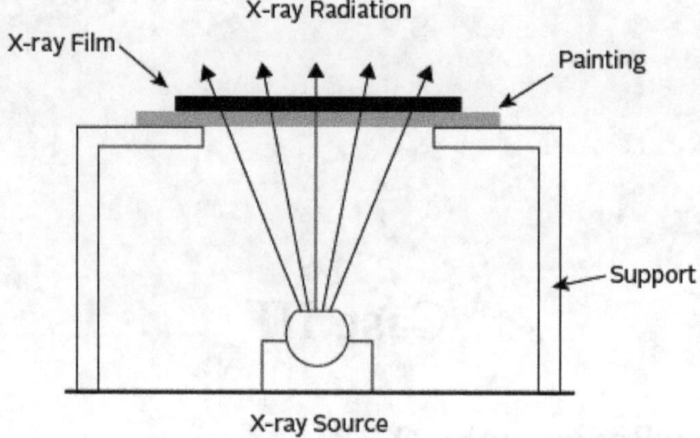



**Fig. 3.1E**   Arrangement for a conventional radiographic analysis.

For that purpose a synchrotron is used, which emits an extremely intense beam of electromagnetic radiation extending from infrared to hard X-ray ranges.

Synchrotron X-rays were discovered in 1947 (Fig. 3.2E), but scientists only began to produce these extremely bright X-rays in the late 1970s, and in the early 1990s the first centralized European Synchrotron Radiation Facility (ESRF) was built. Today, there are numerous synchrotron facilities all over the world.

Such radiation is emitted by electrons accelerating in high vacuum to extremely high velocities close to the speed of light. Powerful magnetic fields cause them to continuously change their direction, allowing them to travel in circular paths. X-rays generated in a synchrotron are several billion times more energetic than those produced by a typical medical X-ray device (Fig. 3.3E).

Synchrotron-produced X-ray images of underdrawings in paintings possess very high resolution and reveal very fine details in the artwork.

Furthermore, minute concentrations of elements can be obtained at sub-microscale resolution and from the smallest of samples by X-ray fluorescence, generated by highly energetic X-rays striking a target. (It will be shown in a later case how synchrotron radiation-based X-ray fluorescence mapping can be applied to visualize hidden paintings).

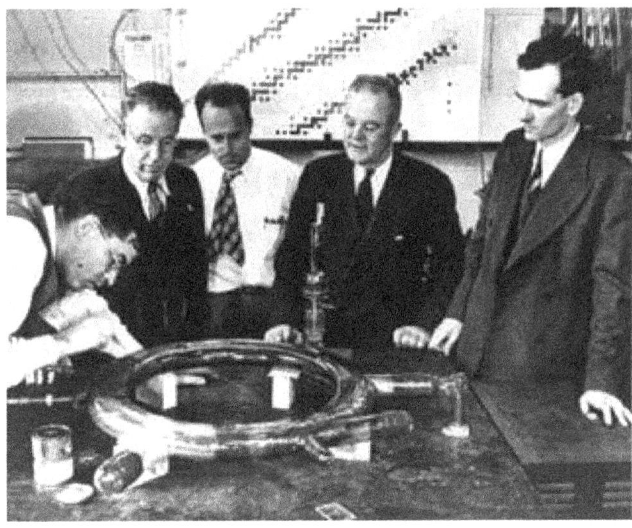

**Fig. 3.2E** Scientists around the vacuum chamber of a 1947 general electric synchrotron (photo courtesy of NSLS, Brookhaven).

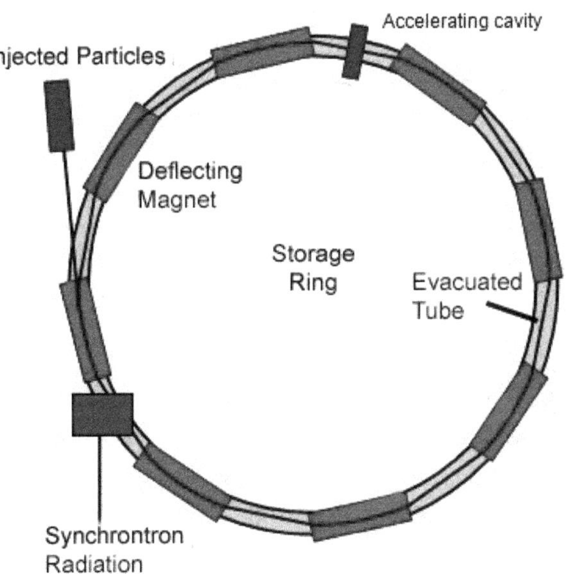


**Fig. 3.3E** A typical synchrotron.

Synchrotrons usually cost millions of dollars to build and span extensive areas, close to the size of a football field. Recently researchers in Palo Alto, California managed to reduce the size of a synchrotron so that it can be contained in a single room. This scaled-down synchrotron allows scientists to undertake high-quality X-ray investigations in their labs.

## 3.  Raman Spectroscopy (RS)

In Raman spectroscopy, a laser beam (generally belonging to the visible region of the electromagnetic spectrum) interacts with the sample.

As a result, light may be totally absorbed, transmitted, reflected, or scattered. Both the type of material and the wavelength of the light affect this interaction (Fig. 3.4E (a)).

Most of the light is generally elastically scattered (i.e., it possesses the same wavelength and energy as the incident light), this process is referred to as a Raleigh scatter (Fig. 3.4E (b)).

Often, a very small fraction of the scattered light would possess a different outgoing wavelength (also frequency and energy) than it had prior to its interaction with matter. This process is referred to as inelastic scattering, and the energy change, which is due to the light interacting with the vibrational modes of the molecules in its path, is called the Raman scattering process.

When the laser beam, *green arrow*, interacts with the molecules in the sample, the energy of the photons is shifted either up, *red arrow,* or down, *blue arrow* (Fig. 3.4E (c)). A sharp filter is used to remove all the elastic scattering, i.e., any radiation received at the same original laser wavelength (or frequency).

This change in energy depends on the frequency of vibration of the molecule so that for light atoms held together with strong bonds the energy change will be more significant than in the case of heavy atoms held together with weak bonds. These vibrations are highly dependent on the exact structure of the molecule and, therefore, comprise a unique vibrational spectrum.

Raman spectroscopy is thus very useful in the identification of organic and inorganic pigments as well as binding media.

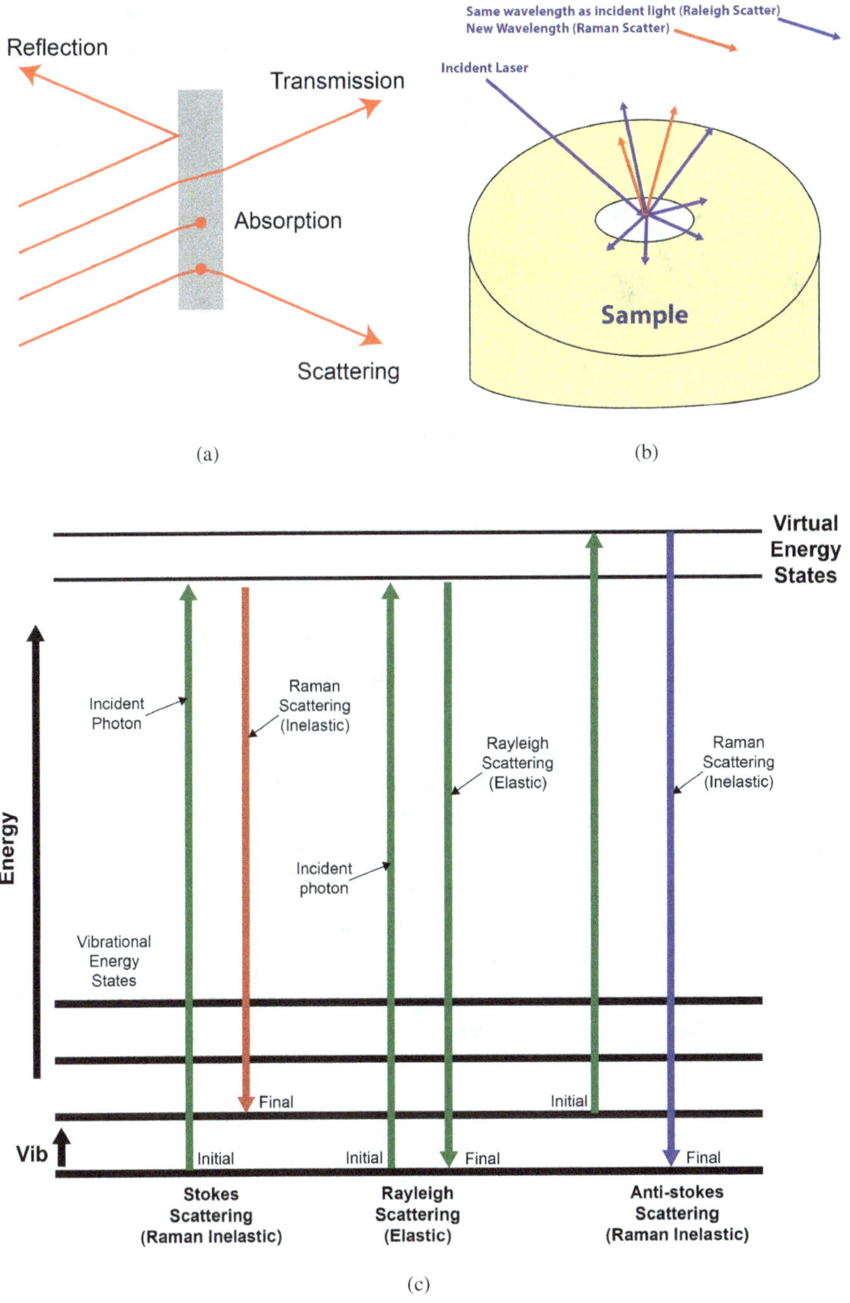


**Fig. 3.4E** Raman and Raleigh scatter.

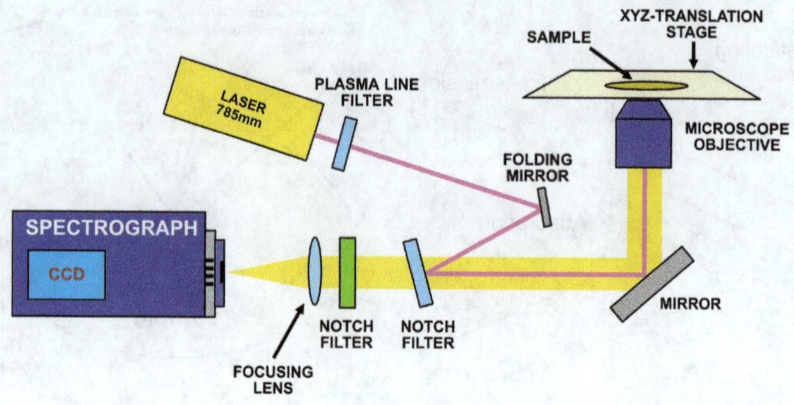


**Fig. 3.5E**   A micro-Raman spectroscope.

This determination is typically achieved through the comparison of the spectrum of an unknown pigment or binder with that of a reference compound. Inorganic pigments are easily identified, as the Raman spectra of classical inorganic compounds are available in the literature, while the spectra of a good number of organic pigments were determined only a decade ago. Raman spectroscopy is thus an ideal tool for substance identification, and the spectrum produced is often referred to as a chemical fingerprint of the molecule.

The recent emergence of micro-Raman spectroscopy has allowed the analysis of artworks in which pigments of less than 1 micrometer in diameter can be identified. The small size of this type of spectroscope (Fig. 3.5E), its non-destructive *in situ* applicability, and ease of transportation give it a comparative advantage over more conventional techniques. It is of particular importance to museums when valuable paintings cannot be transported to laboratories.

# Case IV

## 1. Classification of the Different Types of Craquelure

Natural craquelure is the network of fine cracks formed on painting surfaces as a result of aging and due to the shrinkage of the paint film.

The environmental conditions, the relative concentration of pigment and binder, the action of the drying agent, and the slackening and stretching of the canvas are factors that influence the extent of cracking but not the tendency to crack in a particular pattern.

When an artist uses the same materials put together in a similar fashion, a specific pattern will be produced.

A study of photographed crack patterns taken from 500 paintings was carried out by S. Bucklow at the Hamilton Kerr Institute in Cambridge and A. Varley at the Cambridge University Engineering Department.

The patterns were collected from Italian panels (14th and 15th century), Flemish panels (15th and 16th century), Dutch canvases (17th century), and French canvases (18th century).

The research entailed the statistical classification of cracks and led to a classification of styles or prototypes of craquelure (see Figs. 4.1E (a–d), and examples in Figs. 4.2E and 4.3E).

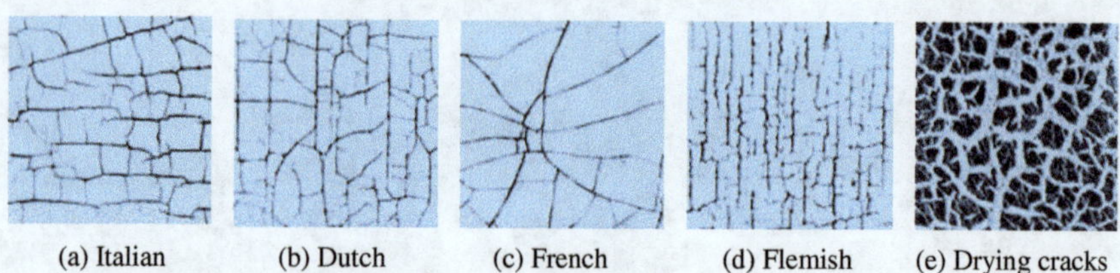

(a) Italian    (b) Dutch    (c) French    (d) Flemish    (e) Drying cracks

**Fig. 4.1E**   Classification of cracks.

Artificial craquelure created by heat or chemical treatments exhibits an unusual maze of tortuous lines Fig. 4.1E (e).

## 2.  Tempera Painting

This word originated from the word "temper," which, when applied to pigments, means tempering them or making them usable by mixing them with a water-soluble binder such as egg yolk, egg white, gum arabic or animal glue.

This was the main medium used in the early Renaissance.

## 3.  Fast Scanning X-ray Fluorescence (XRF) Mapping

The non-invasive X-ray fluorescence mapping technique gives an exciting insight into the inner workings of a painting and to any underlying conceptual modifications.

Such a technique entails, as a start, XRF measurements carried out at a single position, providing an easy tool for pigment discrimination. Next, a complete scan in two dimensions of the image is carried out, and the intensity of the X-ray for each element, (i.e., for each specific energy) is plotted over the entire painting. The result is a single-element X-ray fluorescence intensity map displaying the distribution of a particular metal in the artwork (Fig. 4.4E).

A problem may arise when the artist — in preparing the canvas for re-use — paints over an existing work using, for example, lead paint. In such a case the underlayer is masked by the overlayer of lead white paint. Using conventional XRF would be ineffective in giving any

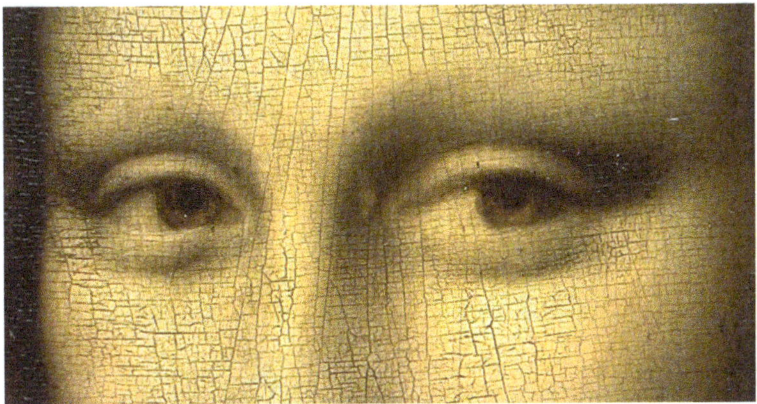

**Fig. 4.2E**   Craquelure with characteristic small Italian rectangular cracks.

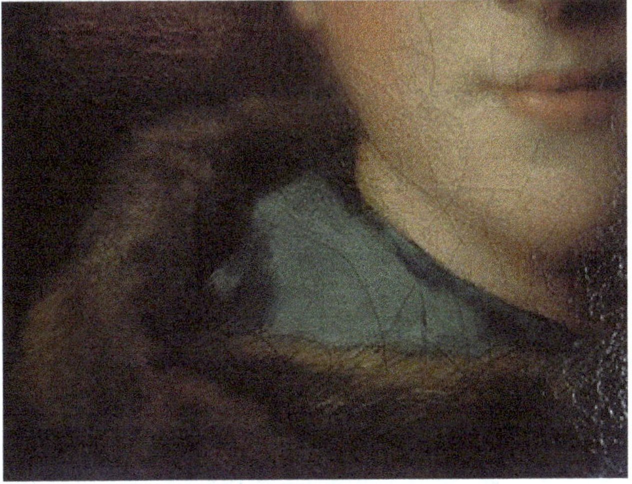

**Fig. 4.3E**   Craquelure with typical French large and somewhat irregular curving cracks.

information on the underlayer as the fluorescence of the lead would mire everything below the overpaint.

To prevent lead fluorescence, a synchrotron X-ray beam is tuned to a lower energy than that needed to remove inner shell electrons from the lead atom (i.e., below the lead edge).

The same X-ray beam could still excite additional elements with absorption edges less than that for lead, such as mercury (Hg), zinc (Zn), cobalt (Co), or iron (Fe).

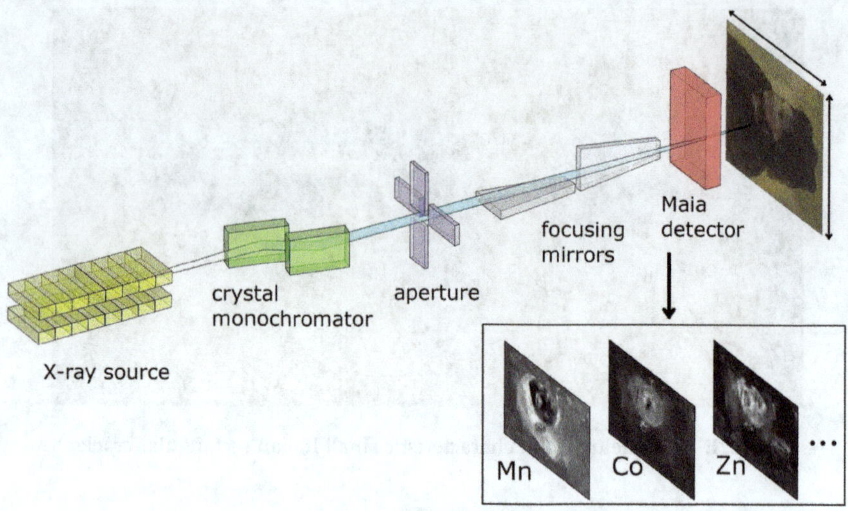


**Fig. 4.4E**　Synchrotron-based scanning X-ray fluorescence microscope.

The images of each element are then digitally combined to give a colored reconstruction of the entire artwork concealed underneath another painting.

X-ray elemental maps allow for the deduction of the different pigments used in a painting. For instance, if iron (Fe) and manganese (Mn) are both located in the hair of a painted figure, then it is probable that umber (a natural mixture of iron and manganese oxides and hydroxides) was used as a pigment, whereas the distribution of cobalt (Co) in a face would suggest cobalt blue as a pigment for establishing flesh tones.

The influence of the overpaint is removed by looking at the image produced by the elastically scattered X-rays (the X-rays that lost no energy in interacting with the painting) for a particular element and subtracting this elastic X-ray image from the obtained image of that element. A much clearer picture of the element is achieved that way as the influence of the overpaint layer is removed.

It is to be noted here that in contrast to other broadband sources, the synchrotron can be tuned to a specific energy.

In the past, one of the major drawbacks of scanning XRF was the slow pixel acquisition rate, leading to a total scan time of several days. Today, the success of this technique is due to the development by scientists at the Brookhaven National Laboratory and Australia's Commonwealth Scientific and Industrial Research Organization (CSIRO) of a special 'Maia' detector that captures details in the artwork with unprecedented speed.

## 4. Principle of Gas Chromatography (GC)

Gas chromatography is an analytical technique that separates and measures the various components of a sample that can be vaporized without decomposition.

The sample solution is injected into the gas chromatograph, transported by a carrier gas (a mobile phase, which is usually helium), and swept into a chromatographic column.

The gaseous compounds subsequently interact with the coating of the column (the stationary phase, which is a microscopic layer of liquid or polymer on an inert solid support) and their separation is based on their elution or removal at different times, referred to as the retention time.

## 5. Mass Spectrometry (MS)

### Atomic number, isotopes, mass number, atomic mass, ions

As mentioned in Endnotes Case I, an atom consists of a central nucleus composed of positively charged protons and neutrons with no charge, surrounded by one or more negatively charged electrons. As the atom is electrically neutral, the number of protons equals the number of electrons (Fig. 4.5E).

(a) **Atomic number**
    The number of protons is called the **atomic number** and determines the identity of the element we are looking at. (Carbon atoms contain six protons, whereas oxygen atoms contain 8 protons).

(b) **Mass number**
    The **mass number** of an element is the total number of protons and neutrons. (A calcium atom has 20 protons and 20 neutrons in its atomic nucleus, so the mass number is 40).

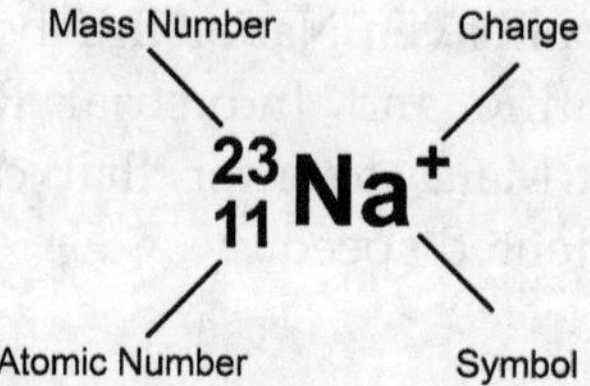



**Fig. 4.5E**   Typical representation of a sodium ion.

(c) **Isotopes**

The number of neutrons in an atom can vary. Forms of the same element that differ only in their number of neutrons are called **isotopes**. (Carbon-14 with 6 protons and 8 neutrons in its nucleus is an isotope of Carbon-12 with 6 protons and 6 neutrons in its nucleus).

(d) **Atomic mass**

The **atomic mass** is closely related to the mass number and is expressed in atomic mass units (amu). Carbon has an atomic mass of 12 amu with a small deviation from its mass number (Fig. 1.2E and some practical examples in Figs. 4.5E and 4.6E).

(e) **Ions**

Ions are produced by giving electrons to an atom or molecule, resulting in a **negatively charged ion**, or by taking electrons away from an atom or molecule, producing a **positively charged ion**. (The oxygen ion $O^{-2}$ has 8 protons in its nucleus and 10 surrounding electrons, whereas the sodium ion Na+ has 11 protons in its nucleus and 10 surrounding electrons).

An ion is typically represented as shown in Fig. 4.5E, some examples are listed in Fig. 4.7E.


## Principle of Mass Spectrometry

Mass spectrometry determines the mass of atoms or molecules by measuring the mass-to-charge ratio of their ions.

**Practical examples**

| Complete Symbol | Name | Number of Protons | Number of Neutrons | Number of Electrons | Atomic Number | Mass Number |
|---|---|---|---|---|---|---|
| $^{12}_{6}C$ | Carbon-12 | 6 | 6 | 6 | 6 | 12 |
| $^{1}_{1}H$ | Hydrogen-1 | 1 | 0 | 1 | 1 | 1 |
| $^{36}_{16}S$ | Sulfur-36 | 16 | 20 | 16 | 16 | 36 |
| $^{15}_{7}N$ | Nitrogen-15 | 7 | 8 | 7 | 7 | 15 |
| $^{46}_{20}CA$ | Calcium-46 | 20 | 26 | 20 | 20 | 46 |

**Fig. 4.6E** Number of protons, neutrons, and electrons in the case of atoms.

| Ions | Protons | Neutrons | Electrons |
|---|---|---|---|
| Carbon ($C^{3-}$) | 6 | 6 | 9 |
| Hydrogen ($H^{1+}$) | 1 | 0 | 0 |
| Oxygen ($O^{2-}$) | 8 | 8 | 10 |
| Lithium ($Li^{3+}$) | 3 | 4 | 0 |
| Sodium ($Na^{1-}$) | 11 | 12 | 12 |

**Fig. 4.7E** Number of protons, neutrons and electrons in the case of ions (Mass number of oxygen (O) is 16, lithium (Li) is 7, and sodium (Na) is 23).

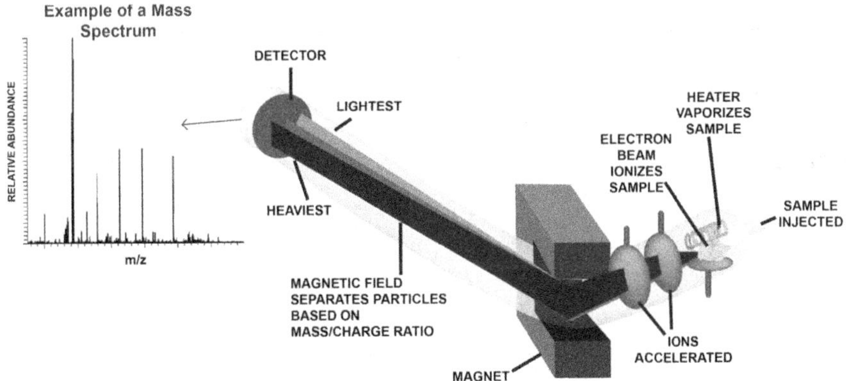


**Fig. 4.8E** Typical ion impact mass spectrometer.

In an electron impact mass spectrometer a heater vaporizes the injected sample, which is ionized by an electron beam in an ionization chamber. Once produced, the ions are accelerated by an external electric field and are deflected according to their masses and charge by a magnetic field (Fig. 4.8E).

The collection of ions could be in the form of simple atomic ions, molecular ions, or, if the latter are too unstable, they can fragment into smaller ions.

The amount of deflection will depend on the mass of the ion and is greatest for the lighter ions and for those with the highest charge.

The results are displayed on a chart referred to as a *spectrum*, and the atoms or molecules in the sample are distinguished through comparison of their determined masses with known masses.

The atoms or molecules in the sample can be identified by correlating known masses of a molecule to identified masses in the spectrum.

## 6. Gas Chromatography in Conjunction with Mass Spectrometry (GC/MS)

Gas chromatography-mass spectrometry (GC/MS) consists of a gas chromatograph (GC) coupled to a mass spectrometer (MS).

After eluting, compounds are converted to ions and pass through a mass analyzer (a filter), which separates the positively charged ions according to mass. The ions then enter a detector that sends information to a computer, which then records all the data produced (Fig. 4.9E).

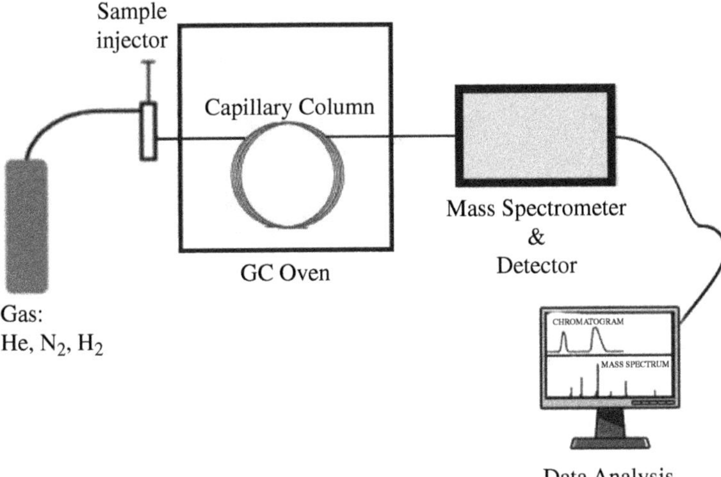


**Fig. 4.9E**   Gas chromatograph coupled to a mass spectrometer.

# Case V

## 1. Polarized Light Microscopy to the Analysis of Paintings

### Usability

The polarized light microscope (Fig. 5.1E) is particularly useful to photograph and observe optically anisotropic pigments (those having unequal physical properties such as refractive index, viscosity, etc. in different directions). It is a contrast-enhancing technique that greatly improves the quality of the image.

Because of its high resolution, it can give greater information than the naked eye or the stereomicroscope and can help identify a single particle among a large number of different ones.

By using the polarized light microscope (PLM), with magnification ranging from 100X to 1000X, additional information can be gleaned on the particle size, color and crystal shape of the pigment as well as on some surface textural characteristics of the painting.

If the sample represents a cross-section, the thickness and order of the layers can be accurately determined with the PLM. Furthermore, it can sometimes help in assessing whether a particular patch in an area of paint is due to an overpaint or is part of the original painting.

In some cases, a ground may be of a uniform color under the stereomicroscope but it can be shown on closer look with the PLM that it is formed of differently colored pigments.

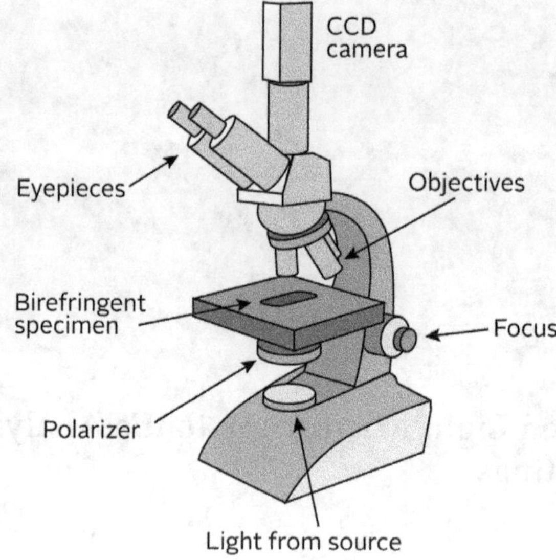


**Fig. 5.1E**   The polarized light microscope.

## Principle of the method

Under normal sunlight, light waves are transmitted in planes that are perpendicular to the direction of propagation. They are said to be plane polarized when they are restricted to one plane (Fig. 5.2E).

In a PLM, light from a source enters from below the sample and passes through a polarizing filter, called a 'polarizer,' before reaching the sample.

If the latter is birefringent (has two refractive indexes that are perpendicular to each other), two polarized and mutually perpendicular wave components will be produced. These are then recombined by a second polarizer or analyzer, which is placed above the sample (Fig. 5.2E).

Image contrast arises from the constructive interference of these light components when they pass through the analyzer. The birefringent samples will appear with a characteristic bright color against a dark background (Fig. 5.3E).

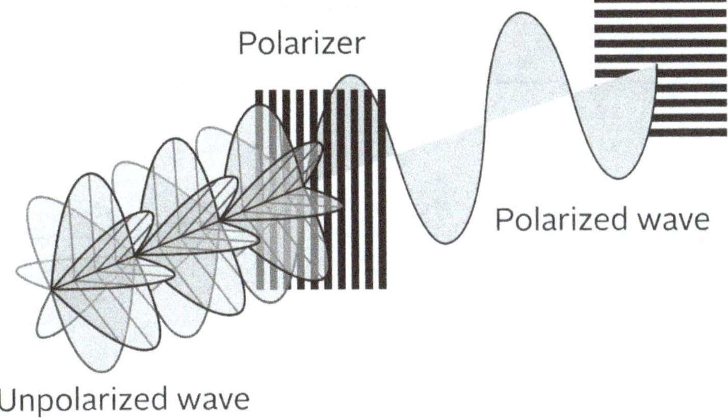



**Fig 5.2E**   Polarizer and polarized wave.

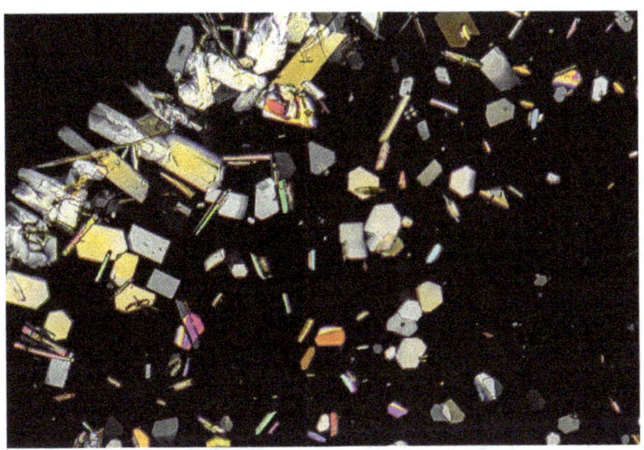

**Fig. 5.3E**   Polarized microscopy image of anisotropic microcrystals.

Wave interference refers to the phenomenon that occurs when two waves meet while traveling along the same medium.

The two types of wave interference are constructive and destructive. Constructive interference arises when the wave amplitudes reinforce each other, resulting in a wave that has greater amplitude. Destructive interference occurs when the crest of one wave meets the

     *Technical Art History*

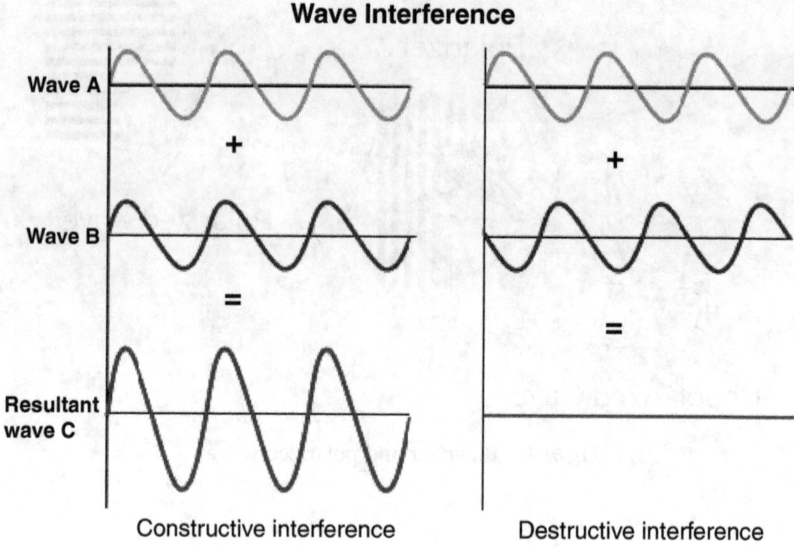


**Fig. 5.4E**   Constructive and destructive interference.

troughs of another, resulting in waves that completely cancel each other out (Fig. 5.4E).

## 2. Infrared Spectroscopy (IR), Fourier Transform Infrared Spectroscopy (FTIR) and Micro-FTIR ($\mu$FTIR)

Infrared spectroscopy is a widely used technique for the identification of organic and inorganic pigments in paintings. Infrared light is an invisible radiation that lies on the low-energy side of the electromagnetic spectrum with wavelengths longer than ordinary light. The energy associated with this part of the spectrum is insufficient to excite electrons but can cause the bonds in molecules to vibrate.

These bonds can be compared to springs than can be stretched or bent (i.e., vibrate), and the frequencies of vibration will depend on the nature of the atoms in the molecule and the strength of the springs (Fig. 5.5E).

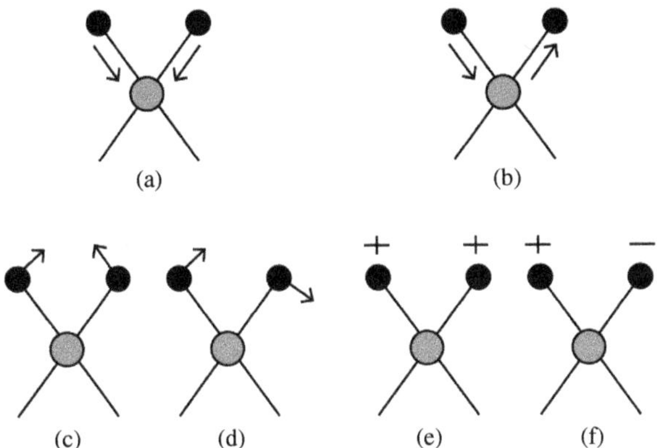

**Fig. 5.5E.** Different vibrational modes in a molecule. (a) Symmetric stretch, (b) asymmetric stretch, (c) scissoring (in-plane bending), (d) rocking (in-plane bending), (e) wagging (out of plane bending), (f) twisting (out of plane bending), + = above the plane, – = below the plane.

Consequently, when infrared light interacts with the sample, part of it is absorbed or transmitted at frequencies that are characteristic of the molecules under investigation. The result is an IR spectrum (plot of the intensity of the absorbed or transmitted radiation against its wavelength) which acts as a fingerprint of the molecule under investigation.

## Instruments

The original infrared spectroscopy instruments relied on a dispersive component (a prism or a grating monochromator) to separate the particular frequencies (or energies) emitted from the infrared source. A detector was then used to measure each energy that passed through the sample at a definite frequency and displayed it as a spectrum. The main problem of this type of instrument was the slowness of the scanning process.

A major technological breakthrough came through the development of FTIR, which allowed the simultaneous measurement of all the transmitted infrared frequencies through the use of an interferometer (consisting of two highly polished mirrors). By means of a mathematical

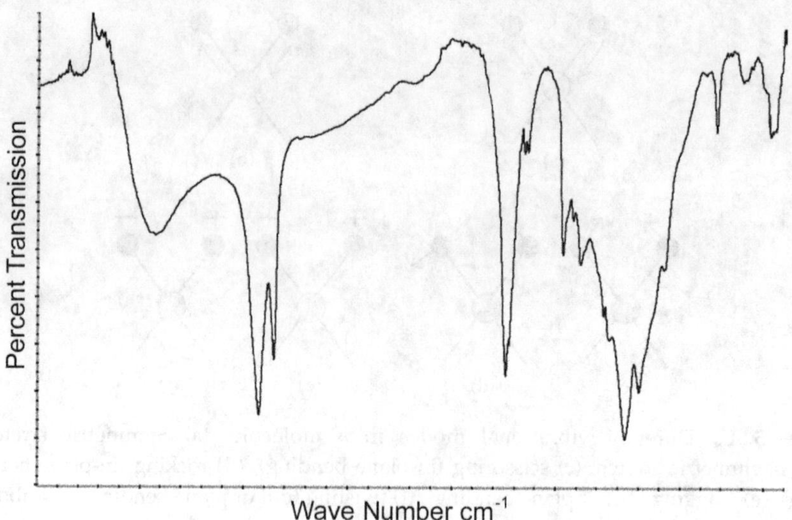



**Fig. 5.6E**   FTIR of cadmium yellow.

process referred to as the Fourier Transform developed by the French mathematician Joseph Fourier, the output could be converted into a spectrum. This technique allowed for a much more rapid scanning process. Example of the FTIR spectrum of cadmium yellow is shown in Fig. 5.6E.

In 1981, an optical microscope was incorporated in the FTIR spectrometer (at McCrone Associates, Inc.) that allowed the analysis of minute samples (of the order of picograms or less) allowing the examination of paintings by a non-destructive approach.

## 3. Pyrolysis-Gas Chromatography-Mass Spectrometry (Py-GC-MS)

Contemporary artists often use organic pigments and synthetic binders. These are challenging to analyze because of their high molecular weight, nonvolatility and low solubility in solvents.

Such challenges have been overcome by the technique of Py-GC-MS.

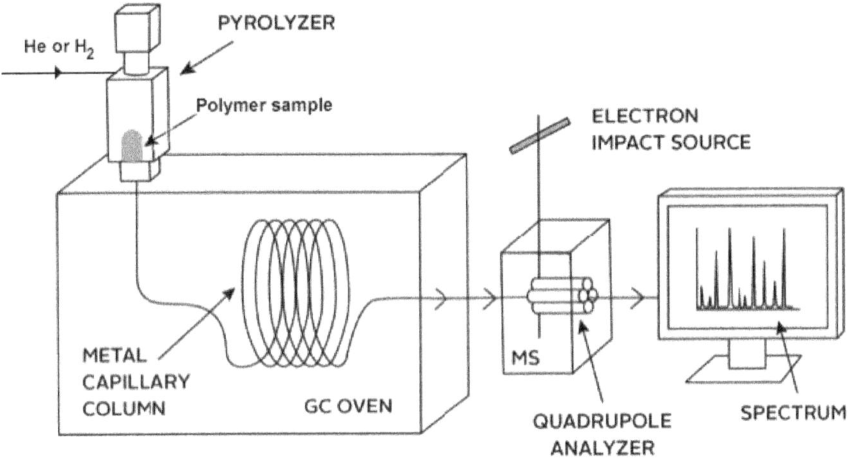


**Fig. 5.7E**   Instrument for pyrolysis-gas chromatography-mass spectrometry.

In a pyrolyzer, materials are heated for a few seconds at around 600°C in a quartz chamber which is under vacuum or under an inert atmosphere (Fig. 5.7E). As a result, large molecules cleave at their weakest bonds forming more volatile fragments that are smaller in size. This mixture of smaller fragments is then swept into the chromatographic column of the GC followed by analysis in the mass spectrometer (GC/MS) (Endnotes page 123).

# Case VI

## 1. Dendrochronology

Dendrochronology has become important to art historians in the dating of panel paintings.

The technique is based on the fact that some species of trees produce growth rings during annual growing seasons. That is as a tree grows, a new growth or tree-ring is produced — typically one ring per year — under the tree's bark (Fig. 6.1E). These growth rings vary in widths based on several factors; the most important among these is the amount of available precipitation and the prevailing temperatures.

Wider rings, therefore, indicate a favorable year for growth and narrower rings indicate an unfavorable year.

Older and younger trees of the same species, of known age and from the same area, are used to create long, chronological growth sequences by overlapping their tree rings, so a long series of rings can be seen. The growth ring pattern of a tree of unknown age is then matched to the reference chronological growth sequences to provide the accurate felling date of the tree.

Dendrochronology has some limitations, however, as it can only be used effectively on trees grown in places with distinct seasons as they produce the distinct tree rings essential for the method to work. This method can also be used when a master reference sequence of the same tree type, and ideally from the same location, as the type to be dated is in existence.

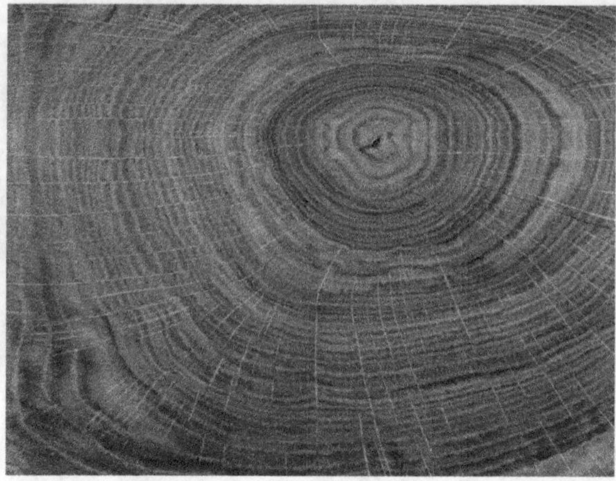

**Fig. 6.1E**    Tree rings (Oak).

In addition, as this technique relies on growth ring patterns, it may only be used for tree species that exhibit consistency in the production of such rings. Oak is the most reliable tree type for this method of dating as its tree ring formation is very consistent, and cases of missing annual growth rings are extremely rare. On the other hand, poplar, elm, and beech typically contain distorted, erratic rings and in some cases missing rings due to fast growth, making applying this dating technique difficult and unreliable for these tree species.

If the sapwood is present in a wooden plank that displays all its rings (or at least rings up to the pith), the possibility of obtaining an exact date for the felling of the tree from which the wooden plank was obtained increases. This is because the sapwood is the last layer of wood right before the phloem and bark, and it contains the latest created growth rings. If the sapwood is missing — as is often the case in trimmed wooden planks used for paintings — it is still possible to make an estimate of the felling time of the tree that produced the plank. To make such an estimate, statistics are used to obtain an estimate of how many growth rings must have been in the sapwood depending on the type and age of the tree (the number of rings determined) as well as its geographic area.

Reliable dating can be obtained with 50–100 rings. Measurement of the width of the ring can be carried out manually using a magnifying glass. For a more precise result, tree-ring series are measured under a x20 stereomicroscope to an accuracy of 0.01mm using a traveling stage based on a microcomputer. Sophisticated measurements have also been carried out by computer tomography (CT). (Computer tomography is an imaging procedure that uses special X-ray equipment to produce detailed pictures).

## 2. Radiocarbon Dating (RD)

Radioactive carbon-14 ($^{14}C$) is continuously formed in the upper atmosphere due to cosmic rays colliding with atoms in the upper atmosphere and producing energetic neutrons. In turn, these atmospheric neutrons interact with atmospheric nitrogen-14 ($^{14}N$), converting it into carbon-14 ($^{14}C$).

This $^{14}C$ constitutes a minuscule proportion of atmospheric carbon compared to the considerably more abundant carbon isotopes carbon-12 ($^{12}C$) and carbon-13 ($^{13}C$) (~1 in a trillion). All carbon isotopes combine with atmospheric oxygen atoms to form carbon dioxide molecules ($CO_2$).

While most of this carbon dioxide enters the oceans, terrestrial plants consume some of the $CO_2$ through the process of photosynthesis, fixing the carbon in their tissues. Animals that eat these plants in turn also fix the plant's carbon in their tissues. As long as the plant or animal is alive, it continually rejuvenates the carbon in its tissues, exchanging old carbon for newly consumed carbon (Fig. 6.2E).

The ratio of $^{14}C$ to all other isotopes of carbon is stable throughout the lifetime of living organisms; however, when an organism dies, it cannot rejuvenate the carbon in its body. The $^{14}C$ starts decaying at a constant rate without being replenished, and the standard ratios of $^{14}C/^{12}C$ and $^{14}C/^{13}C$ at death are changed as a result of such decay. Through a comparison of these ratios in modern samples to those in the dead organism, it is possible to determine the age of the sample. In other words, this will allow us to estimate the amount of time elapsed between the organism's death and the present. However, radiocarbon dating can be applied to any organic material.

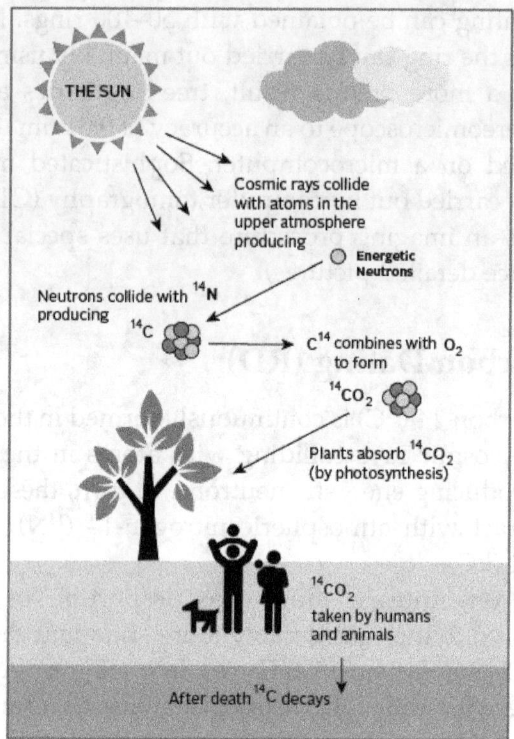



**Fig. 6.2E**  Formation and decay of $^{14}C$.

This technique has, however, a practical limit in that it can only be applied to objects that are no older than 50,000 to 60,000 years. The reason being that the older the object, the less $^{14}C$ there is to carry out measurements and thus at that age limit of 50 to 60 thousand years the amount of $^{14}C$ remaining in the object is just at or below the instrumental limit of detection for this technique.

## 3.  Accelerator Mass Spectrometry (AMS)

AMS is used to detect long-lived radioisotopes like $^{14}C$ and enables the analysis of samples of the order of 1–2mg.

It is the method of choice for the analysis of $^{14}C$ as it has much higher precision than the standard radiometric method that necessitates about 10mg of sample. It is also a much more rapid procedure

**Separation of carbon isotopes**

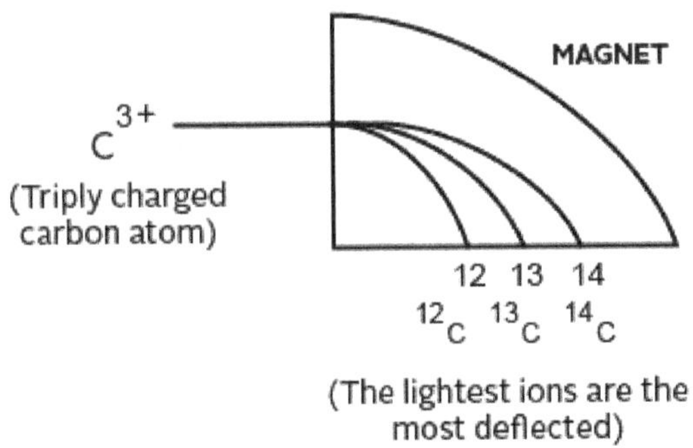



**Fig. 6.3E**  Principle of mass spectrometry of carbon isotopes.

that is carried out in a few hours as compared to one or two days in a conventional radiometric technique.

Samples are initially changed into a solid graphite form, which by a number of steps, will eventually be converted to a triply charged carbon ion and accelerated to extraordinarily high kinetic energies (Fig. 6.3E). The latter allows the elimination of isobaric interference (atomic and molecular isobars with $^{14}C$ like $^{14}N$ and $^{13}CH-$, respectively).

## 4. Laser Ablation Multiple Collector Inductively Coupled-Mass Spectrometry (LA-MC-ICP-MS)

### i. Isotopes (revisited), radioisotopes, atomic isobars, and molecular isobars

**Isotopes**, as we have already seen , are atoms of an element that have the same atomic number but a different mass number; that is, they have the same number of protons and, therefore, similar chemical properties, but a different number of neutrons.

**Radioisotopes** are unstable isotopes as their nuclei spontaneously decay and emit energy in the form of radiation to attain a stable form.

**Atomic isobars** are atoms of different elements with the same mass number but different atomic number (or number of protons) e.g., $^{14}N$ and $^{14}C$.

**Molecular isobars** of $^{14}C$. These are molecules such as $^{13}CH-$ and $^{12}CH_2-$, which have the same mass as $^{14}C$.

## ii. The technique

LA-MC-ICP-MS allows for the elemental analysis of the artist's paints down to parts per billion (ppb) and can be performed on solid samples without prior sample preparation. It is ideal for the analysis of radioisotopes.

In this technique, a laser beam — a very intense source of light energy — strikes the sample to be analyzed, in our case, a spot on the painting containing the pigment to be examined, causing minute amounts of the sample to be transformed into a fine spray as an aerosol. The process of removing material from a solid surface by irradiating with a laser beam is referred to as laser ablation.

The aerosol is carried by helium and ionized in a plasma torch. These ions are subsequently extracted from the plasma into the high vacuum of the mass spectrometer, where they are separated based on their mass to charge ratio. Multiple collectors receive the mass resolved beams of ions, which are then converted into voltage. By comparing the voltages in different collectors, isotopic ratios can be determined. Such a technique has been recognized as very useful in the determination of lead isotope in pigments. Because of the minute amount of sample being transformed into a spray, the technique entails virtually no damage to the painting.

## iii. Lead isotope ratios and the locality of the lead ore

Lead isotope ratios in paintings are useful in authenticity matters. They can help in identifying the locality of the lead ore from which the lead was extracted before being transformed to lead carbonate.

Lead has four natural isotopes, which are $^{204}Pb$, $^{206}Pb$, $^{207}Pb$, and $^{208}Pb$. The last three isotopes originate in part from the radioactive decay of $^{238}U$, $^{235}U$, and $^{232}Th$, so that their concentrations vary depending on the localities of the rocks from which they were extracted.

$^{204}Pb$, which does not result from any radioactive decay, is stable, with its concentration remaining unchanging with time. Consequently, a plot of the ratios $^{206}Pb/^{204}Pb$ on the x-axis and of $^{207}Pb/^{204}Pb$ on the y-axis indicates the origin of the lead ore from which the lead was extracted (Fig. 6.5).

Due to the small sample sizes involved, contaminants are difficult to control. The samples, therefore, need rigorous pretreatment to ensure that all contaminants have been eliminated.

Rare isotopes like $^{14}$C are generally measured as a ratio of a stable, more abundant isotope like $^{12}$C or $^{13}$C and are represented as $^{14}$C/$^{13}$C or $^{14}$C/$^{12}$C.

# Case VII

## 1. Raking Light

In raking light, the painting is illuminated from one side only, and at an acute or nearly parallel angle with respect to its surface (Fig. 7.1E).

It is useful in detecting retouches and revealing the subtle surface textures and brushwork in the paint. The effects of impasto are accentuated through the exaggeration of shadows and by an increased illumination of the surface facing the light (Figs. 7.2E and 7.3E). Irregularities are highlighted, documentation on craquelure is obtained, and uneven warping can be detected by this method.

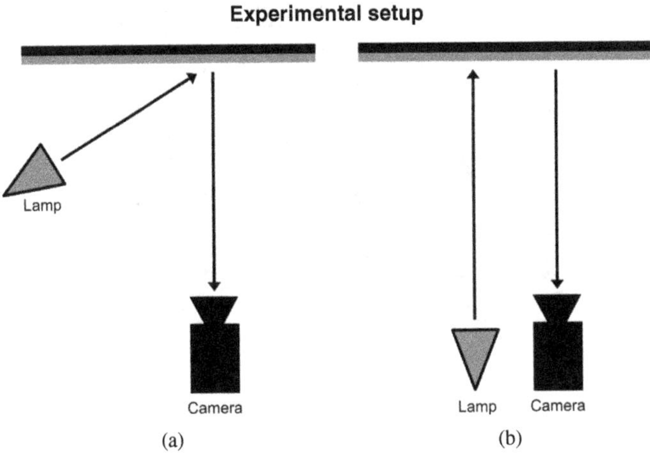


**Fig. 7.1E**  (a) Raking light imaging. (b) Normal light imaging.

 *Technical Art History*

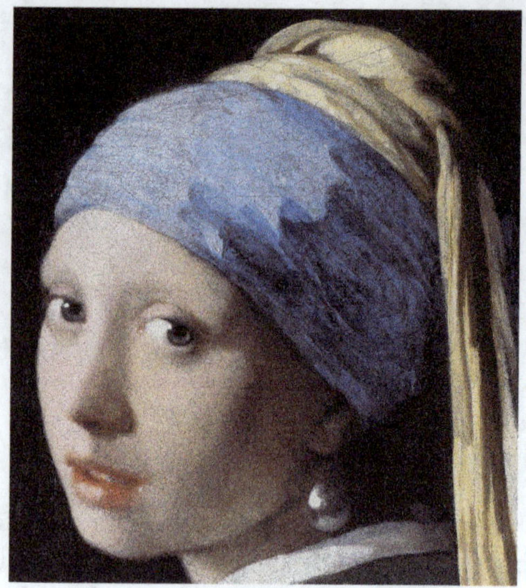

**Fig. 7.2E**  *Girl with a Pearl Earring* (1665).

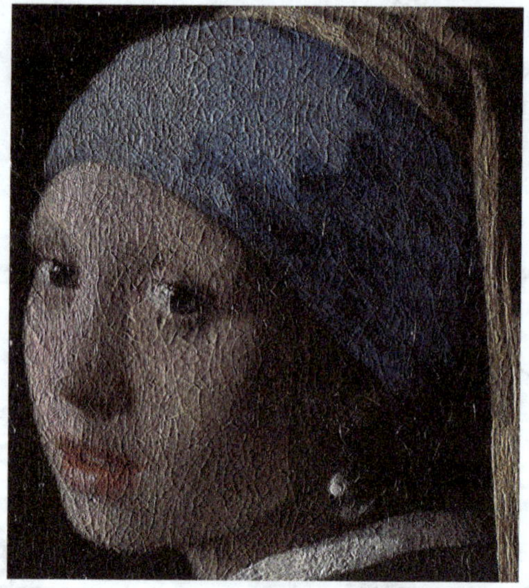

**Fig. 7.3E**  *Girl with a Pearl Earring* under raking light.

Raking light allows art historians to successfully study the manner of the stroke as well as stroke patterns. It also helps in identifying retouches.

In a study of a Van Gogh painting, raking light indicated that he used random strokes to suggest movement and more direct strokes to pursue forms.

## 2. Canvas Weave Thread Counting

Not too long ago, the standard technique in weave analysis was to cut as non-invasively as possible a small square of canvas from a safe location in the painting — such as the tacking margin — and to manually count the number of threads using a ruler in both the vertical and horizontal directions. A sample of a weaved canvas is shown in Fig. 7.4E.

The latter technique was superseded by the use of X-ray radiographs of the painting, which revealed the canvas weave and individual threads. In this method, the X-ray films were mounted on a lightbox, and a ruler was used to count threads.

Both approaches are not very reliable with regard to authenticity as the horizontal threads frequently slightly deviate from a straight line and give unreliable thread counts.

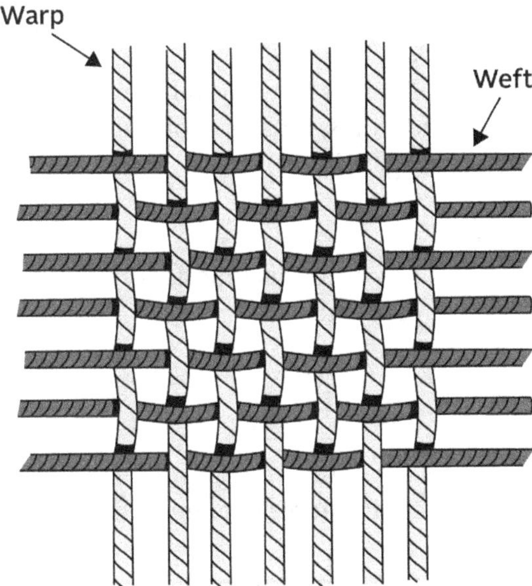


**Fig. 7.4E**  Weaving in a canvas. The *warp* refers to the vertical threads and the *weft* to the horizontal threads.

The most reliable technique is the one introduced by Professors C. Richard Johnson, Jr. and Don H. Johnson from Cornell and Rice Universities, respectively.

It relies on developed computer algorithms for the automatic counting of canvas threads from digitized X-ray images of paintings. By this method, it is possible to map the thread density of both the vertical and horizontal threads everywhere across the painting.

These weave maps are visualized as color-coded patterns of stripes. If one painting's pattern of stripes matches another painting's, this suggests that the canvases used for the two artworks originate from the same bolt.

A computer software performs searches to determine whether a painting's canvas has a thread density pattern that matches another.

## 3. X-ray Diffraction (XRD) and Micro X-ray Diffraction ($\mu$XRD)

### i. Crystalline versus amorphous solid

A crystal is a solid composed of atoms, ions, or molecules arranged in a highly ordered microscopic structure that is periodic in three dimensions (see Fig. 7.5E (a)).

An amorphous solid is a non-crystalline solid that lacks long-range order because the atoms, ions, or molecules are not organized in a definite pattern (see Fig. 7.5E (b)).

### ii. X-ray diffraction

X-ray diffraction is an important technique for identifying crystalline organic and inorganic pigments.

### Principle of the method

X-rays generated from an X-ray tube are directed toward a sample, and upon encounter with its atoms change direction, i.e., they are diffracted (Fig. 7.6E).

When the conditions of a particular law (Bragg's law) are satisfied, and the diffracted X-rays constructively interfere (Endnotes page 132)

## What is Crystalline Structure?

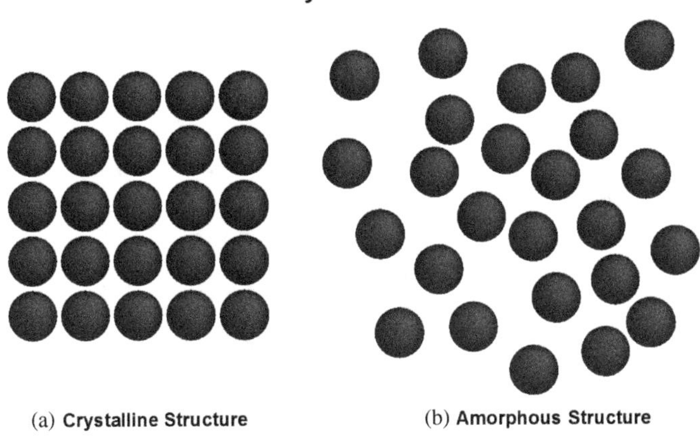


**Fig. 7.5E**  Difference in the atomic arrangements between an amorphous and a crystalline solid.

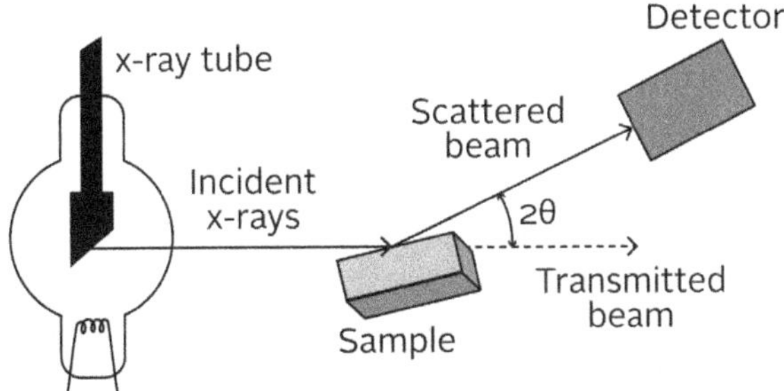


**Fig. 7.6E**  Experimental set up for an X-ray diffractometer.

with each other, X-ray peaks are observed in a pattern referred to as the X-ray diffraction pattern (Fig. 7.7E).

Crystalline structures diffract X-rays to give a distinct fingerprint pattern characteristic for that particular crystal structure.

X-ray diffraction, as opposed to X-ray fluorescence, is sometimes useful in differentiating between two crystalline solids with different structures. For instance, X-ray diffraction would give two different diffraction patterns in the case of both carbonates of lead (Cerussite of formula $PbCO_3$, composed of the elements lead, carbon and oxygen, and Hydrocerussite $Pb_3(OH)_2(CO_3)_2$, composed of the elements lead,

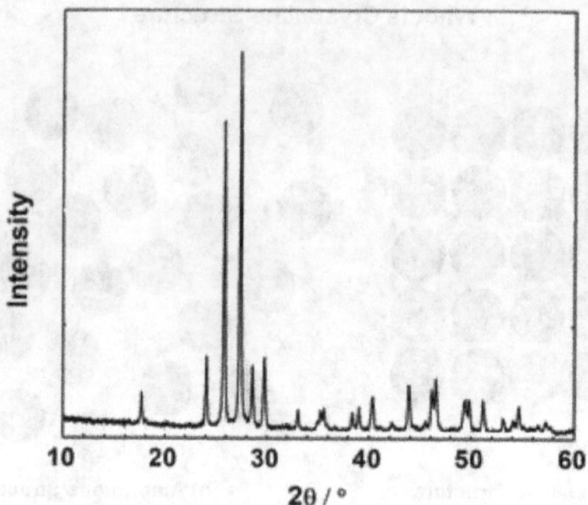

**Fig. 7.7E**   X-ray diffraction pattern of Strontium chromate ($\theta$ is the angle between the incident beam and the crystallographic reflecting plane).

carbon, oxygen, and hydrogen). X-ray fluorescence would also indicate the presence of lead for these two carbonates without differentiating between them.

Inorganic pigments can occur in different crystallographic modifications in the various layers requiring identification by X-ray diffraction. Because of the narrow thickness of the paint layers, in the range of several tens of micrometers or even less, this conventional X-ray diffraction technique is inconvenient.

Alternatively, the most appropriate technique is micro X-ray diffraction ($\mu$XRD).

### iii. Micro X-ray diffraction ($\mu$XRD) and limits of application

Micro X-ray diffraction enables the identification of the crystalline constituents within the different paint layers as well as the examination of small sample areas.

This technique requires the generation of a very narrowly focused X-ray beam to cut across the sample or to focus on a small spot on the sample surface. The resulting increased intensity delivered to the sample in a small focal spot allows for enhanced diffraction measurements of tiny specimens on the order of 2–5 micrograms or of a paint cross-section $100\mu$m $\times$ $200\mu$m in size.

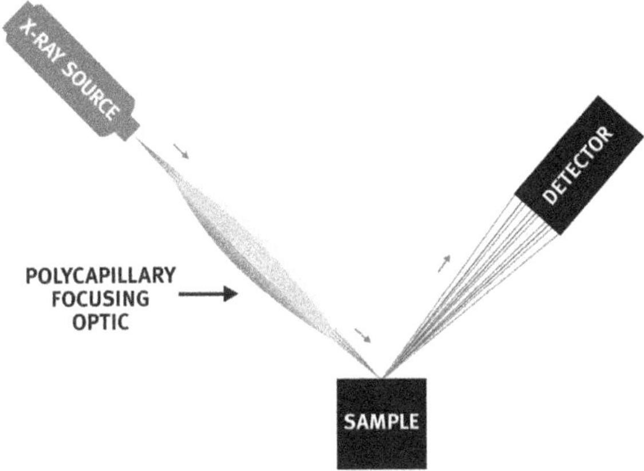



**Fig. 7.8E**  Polycapillary focusing optic.

To achieve such a goal, the very narrowly focused X-ray beam that needs to be generated can be obtained by either using synchrotron X-rays (which cannot always readily be available in labs) or through the use of polycapillary focusing optics (Fig. 7.8E).

In the latter case, X-rays are collected from the divergent X-ray source and directed as a small, focused beam to parts of the sample surface with diameters as small as tens of micrometers. The focused beam is obtained by means of special capillaries, and the diffracted beam reaches a specially designed sensitive detector.

# Case VIII

## 1. Infrared Transmitted (IRT) Imaging

Infrared transmitted (IRT) photography has recently gained importance as a very effective imaging technique for paintings. Such a method allows for better detection of pentimenti and provides greater details in the underdrawings. It can also give information on the actual buildup by the painter in shaping the figures in the artwork.

In such a technique, the camera faces the front of the painting while the lamp providing the IR faces its back (Fig. 8.1E (a)). This is different from the conventional infrared reflected imaging where both the light source and the camera face the front of the painting (Fig. 8.1E (b)). It is important to bear in mind that both techniques use the same source of radiation, an infrared source, and the same infrared detector. The only difference is that in one case the source is at the front of the painting and in the other case the source is at the back of the painting.

In IRT, the infrared light penetrates the canvas, ground and paint layers and diminishes the ability of materials in different layers to scatter or absorb infrared radiation.

Halogen lamps can be used as sources of infrared radiation; however, an LED is preferable as it avoids the heating of the canvas. It is important that any other source of infrared radiation in the laboratory be turned off to avoid diffused light, which would interfere with the experimental results. An example of a painting seen through visible light, an infrared image, and infrared transmitted image is shown in Fig. 8.2E.

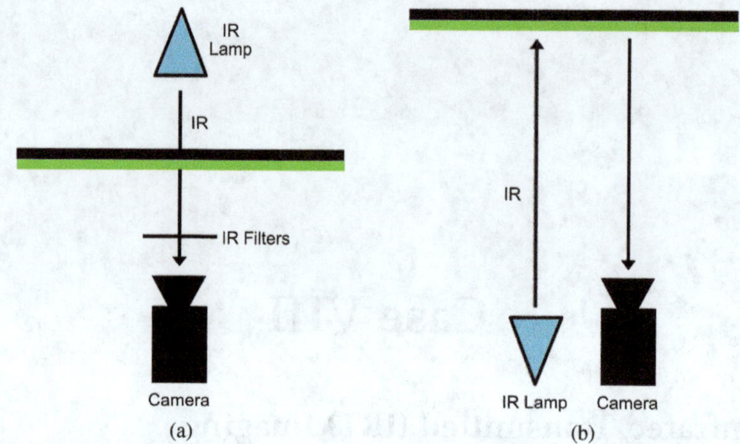



**Fig. 8.1E** (a) Infrared transmission (IRT) imaging. (b) Infrared reflected (IRR) imaging.

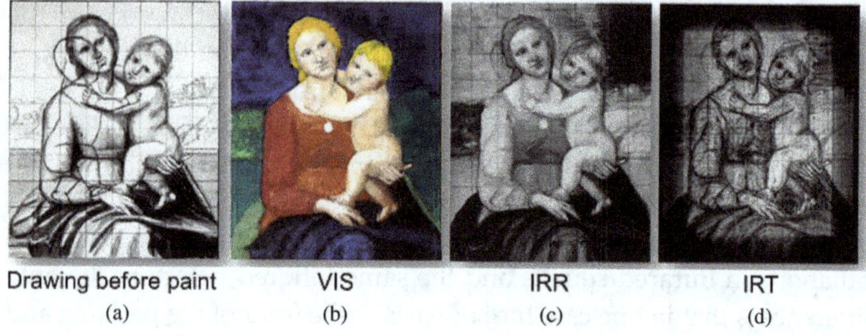



**Fig. 8.2E** Infrared transmitted imaging: Example given through a mockup painting containing some historical pigments. (a) Initial drawing before paint is applied to produce a mockup painting (number of changes are visible). (b) Mockup painting with different historical pigments seen under visible light. (c) Infrared image (d) Infrared transmitted image (more details in the underdrawing and greater contrast). It is also noted that a part of the sky, which was painted with azurite, is quite opaque in the IRR image but becomes transparent in the IRT photograph. The frame is responsible for the dark border observed in the IRT image.

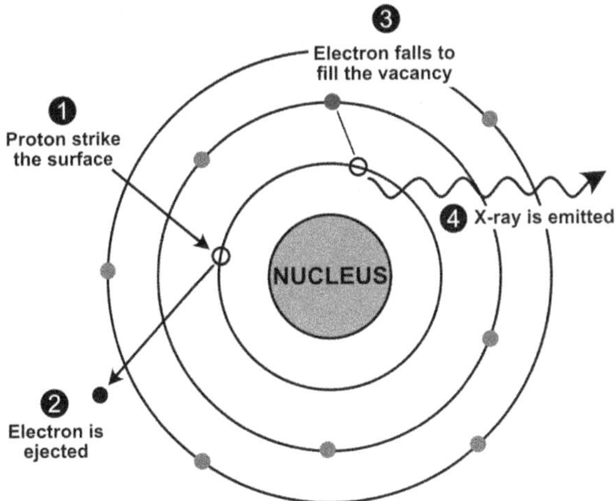


**Fig. 8.3E**  Process of X-ray emission.

## 2. Proton-induced X-ray Emission (PIXE)

Proton-induced X-ray emission (PIXE) is a non-invasive elemental analysis technique that has gained popularity in the last decade for the analysis of paintings. It is a sensitive technique that allows elemental measurement levels down to a few parts per million and is rapid as it necessitates an irradiation time of less than a minute. An additional advantage of PIXE is that it enables the detection of all elements heavier than sodium.

X-ray emission is induced by a low-intensity beam of accelerated subatomic charged particles that interact with the atoms of the material under study. Upon interaction, some electrons are ejected from the inner shells of the atoms, leaving vacancies that are filled by outer shell electrons. This process is accompanied by X-ray emission at a unique set of energies that are characteristic of each element. (Fig. 8.3E).

The spectra obtained are quite complex, with a large number of peaks and some interference, making their interpretation by hand an almost impossible job. The development of computer codes allows the determination in a non-invasive way of the sample elemental composition within minutes after irradiation.

A typical experimental setup for PIXE with a typical spectrum is shown in Fig. 8.4E.

# Proton Induced X-ray Emission (PIXE)

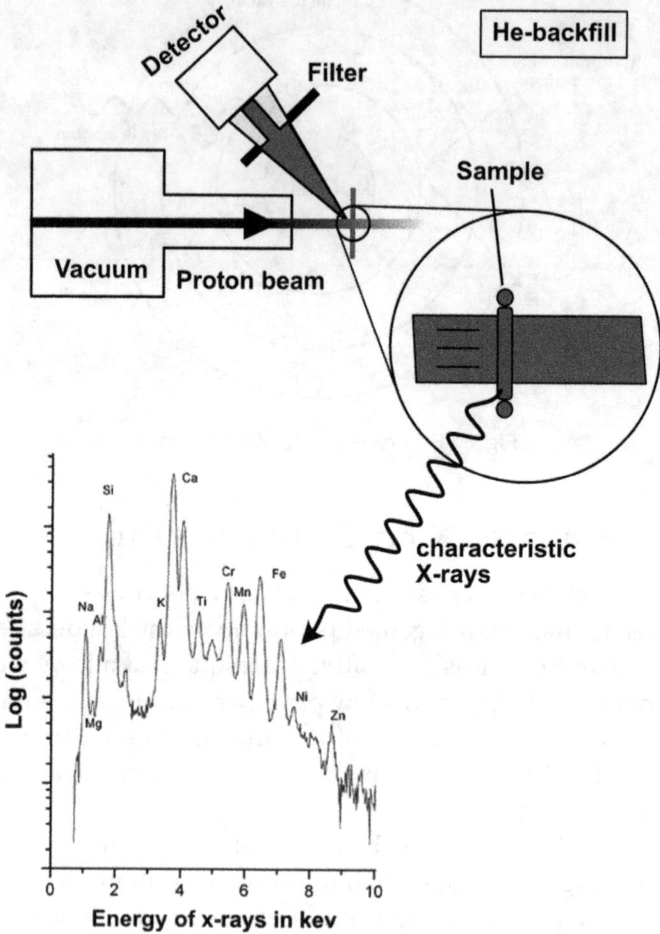


Fig. 8.4E   Experimental setup for PIXE with typical spectrum.

# Case IX

## 1. Multispectral Imaging (MSI) of a Painting

Multispectral imaging entails the observation of a painting using a selected range of wavelengths in the electromagnetic spectrum. Many images of the same scene are taken, each at a different wavelength. Each range reveals different information.

In the visible range, a photographic image of the painting is obtained, which is in keeping with that observed with the naked eye. Also in the same wavelength range, a grazing light image results through the use of raking light, which reveals the subtle surface textures, the shape of the cracks and the brushwork in the paint.

In the ultraviolet range (UV), UV fluorescence (UVF) and UV reflected (UVR) images are produced. UVF reveals recent retouchings applied over a layer of varnish. Recent retouchings prevent the UV light from reaching the varnish and appear as dark patches compared to the fluorescent area. The UVR images enhance the reading of faded paints and are also useful to identify certain pigments.

The infrared range which is closest to the visible range yields infrared charge coupled device (IRCCD), infrared false color (IRFC) and infrared reflectography (IRR) images. IRCCD images yield information below the painting's surface, such as the revelation of underdrawings. IRFC helps in the rapid detection of retouches, in the tentative identification of pigments and in differentiating between paint materials. A more sophisticated scientific camera is used for IRR.

This yields greater information on underdrawings and pentimenti than in the case of IRCCD.

## 2. Infrared False Color (IRFC)

The infrared false color method — sometimes referred to as infrared pseudo-color, is a practical and rapid method for the detection of retouches. It is also useful for the provisional identification of pigments; however, these need to be confirmed by more sophisticated analytical methods.

Photo-editing software mixes the channels (wavelength bands) of a visible and infrared image to digitally produce the IRFC image (Fig. 9.1E).

Pigments with similar colors under visible light have different IRFCs if they behave differently under Infrared light.

A case in point is the green pigment malachite which absorbs the infrared, red and blue light, with only its green component partaking in the IRFC picture, providing a blue color for malachite. Another green pigment veridian, reflects the infrared light and through the mixing of the red and blue channels acquires in the IRFC image a purple color (Fig. 9.2E).

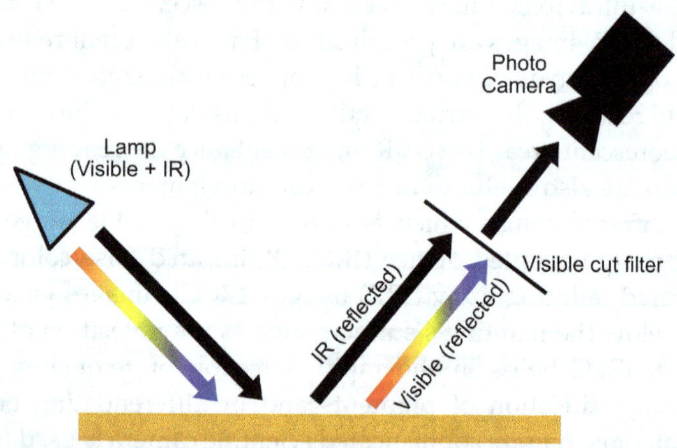


**Fig. 9.1E.**   IRFC (mixing of the channels of a visible and infrared image).

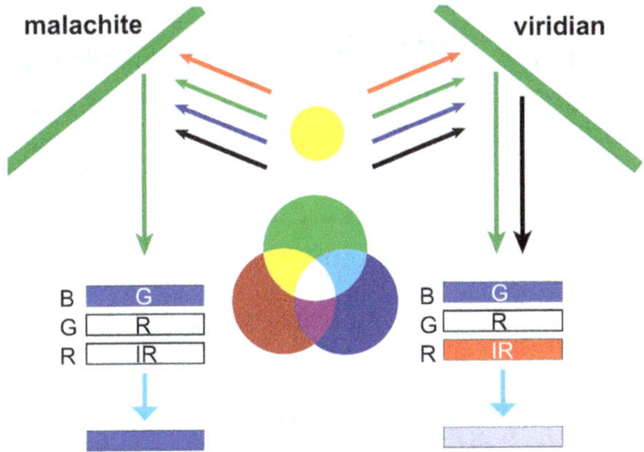



**Fig. 9.2E.** Malachite and viridian behave differently under infrared light.

## 3. Terahertz (THz) Imaging and Spectroscopy

One part of the electromagnetic spectrum that is steadily gaining importance is the THz region ($10^{12}$ Hz), which lies between the microwave and infrared regions of the spectrum (Fig. 9.3E).

Commercial equipment that allows the generation and detection of THz rays is now readily available, overcoming the initial difficulties encountered in producing suitably compact THz sources. This technique has led to a more thorough approach to the analysis of paintings.

Pigments under THz radiation yield distinctive spectra that can act as fingerprints for such colorants. The characterization of materials in different layers can be carried out by this method.

Furthermore, analyses carried out at the interface of each layer indicate the nature of the binding medium.

In THz imaging, a source produces pulses of THz radiation, which shine upon the painting. Use is made of a commercial THz scanner that moves across the artwork in a raster pattern. A computerized signal processing technique separates the signals transmitted from each successive layer of the artwork, producing a three-dimensional map of the image. The method enables the detection of underdrawings, pentimenti as well as hidden previous compositions.

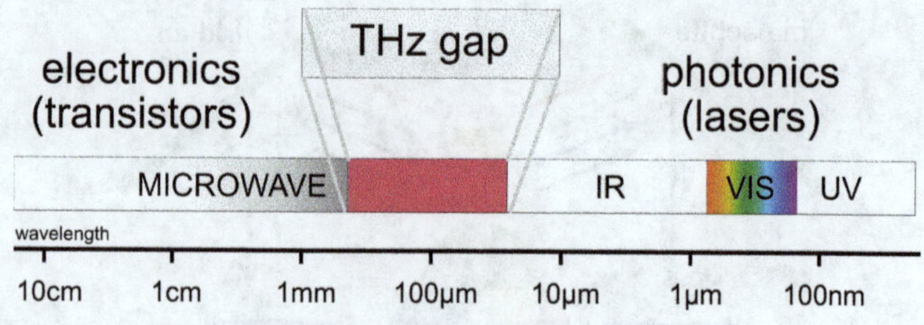


**Fig. 9.3E.**    The terahertz region.

The advantage of the THz approach when compared to other imaging techniques (infrared and X-ray) is further penetration together with depth resolution.

The level of detail obtained by THz imaging plays a crucial role in the authentication of paintings.

The low energy and low density of THz radiation, together with the fact that there is no contact made with the artwork, makes it a non-invasive technique. Furthermore, the nonionizing nature of THz radiation renders it a preferred option to X-ray radiography (where radiation-shielded rooms) when necessary.

# Further Readings

**Accelerator mass spectrometry with radiocarbon dating**
1. Hodgins, W. L. (2019). 'Identifying art forgeries by radiocarbon dating microgram quantities of artists' paints', *Proceedings of the National Academy of Sciences of the United States of America PNAS*, **116**(27), pp. 13158–13160.
2. Hajdas, I. (2019). 'Radiocarbon dating method', in *Technical Art History: A Handbook of Scientific Techniques for the Examination of Works of Art*, Authentication in Art Foundation, p. 114.
3. Hajdas, I. (2019). 'Radiocarbon dating using Bomb Peak C-14', in *Technical Art History: A Handbook of Scientific Techniques for the Examination of Works of Art*, Authentication in Art Foundation, pp. 112–113.
4. Craddock, P. (2009). *Scientific Investigation of Copies, Fakes and Forgeries*, Elsevier Ltd., pp. 87–93 and p. 290.

**Canvas**
1. Den Leeuw, M. (2019). 'Canvas weave thread counting', in *Technical Art History: A Handbook of Scientific Techniques for the Examination of Works of Art*, Authentication in Art Foundation, pp. 118–119.
2. Ragai, J. (2015). *The Scientist and the Forger, Insights into the Scientific Detection of Forgery in Paintings* (1st Ed.), Imperial College Press, pp. 125–129.

3. Young, C. and Katlan, A. W. (2012). 'History of fabric supports', in Stoner, J. H. and Rushfeld, R. (eds.), *Conservation of Easel Paintings*, Routledge (Taylor and Francis Group), pp. 124–133.
4. Hendriks, E., Johnson, D. H. and Johnson, C. R. Jr. (2010). 'Interpreting canvas weave matches', *Art Matters*, **5**, pp. 53–61.
5. Craddock, P. (2009). *Scientific Investigation of Copies, Fakes and Forgeries*, Elsevier Ltd., pp. 291–292.

**Craquelure**
1. Bucklow, S. (2012). 'The classification of craquelure patterns', in Stoner, J. H. and Rushfeld, R. (eds.), *Conservation of Easel Paintings*, Routledge (Taylor and Francis Group), pp. 285–290.
2. Wieseman, M. E. (2010). *A Closer look: Deceptions and Discoveries*. National Gallery, London, p. 10.
3. Craddock, P. (2009). *Scientific Investigation of Copies, Fakes and Forgeries*, Elsevier Ltd., pp. 305–307.
4. Varley, A. J. (1999). *Statistical Image Methods for Line Detection*. PhD Thesis, University of Cambridge.
5. Bucklow, S. (1996). *Formal Connoisseurship and the Characterization of Craquelure*. PhD Thesis, University of Cambridge.

**Cross-section analysis**
1. Bracci, S. (2019). 'Cross-section microanalysis using UV/Vis microscopy', in *Technical Art History: A Handbook of Scientific Techniques for the Examination of Works of Art*, Authentication in Art Foundation, pp. 76–77.
2. Ragai, J. (2015). *The Scientist and the Forger, Insights into the Scientific Detection of Forgery in Paintings* (1st Ed.), Imperial College Press, pp. 37–39.
3. Wolbers, W. C., Buck S. L. and Olley, P. (2012). 'Cross-section microscopy analysis and fluorescent staining', in Stoner, J. H. and Rushfeld, R. (eds.), *Conservation of Easel Paintings*, Routledge (Taylor and Francis Group), pp. 326–290.
4. Townsend, J. H. and Keune, K. (2006). 'Microscopical techniques applied to traditional paintings', *Infocus Magazine*, **41**(1), pp. 58–61.

**Dendrochronology**

1. Den Leeuw, M. (2019). 'Dendrochronology', in *Technical Art History: A Handbook of Scientific Techniques for the Examination of Works of Art*, Authentication in Art Foundation, pp. 118–119.
2. Andreu-Hayles, L. and Leland, C. (2014). 'Dendrochronology, Progress', in Rink W., Thompson J. (eds.), *Encyclopedia of Scientific Dating Methods*, Springer, Dordrecht.
3. Kuniholm, P. I. (2002). 'Dendrochronology (tree-ring dating) of panel paintings', in Taft, W. S. JR. and Mayer, J. (eds.), *The Science of Paintings*, Springer-Verlag, New York, pp. 206–214.
4. Sutherland, E. K. (1999). 'Dendrochronology', in *Environmental Geology, Encyclopedia of Earth Science*, Springer, Dordrecht.

**Gas chromatography-mass spectrometry (see Pyrolysis-gas chromatography-mass spectrometry)**

**Infrared radiation**

1. Den Leeuw, M. (2019). 'Infrared reflectography', in *Technical Art History: A Handbook of Scientific Techniques for the Examination of Works of Art*, Authentication in Art Foundation, p. 11.
2. Den Leeuw, M. (2019). 'False color infrared' in *Technical Art History: A Handbook of Scientific Techniques for the Examination of Works of Art*, Authentication in Art Foundation, p. 14.
3. Cosentino, A. (2016). 'Infrared technical photography for art examination', *e-Preservation Science*, **13**, pp. 1–6.
4. MacBeth, R. (2012). 'The technical examination and documentation of easel paintings', in Stoner, J. H. and Rushfeld, R. (eds.), *Conservation of Easel Paintings*, Routledge (Taylor and Francis Group), pp. 296–300.
5. Wieseman, M. E. (2010). *A Closer Look: Deception and Discoveries.* National Gallery, London, p. 41.
6. Craddock, P. (2009). *Scientific Investigation of Copies, Fakes and Forgeries*, Elsevier Ltd., p. 58, pp. 287–288.

**Laser-ablation-inductively coupled plasma-mass spectrometry**

1. Fabian, D. (2019). 'Lead isotope analysis' in *Technical Art History: A Handbook of Scientific Techniques for the Examination of Works of Art*, Authentication in Art Foundation, pp. 107–109.

2. Doronila, A. (2019). 'Laser ablation inductively coupled plasma mass spectrometry', in *Technical Art History: A Handbook of Scientific Techniques for the Examination of Works of Art*, Authentication in Art Foundation, p. 102.
3. Fabian, D. and Fortunato, G. (2010). 'Tracing white: A study of lead white pigments found in seventeenth-century paintings using high precision lead isotope abundance ratios', in Kirby, J., Nash, S. and Cannon, J. (eds.), *Trade in Artists' Materials: Markets and Commerce in Europe to 1700*, London: Archetype Publications, pp. 426–443.
4. Smith, K., Horton, K., Watling, R. J. and Scoullar, N. (2006). 'Detecting art forgeries using LA-ICP-MS in corporating the *in situ* application of laser-based collection technology', *Talanta*, **67**(2), pp. 402–413.
5. Fortunato, G., Ritter, A. and Fabian, D. (2005). 'Old Masters' lead white pigments: Investigations of paintings from the 16th to the 17th century using high precision lead isotope abundance ratios'. *Analyst*, **130**(6), pp. 898–906.

**Multispectral imaging**

1. Cosentino, A. (2015). 'Multispectral imaging of pigments with a digital camera and 12 interferential filters', *e-Preservation Science*, **12**, pp. 1–7.
2. Cosentino, A. (2015). 'Multispectral imaging and the art expert', *Spectroscopy Europe*, **27**(2), pp. 6–9.
3. MacBeth, R. (2012). 'The technical examination and documentation of easel paintings', in Stoner, J. H. and Rushfeld, R. (eds.), *Conservation of Easel Paintings*, Routledge (Taylor and Francis Group), p. 291.
4. Pelagotti, A., Del Mastio, A., De Rosa, A. and Piva, A. (2008). 'Multispectral imaging of paintings: A way to material identification', *IEEE Signal Processing Magazine*, **25**(4), pp. 27–36.
5. Delaney, J. K., Walmsley, E., Berrie, B. H. and Fletcher, C. F. (2005). 'Multi-spectral imaging of paintings in the infrared to detect and map blue pigments', in The National Academies Press, *Scientific Examination of Art: Modern Techniques in Conservation and Analysis*, pp. 162–183.

**Polarized light microscopy**

1. Eastaugh, N. and Walsh, V. (2012). 'Optical microscopy', in Stoner, J. H. and Rushfeld, R. (eds.), *Conservation of Easel Paintings*, Routledge (Taylor and Francis Group), pp. 311–316.
2. Townsend, J. H. and Keune, K. (2006). 'Microscopical techniques applied to traditional paintings', *Infocus Magazine*, **41**(1), pp. 54–65.
3. Bonanni, L. Xiao, X., Hockenberry, M., Subramani, P., Ishii, H., Seracini, M. and Schulze, J. (2009). 'Wetpaint: Scraping through multi-layered images', in *Proceedings of the 27th International Conference on Human Factors in Computing Systems (CHI '09)*, ACM, New York, NY, USA, pp. 571–574.
4. Boime, A. and Kossolapov, A. (2003). 'Manet's lost Infanta', *Journal of the American Institute for Conservation*, **42**(3), pp. 407–418.
5. McCrone, W. C. (2001). 'Artful dodgers: Virtuosos of art forgery meet the masters of scientific detection', *The Sciences*, **41**(1), pp. 32–37.

**Proton-induced or particle-induced X-ray emission**

1. Giunti, L., Mathot, S., Taccetti, F. and Vretenar, M. (2019). 'Proton Induced X-ray Emission-PIXE', in *Technical Art History: A Handbook of Scientific Techniques for the Examination of Works of Art*, Authentication in Art Foundation, p. 68.
2. Collon, P. and Wiescher, M. (2012). 'Accelerated ion beams for art forensics', *Physics Today*, **65**(1), pp. 58–59.
3. Craddock, P. (2009). *Scientific Investigation of Copies, Fakes and Forgeries*, Elsevier Ltd., pp. 50–51.
4. Neelmeijr, C. and Mader, M. (2002). 'The merits of particle induced X-ray emission in revealing painting techniques', *Nuclear Instruments and Methods in Physics Research B*, **189**, pp. 293–302.

**Pyrolysis-gas chromatography-mass spectrometry (Gas chromatography-mass spectrometry)**

1. Colombini, P. C. (2019). 'Pyrolysis gas chromatography coupled with mass spectrometry Py-GC/MS' in *Technical Art History: A Handbook of Scientific Techniques for the Examination of Works of Art*, Authentication in Art Foundation, pp. 90–95.

2. Hussein., S. Z. and Maqbool, K. (2014). 'GC-MS: Principle, technique and its application in food science', *International Journal of Current Science*, **13**, pp. 116–118.
3. Peggie, D. A. (2014). 'The chemistry and investigation of the transition from egg tempera painting to oil in Italy in the 15th century', in Sgamellotti, A., Brunetti, B. G. and Miliani, C. (eds.), *Science and Art, The Painted Surface*, Royal Society of Chemistry, pp. 221–225.
4. Hutanu, D., Woods, A. G. and Darie, C. C. (2013). 'Recent applications of mass spectrometry in paint analysis', *Modern Chemistry & Applications*.
5. Kusch, P. (2012). *'Pyrolysis-gas chromatography/mass spectrometry* of polymeric materials', in Mohd, M. A. (ed.), *Advanced Gas Chromatography-Progress in Agricultural, Biomedical and Industrial Applications*, pp. 343–362.
6. Russell, J., Singer, B. W., Perry, J. J. and Bacon, A. (2011). 'The identification of synthetic organic pigments in modern paints and modern paintings using pyrolysis-gas chromatography–mass spectrometry', *Analytical and Bioanalytical Chemistry*, **400**(5), pp. 1473–1491.

**Raking light**

1. Cosentino, A., Gil, M., Ribeiro, M. and Di Mauro, R. (2014). 'Technical photography for mural paintings: The newly discovered frescoes in Aci Sant'Antonio (Sicily, Italy)', *Conservar Património*, **20**, pp. 23–33.*
2. MacBeth, R. (2012). 'The technical examination and documentation of easel paintings', in Stoner, J. H. and Rushfeld, R. (eds.), *Conservation of Easel Paintings*, Routledge (Taylor and Francis Group), pp. 292–293.

**Raman microscopy**

1. Pinna, D. (2019). 'Raman spectroscopy', in *Technical Art History: A Handbook of Scientific Techniques for the Examination of Works of Art*, Authentication in Art Foundation, pp. 43–44.

---

*This article deals with a number of techniques including raking light.

2. Scherrer, N. C., Stefan, Z., Francoise, D., Annette, F. and Renate, K. (2009). 'Synthetic organic pigments of the 20th and 21st century relevant to artist's paints: Raman spectra reference collection', *Spectrochimica Acta, Part A: Molecular and Biomolecular Spectroscopy*, **73**(3), pp. 505–524.

3. Craddock, P. (2009). *Scientific Investigation of Copies, Fakes and Forgeries*, Elsevier Ltd., pp. 288–289.

4. Clark, R. J. H. (2005). 'Raman microscopy in the identification of pigments on manuscripts and other artwork', in The National Academies Press, *Scientific Examination of Art: Modern Techniques in Conservation and Analysis*, pp. 162–183.

5. Smith, G. D. and Clark, R. J. H. (2004). 'Raman microscopy in archaeological science', *Journal of Archaeological Science*, **31**(8), pp. 1137–1160.

## Scanning electron microscopy and energy dispersive X-ray fluorescence

1. Pinna, D. (2019). 'Scanning electron microscopy — SEM — coupled with energy dispersive X-ray spectroscopy — EDS or EDX', in *Technical Art History: A Handbook of Scientific Techniques for the Examination of Works of Art*, Authentication in Art Foundation, pp. 52–54.

2. Wieseman, M. E. (2010). *A Closer Look: Deception and Discoveries*. National Gallery, London, pp. 24–25.

3. Bower, N. W., Stulik, D. C. and Doehne, E. (1994). 'A critical evaluation of the environmental scanning electron microscope for the analysis of paint fragments in art conservation', *Fresenius J Anal Chem*, **348**, pp. 402–410.

4. Stulik, D. and Doehne, E. (1991). 'Applications of environmental scanning electron microscopy in art conservation and archaeology', *MRS Proceedings*, **185**, pp. 23–29.

## Terahertz spectroscopy

1. Lewis, R. (2019). 'Terahertz spectroscopy and imaging' in *Technical Art History: A Handbook of Scientific Techniques for the Examination of Works of Art*, Authentication in Art Foundation, pp. 110–111.

2. Squires, A. D., Lewis, R. A., Zaczek, A. J. and Korter, T. M. (2017). 'Distinguishing quinacridone pigments via terahertz spectroscopy: Absorption experiments and solid-state density functional theory simulations', *J. Phys. Chem.*, **121**, pp. 3423–3429.

3. Abraham., E., Younes, A., Delagnes, J. C. and Mounaix, P. (2010). 'Non-invasive investigation of art paintings by terahertz imaging', *Applied Physics*, **100**, pp. 585–590.

4. Seracini, M., Gallerano, G. P., Morelli, G. and Kuester, F. (2008). 'Infrared, millimeter, and terahertz waves: New innovations and applications for cultural heritage', *33rd International Conference on Infrared, Millimeter and Terahertz Waves*, Pasadena, CA, pp. 1–1.

5. Koori, F., Ogawa, Y. and Hayashi, S. (2007). 'Terahertz spectroscopy for art conservation', *Electronics Express*, **4**(8), pp. 258–263.

**Transmitted light**

1. Den Leeuw, M. (2019). 'Transmitted infrared', in *Technical Art History: A Handbook of Scientific Techniques for the Examination of Works of Art*, Authentication in Art Foundation, p. 15.

2. Cosentino, A. (2016). 'Transmittance spectroscopy and transmitted multispectral imaging to map covered paints', *Conservar Patrimonio*, **24**, pp. 37–44.

3. MacBeth, R. (2012). 'The technical examination and documentation of easel paintings', in Stoner, J. H. and Rushfeld, R. (eds.), *Conservation of Easel Paintings*, Routledge (Taylor and Francis Group), Routlege, pp. 293–294.

**UV radiation and UV fluorescence**

1. Mass, J. (2019). 'Ultraviolet-induced infrared fluorescence' in *Technical Art History: A Handbook of Scientific Techniques for the Examination of Works of Art*, Authentication in Art Foundation, pp. 54–56.

2. Cosentino, A. (2015). 'Practical notes on ultraviolet technical photography for art examination', *Conservar Patrimonio*, **21**, pp. 53–62.

3. Eastaugh, N. and Walsh, V. (2012). 'Optical microscopy', in Stoner, J. H. and Rushfeld, R. (eds.), *Conservation of Easel Paintings*, Routledge (Taylor and Francis Group), p. 317.

4. MacBeth, R. (2012). 'The technical examination and documentation of easel paintings', in Stoner, J. H. and Rushfeld, R. (eds.), *Conservation of Easel Paintings*, Routledge (Taylor and Francis Group), pp. 294–296.

**X-ray diffraction and scanning X-ray powder diffraction**
1. Mass, J. (2019). 'Laboratory-based micro X-ray diffraction — XRD', in *Technical Art History: A Handbook of Scientific Techniques for the Examination of Works of Art*, Authentication in Art Foundation, p. 17.
2. Pinna, D. (2019). 'Scanning X-ray powder diffraction — XRPD imaging', in *Technical Art History: A Handbook of Scientific Techniques for the Examination of Works of Art*, Authentication in Art Foundation, pp. 33–34.
3. Simova, V., Bezdicka, P., Hradilova, D. and Grygar, T. (2005). 'X-ray powder micro-diffraction for routine analysis of paintings', *Powder Diffraction*, **20**(3), pp. 224–229.
4. Schreiner, M., Frühmann, B., Jembrih-Simbürger, D. and Linke, R. (2004). 'X-rays in art and archaeology — An overview', *Powder Diffraction*, **19**(1), pp. 3–11.

**X-ray fluorescence and energy dispersive X-ray fluorescence**
1. Mass, J. (2019). 'Portable X-ray fluorescence-PXRF-spot analysis', in *Technical Art History: A Handbook of Scientific Techniques for the Examination of Works of Art*, Authentication in Art Foundation, pp. 62–64.
2. Ragai, J. (2018). *The Scientist and the Forger, Probing a Turbulent Art World* (2nd Ed.), World Scientific Publishing, pp. 149–151.
3. Thurrowgood, D., Paterson, D., de Jonge, M. D., Kirkham, R., Thurrowgood, S. and Howard, D. L. (2016). 'A hidden portrait by Edgar Degas', *Sci Rep*, **6**, p. 29594.
4. Craddock, P. (2009). *Scientific Investigation of Copies, Fakes and Forgeries*, Elsevier Ltd., pp. 47–50.
5. Pessanha, S., Guilherme, A., Manso, M. and de Carvalho, M. L. (2008). 'X-ray fluorescence applications to art and cultural heritage: study of a Japanese print', *Spectroscopyeurope*, **20**(8), pp. 9–11.

**X-ray radiography**

1. Den Leeuw, M. (2019). 'X-Radiography', in *Technical Art History: A Handbook of Scientific Techniques for the Examination of Works of Art*, Authentication in Art Foundation, p. 21.
2. Janssens, K., Alfeld, M., Van derSnickt, G., De Nolf, W., Vanmeert, F., Radepont, M., Monico, L., Dik, J., Cotte, M., Falkenberg, G., Miliani, C. and Brunetti, B. G. (2013). 'The use of synchrotron radiation for the characterization of artists' pigments and paintings', *Annual Review of Analytical Chemistry*, **6**, 399–425.
3. MacBeth, R. (2012). 'The technical examination and documentation of easel paintings', in Stoner, J. H. and Rushfeld, R. (eds.), *Conservation of Easel Paintings*, Routledge (Taylor and Francis Group), Routlege, pp. 301–304.
4. Wieseman, M. E. (2010). *A Closer Look: Deception and Discoveries*. National Gallery, London, pp. 16-17, 21–22.
5. Dik, J., Janssens, K., Van Der Snickt, G., Van DerLoeff, L., Rickers, K. and Cotte, M. (2008). 'Visualization of a lost painting by Vincent Van Gogh using synchrotron based X-ray fluorescence elemental mapping', *Analytical Chemistry*, **80**(16), pp. 6436–6442.

**Additional readings combining a number of techniques**

1. Gołębiowski, M., Doleżyńska-Sewerniak, E. and Zygier, E. (2014). 'Chemical analysis of historic art and painting conservation materials (19th and 20th centuries) from the national museum in Krakow by gas chromatography–mass spectrometry and Fourier transform infrared spectroscopy', *Spectroscopy Letters*, **47**(1), pp. 57–75.
2. Eastaugh, N. and Walsh, V. (2012). 'Optical microscopy', in Stoner, J. H. and Rushfeld, R. (eds.), *Conservation of Easel Paintings*, Routledge (Taylor and Francis Group), pp. 306–317.
3. Vander Snickt, G., Janssens, K., Dik, J., De Nolf, W., Vanmeert, J. J., Cotte, M., Falkenberg, G. and Van der Loeff, L. (2012). 'Combined use of synchrotron radiation based micro-X-ray fluorescence, micro-X-ray diffraction, micro-X-ray absorption near-edge and micro Fourier transform infrared spectroscopies for revealing an alternative degradation pathway of the pigment cadmium yellow in a painting by Van Gogh', *Analytical Chemistry*, **84**, pp. 10221–10228.

4. Brostoff, L. B., Centeno, S. A., Ropret, P., Bythrow, P. and Pottier, F. (2009). 'Combined X-ray diffraction and Raman identification of synthetic organic pigments in works of art: From powder samples to artists' paints', *Analytical Chemistry*, **81**(15), pp. 6096–6106.
5. Townsend, J. H. and Keune, K. (2006). 'Microscopical techniques applied to traditional paintings', *Infocus Magazine*, **41**(1), pp. 54–65.
6. Hochleitner, B., Schreiner, M., Drakopoulos, M., Snigireva, I. and Snigirev, A. (2005). 'Analysis of paint layers by light microscopy, scanning electron microscopy and synchrotron induced X-ray micro-diffraction', in Van Grieken, G. and Janssens, K. (eds.), *Cultural Heritage Conservation and Environmental Impact Assessment by Non-Destructive Testing and Micro-Analysis*, Taylor & Francis, London, pp. 171–182.
7. Dredge, P., Wuhrer, R. and Phillips, M. R. (2003). 'Monet's painting under the microscope', *Microscopy and Microanalysis*, **9**(02), pp. 139–143.
8. King, A. (1994). *An Evaluation of Selected Methods of Technical Examination in the Detection of Forgeries*, Research Project, Department of Conservation and Technology, Courtauld Institute of Art, London, pp. 8–13.

## Teacher Guide

Resources are available to instructors who adopt this textbook for their courses. These include:

- Selected questions and answers from *Technical Art History*
- Tips for active learning
- Curated repository of video resources and questions

To access the materials, please visit: https://www.worldscientific.com/worldscibooks/10.1142/q0276-sm.

# Picture Credits

**Art Roster, Mt Shasta**
Fig. 1.1. *View from the Sea* attributed to Salvador Dalí.


**Badrawi, Fadia**
Figs: 6.4 Principle of LA-MC-ICP-MS, 1.3E An electromagnetic wave, 1.5E (b) The optical microscope, 1.9E Principle of XRF, characteristic spectra, 1.11E Principle of Infrared Reflectography (IRR), 2.3E A raster scan, 3.1E Arrangement for a conventional radiographic analysis, 4.6E The atom, 5.1E The polarized light microscope, 5.2E Polarizer and polarized wave, 5.5E Different vibrational modes in a molecule, 5.7E Instrument for pyrolysis-gas chromatography-mass spectrometry, 6.2E Formation and decay of $^{14}$C, 6.3E Principle of mass spectrometry of carbon isotopes, 7.4E Weaving in a canvas, 7.6E Experimental set up for an X-ray diffractometer.


**Bersani, Danilo**
Fig. 4.5 Detection of proteinaceous materials by GC/MS.


**Bocchetti, Gaby**
Figs: 1.2 *View from the Sea* under UV light (with permission from ArtRoster Mt Shasta), 1.3 Infrared reflectogram of *View from the Sea* (with permission from ArtRoster Mt Shasta), 1.6 (b) and 1.6 (c) (modified from open access picture 1.6 (a)), 1.7 (b) Image obtained by infrared reflectography, 2.1 Is it a Monet? (modified from open access

     *Picture Credits*

picture), 3.1 Fourth version of *The Bedroom* (modified from open access picture), 4.2 *Discovered painting* (modified from open access), 4.3 (a) Fluorescence from darker area, 4.3 (b) Fluorescence from Madonna's blue gown, 4.4 Underpainting, 5.1 Painting purported to be by Willem de Kooning, 5.2 Paint cross-section, 5.3 $\mu$FTIR of copper phthalocyanine (modified from open access), 5.4 $\mu$FTIR of linseed oil (modified from open access), 6.1 Painting purported to be part of *The Seasons* by Pieter Bruegel the Elder (modified from open access picture), 7.1 Painting found at San Telmo (modified from open access picture), 1.1E Different layers in a painting, 1.2E The atom, 1.5E (a) The optical microscope, 1.7E UV fluorescence, 1.8E Characteristic spectra of UV-induced visible fluorescence, 1.12E (a) Craquelure, 1.12E (b) UV fluorescence and detection of a retouch (modified from open access picture 1.6 (a)), 2.1E Top picture: Pigment embedded in a resin and bottom picture: Cross-section, 3.3E A typical synchrotron, 3.4E (b), 3.4E (c) Raman and Raleigh scatter, 4.6E and 4.7E (modified from open access Tables), 4.8E Typical mass spectrometer (modified from open access picture), 4.9E Gas chromatograph coupled to a mass spectrometer, 7.3E (b) Normal light imaging, 7.5E Difference in the atomic arrangements between an amorphous and a crystalline solid, 8.3E Process of X-ray emission, 8.4E Experimental set-up for PIXE with typical spectrum obtained, 9.1E IRFC (mixing of the channels of a visible and infrared image).

**Bucklow, Spike**
Figs. 4.1E (a, b, c, d, e) Classification of cracks.

**Cosentino, Antonio**
Figs: 7.1E (a) Raking light imaging, 8.1E (a) Infrared transmission, 8.2E (a) Initial drawing, 8.2E (b) Mockup painting, 8.2E (c) Infrared image, 8.2E (d) Infrared transmitted image, 9.2E Malachite and Viridian behave differently under infrared light.

**Dredge, Paula and Art Gallery of New South Wales**
Figs. 2.2E Optical micrographs of chips removed from a painting by Claude Monet. (a) No separation, (b) clear separation.

**Fortunato, Giuseppino (Swiss Federal Laboratories for Materials Science and Technology)**
Fig. 6.5 Origin of lead ores from which lead was extracted in case of authenticated Flemish and Italian artists.

**Mauritshuis, The Hague**
Figs: 7.1E *Girl with a Pearl Earring*, 7.2E *Girl with a Pearl Earring* under raking light.

**Ming, Aquilar, Huntington Library Art Museum, L.A**.
Fig. 3.4 *The Blue Boy* (ca. 1770) by Thomas Gainsborough (1727–1788).

**National Synchrotron Light Source (NSLS), Brookhaven**
Fig. 3.2E Scientists around the vacuum chamber of a 1947 General Electric synchrotron.

**Public Domain, Open Access**
Figs: 1.4 XRF obtained from the darkened under UV light of the yellow area, 1.5 XRF obtained for the yellow area with no restoration, 1.6 (a) Berthe Morisot, *The Psyche Mirror*, 1.7 (a) *Two Acrobats with a Dog*, 2.2 Layered structure of a painting, 3.2 Top panel XRF spectrum from the yellowish orange area of the painting. Bottom panel XRF spectrum of a cadmium salt, 3.3 Top panel Raman spectrum obtained from the blue area of the painting. Bottom panel is a reference Raman spectrum of copper phtalocyanine, 4.1 *The Virgin Adoring the Sleeping Christ Child by Botticelli*, 4.6 Mass spectrum of carbon dioxide, 6.2 Butterfly joints, 6.6 Cross-section of a tree, 8.1 Painting alleged to be Poussin's *Flight into Egypt*, 9.3 Terahertz spectrum of indigo, 1.4E Electromagnetic spectrum, 1.6E The stereo-microscope, 1.10E Energy dispersive X-ray fluorescence of a material containing a number of different elements, 2.4E Bellini's *Feast of the Gods*, 3.5E A micro-Raman spectroscope, 4.2E Craquelure with characteristic small Italian rectangular cracks, 4.3E Craquelure with typical small French large and somewhat irregular curving cracks (belongs to a portrait 1750), 4.4E Synchrotron-based scanning X-ray fluorescence microscope

(Thurrowgood, D., Paterson, D., de Jonge M.D., Kirkham, R., Thurrowgood, S., Howard, D.L., doi:10.1038/srep29594(2016), reproduced under Creative Commons Attribution 4.0 International License.), 5.3E Polarized microscopy image of anisotropic microcrystals, 5.4E Constructive and destructive interference, 5.6E FTIR of cadmium yellow, 6.1E Tree rings (Oak tree), 7.7E X-ray diffraction pattern of Strontium chromate, 9.3E The terahertz region.

**Reece David, Renishaw Center**
Fig. 3.4E Raman and Raleigh scatter.

**Wadum Art Technological Studies**
Fig. 6.3 An example of a reverse side of a panel showing the Coat of Arms of Antwerp.

**XOS Company**
Fig. 7.8E Polycapillary focusing optics.

# Glossary

**Accelerator Mass Spectrometry (AMS):** Technique used to detect long-lived radioisotopes like $^{14}$C and enabling the analysis of samples of the order of 1–2 mg.

**Anachronistic:** It is a chronological inconsistency in some respect. In a painting, this may be the juxtaposition of persons, objects, pigments, material, clothing, hairstyle, etc., generally belonging to a period not in the correct historical time of the artist.

**Art Historian:** A person who studies the different types and styles of art and artists throughout history. Art historians may advise others about selling and buying art and often help art curators put together important exhibitions.

**Art Institute of Chicago:** Founded in 1879 and located in Chicago's Grant Park, it is one of the oldest and largest art museums in the United States.

**Axis Powers:** One of two major military alliances during World War II consisting of Germany, Japan and Italy. The opposite side, the Allies, consisted of many countries including the USA, UK, France, and Poland.

**Binding Medium:** An ingredient used to bind the dry pigments together. Types include egg and plant oil, such as linseed oil.

**Botticelli, Sandro (1445–1510):** One of the greatest Italian painters of the Early Renaissance. Botticelli's name is derived from his elder brother Giovanni, a pawnbroker who was called Botticello ("Little Barrel"). Botticelli painted a gamut of religious themes, a few portraits and a small number of mythological subjects.

**Bruegel the Elder, Pieter (ca. 1525–1569):** The most distinguished member of a large Netherlandish family of artists (and in some cases copyists) active for four generations in the 16th and 17th centuries. Residing in Antwerp, he became a master in the painters' Guild of Saint Luke between 1551 and 1552. Many of Bruegel's paintings focus on the lives of Flemish commoners and combine landscapes and peasant scenes.

***Burning Giraffes and Telephones* (1937):** It is one of Salvador Dalí's most famous paintings. It was created in 1937, when the artist, who was at the time the most famous Surrealist, was still in Europe, before his 8-year exile in the United States.

**Cadmium Yellow:** It is a pigment prepared with an acid solution of cadmium sulfide (solid inorganic compound) used in both oil and watercolor but seldom mixed with copper-based pigments. This pigment was used sparingly due to the scarcity of cadmium metal that made it more expensive.

**Carmine Red:** Also called cochineal. It is a pigment of a bright-red color obtained from the aluminum salt of carminic acid.

***Catalan Bread* (1932):** A centralized composition in which a single loaf of bread is brightly illuminated against a dark, relatively monotonic ground. Without any other points of reference, the size and scale of the bread is ambiguous, which adds to the air of mystery in the painting. The shape and position of the loaf of bread is a rather suggestive phallic reference. While the inkwell is an established Dalinian symbol for intercourse, the presence of the rope and the limp watch allude to sexual dysfunction.

**Catalogue Raisonné:** Comprehensive, annotated listing of all the known artworks by an artist with explanations and scholarly comments. The works are typically described in such a way that they may be reliably identified by third parties.

**Christie's:** British auction house founded in 1766 by James Christie. This leading auctioneer of Fine Arts operates globally with main sites at St James's, central London, and in New York City at the Rockefeller Center.

**Coat of Arms:** Special design, generally in the form of a shield, used as a symbol of identity.

**Cobalt Blue:** It is cobalt aluminum oxide, an expensive and stable blue pigment first used in 1802. Vincent van Gogh famously described this pigment as "a divine color and there is nothing so beautiful for putting atmosphere around things…".

**Cochineal Lake:** Red pigment extracted from the cochineal beetle that is native to North America. Archeological evidence suggests its use by the Aztecs for dyeing and painting. This pigment was brought to Europe in the 16th century following the Spanish conquest.

**Colorito:** Term usually applied to a painting in which color is employed in a dominant manner, as an important compositional element and for sensual expressive purposes.

**Compositional Differences (in a painting):** Term used to describe differences in the arrangement of the visual elements such as figures, trees, and so on, in a painting or other artwork. Composition is different from the subject matter of a painting. Every painting, whether abstract, surrealistic or representational, regardless of subject matter, has a composition.

**Connoisseur:** A discerning well-learned expert who is especially competent to pass critical judgments on a work of art.

**Conservation Scientist (as it pertains to art in a museum, gallery or an archive):** Museum, gallery or archive professional who works in the field of conservation science and whose focus is on research and preservation of cultural heritage objects through scientific techniques.

**Copper Phthalocyanine:** Bright blue synthetic pigment first prepared in 1927 and belonging to a group of phthalocyanine dyes.

**Craquelure:** A network of fine cracks in the paint or varnish of a painting. It can be a result of drying, aging, intentional patterning, or a combination of all three.

**Cross-section:** Slice through any object, which shows its layered structure. In the context of the technical examination of a painting, it is a slice of a small sample of paint impregnated in a block of resin and polished.

**Crown of Thorns:** Placed on the head of Jesus during the events leading up to the crucifixion. It was used both to cause Jesus pain and to mock his claim of authority. Received by Saint Louis IX from Baldwin II, the relic is preserved in a gilded, crystalline reliquary and kept in Notre-Dame de Paris. There, it was presented to the faithful every year for a special service on Good Friday until 15 April 2019, when it was rescued from a fire at the cathedral.

**Cystic Fibrosis:** Life-threatening hereditary disease that affects the lungs and digestive system.

**Dalí, Salvador (1904–1989):** Salvador Domingo Felipe Jacinto *Dalí* was a Spanish surrealist artist renowned for his technical skill, precise draftsmanship and the striking and bizarre images in his work.

**de Kooning, Willem (1904–1977):** Dutch-American pioneer of 20th-century art who immigrated to the USA illegally, as a secret stowaway on a ship in 1926. He was a prominent and celebrated abstract expressionist painter. Unlike some of his contemporaries like Jackson Pollock and Mark Rothko, de Kooning never fully abandoned the depiction of the human figure. His series of paintings Woman I-VI (1950–53) caused a sensation with its violent imagery featuring a unique blend of gestural abstraction and figuration, which was largely at odds with the tenets of Abstract Expressionism and his previous work.

**Dendrochronology:** Scientific method of dating trees (obtaining a felling date of a tree) by examining tree growth rings.

**Designo:** Comes from the Italian word for drawing or design. It carries a more complex meaning in art, entailing both the intellectual capacity to invent design and the ability to execute an anatomically correct drawing.

**EDXRF and EDX:** EDXRF (Energy dispersive X-ray fluorescence) is a simple and accurate technique for the determination of the chemical composition of pigments through the interaction of X-rays with the sample, with subsequent emission of X-rays specific to the type of atoms present in the sample. All the elements are excited simultaneously and subsequently separated and identified individually. EDX works on the same principle as EDXRF but is so referred to when used in conjunction with a scanning electron microscope.

**Electromagnetic Radiation (EM radiation or EMR):** It refers to the waves of the electromagnetic field, propagating through space. These include radio waves, microwaves, infrared, (visible) light, ultraviolet, X-rays, and gamma rays.

**En Plein Air:** French term predominantly used in reference to a painting executed in the open air as opposed to a studio.

***Flowers in a Blue Vase (1887):*** Painting by Vincent van Gogh (not to be confused with *Flowers in a Blue Vase* painted in 1875 by Paul Cézanne). It is housed in the van Gogh Museum in Amsterdam and was painted during his time in Paris.

**Fourier Transform Infrared Spectroscopy (FTIR) and Micro-FTIR ($\mu$FTIR):** A technique which is used to obtain the infrared spectrum of a minute sample of organic and certain inorganic materials, over a wide spectral range, thereby providing specific information about chemical bonding and molecular structure.

**French Baroque Period:** The Baroque period was a time in history that followed the Renaissance and was defined by elaborate and highly ornamented expressions. This stylistic movement first started in Rome in the 1600s and spread throughout the majority of Europe. In France, the Baroque period covered the time of the reigns of Louis XIII, Louis XIV and Louis XV.

**French Ultramarine:** Blue pigment made from natural lapis lazuli, or its synthetic equivalent.

**Garden in Argenteuil (1873):** Also known as *The Garden of Monet at Argenteuil*, it is a painting by Claude Monet in his famous impressionism style, of his water-garden and water-lilies at his house in Giverny.

**Gas Chromatography:** Analytic technique used to separate and identify compounds that can be vaporized without decomposition in a mixture. This technique can be used to determine the type of binder used in paint or the type of resin used in a varnish.

**Gauguin, Paul (1848–1903):** French post-Impressionist painter. Much like his friend van Gogh, he is recognized for his experimental use of color and was unappreciated until after his death. He spent the last ten years of his life in French Polynesia, which had a clear influence on most of his paintings from this period.

**Gothic Architecture:** Architectural style that flourished in Europe during the Middle Ages between the mid-12th and the 16th century. Originating in northern France and England, this style of architecture is characterized by impressive stone structures, intricate sculptures, clustered columns and sharply pointed spires.

**Greenhalgh, Shaun (1960–present):** British artist and former master art forger. Greenhalgh produced over a seventeen-year period, between 1989 and 2006 produced many forgeries over. With the help of his family, these were passed through major auction houses and sold to internationally renowned museums as well as private collectors. In 2007, Bolton Crown Court sentenced Shaun Greenhalgh to four years and eight months in prison for the crime of producing artistic forgeries. In early 2010, the Victoria and Albert Museum in London held an exhibition of Greenhalgh's works.

**Impasto:** Painting technique, where paint is employed in very thick layers, in which the brush or painting-knife strokes are typically visible.

**Imperial Academy of Arts:** Initially named *Academy of the Three Noblest Arts* by its founder Ivan Shuvalov in 1757, the institution later adopted the name *Russian Academy of Arts* and was informally called the *St. Petersburg Academy of Arts*. Catherine the Great renamed it the *Imperial Academy of Arts* and commissioned a new building, completed 25 years later in 1789 by the Neva River. In 1947, it was moved to Moscow, and much of its art collection was placed in The State Hermitage Museum. The Academy promotes neoclassical styles and techniques and is arguably one of the best art schools in the world.

**Indigo:** Deep blue pigment extracted from plants. Species of *Indigofera* were cultivated in East Asia, Egypt, India, and Peru since antiquity. The earliest direct evidence for the use of indigo dates around 4000BC and comes from Huaca Prieta, in contemporary Peru. Indigo was used by the Romans and figured prominently in European easel painting. Since 1870, it has been manufactured synthetically.

**Infrared False Color (IRFC) Imaging:** This technique produces an image created by digitally editing the visible and infrared images of the same subject. IRFC is helpful to detect retouches and for the tentative identification of pigments. IRFC often does not provide conclusive results; however, it is recognized as a valid tool to identify areas of interest for further analysis.

**Infrared Radiation (IR):** Electromagnetic radiation of longer wavelength than visible light, and invisible to the human eye. Infrared radiation is given off by all warm objects.

**Infrared Reflectography (IRR):** Non-invasive method of studying a painting by looking beneath the visible layers of paint. This allows the examination of underdrawings and is particularly useful in the case of charcoal underdrawings.

**Infrared Spectroscopy:** Technique that involves the interaction of infrared radiation with matter. It is excellent for the identification of organic materials, including paints, resins, adhesives, oils. It is also used by chemists to determine functional groups in a molecule.

**Infrared Transmission (IRT) Imaging:** In this imaging technique, a source of infrared radiation is placed facing the back of the painting and a detector (often a modified camera) is placed at the front of the painting. IRT often provides better images compared to normal IRR for detecting underdrawings and underpaintings. However, this method is useful only for art on translucent supports, such as paintings on canvas, drawings on paper and historical documents and manuscripts.

**InGaAs Sensor:** Indium gallium arsenide is an alloy image *sensor* used in the visible and infrared regions of the electromagnetic spectrum.

***In Situ:*** Latin phrase typically italicized to mean 'on-site' or 'locally'.

**Isotopes:** Atoms of the same element that have a different number of neutrons but the same number of protons and electrons.

**Kröller-Müller Museum:** National art museum and sculpture garden, located in the Hoge Veluwe National Park in Otterlo, the Netherlands.

**Kustodiev, Boris Mikhailovich (1878–1927):** A talented Russian painter. He was admitted to the Imperial Academy of Arts in 1896. Upon graduating in 1903, he obtained the right to travel abroad on a grant from the Imperial Academy to further his education and left in 1903 for France, Spain, Italy, Austria and Germany. Upon his return to Russia in 1909, Kustodiev was awarded the title of Academician of Art.

**Lapis Lazuli:** Deep-blue rock used for pigmentation and at times as a semi-precious stone prized since antiquity for its intense blue color.

**Laser Ablation-Inductively Coupled Plasma-Mass Spectrometry (LA-ICP-MS):** An elemental and isotopic analytical technique that can be performed directly on solid samples involving the direct conversion of a sample into an aerosol of fine particles, which are carried by helium, ionized in a plasma torch, and analyzed using a mass spectrometer.

**Lazurite:** Deep-blue to greenish-blue component of lapis lazuli, which is used as a pigment.

**Lead White:** Carbonate of lead that occurs naturally as a mineral. This pigment was in use since antiquity and was the only white pigment used in European paintings until the 19th century when it was replaced with a less toxic substitute (zinc white and then titanium white).

**Light Emitting Diode (LED):** Semiconductor light source that emits light when a current flows through it. Electrons in the semiconductor release energy in the form of photons (i.e., light).

**Linseed Oil:** Oil extracted from flax seeds.

**Lobkowicz Palace:** The only privately owned building of the 16th century Prague Castle complex in the Czech Republic. The building owned by the Lobkowicz Czech noble family houses their family collection, which includes works by masters such as Canaletto, Bruegel the Elder, Cranach, and Velázquez, as well as original scores and manuscripts by Beethoven and Mozart.

**Longwave Ultraviolet Light:** Ultraviolet light can be split into UVA (345–300 nm) referred to as Near or Longwave UV light, UVB (280–315 nm) referred to as Middle or Middlewave UV light, and UVC (180–280 nm) referred to as Far or Shortwave UV light.

**Louvre:** Musée du Louvre or the Louvre Museum is the world's largest art museum located in central Paris. The Louvre is also arguably the most visited art museum in the world.

**Malachite:** Bright green mineral and the oldest known green pigment. It was used in Egyptian tomb paintings as early as the Fourth Dynasty (~2700 B.C.).

**Manganese Blue:** Modern, inorganic synthetic blue pigment first produced in 1907 and patented in 1935.

**Mass Spectrometry (MS):** An analytical technique that measures the mass-to-charge ratios as well as the relative abundance of ions in the gas phase.

**Metropolitan Museum of Art in New York (colloquially known as 'the Met'):** It is the largest art museum in the United States. It houses over two million works of art from around the globe.

**Micro Raman Spectroscopy:** Useful technique for the identification of individual components in pigment mixtures. It uses a Raman microscope specially designed for Raman spectroscopy.

**Micro X-ray Diffraction ($\mu$XRD):** Type of analysis that uses a very narrow beam of X-rays to carry out localized X-ray diffraction measurements on a very small area. It allows the study of the nature and structure of the material under investigation.

*Modus Operandi*: Latin phrase, approximately translated as mode of operating or habitual method or procedure.

**Monet (1840–1926):** Oscar-Claude Monet was a prolific French painter and one of the founders of the impressionism movement.

**Multispectral Imaging Digital Camera:** Specialized digital camera with a set of bandpass interferential filters that are used to examine works of art.

**Multispectral Imaging in Art:** Non-destructive technique that reveals underdrawings, detects alterations and allows the identification of certain materials and pigments used in the composition of a painting. Conservators can use this technique to differentiate between original sections from later additions or restorations to help in the selection of the best conservation procedures.

**National Galleries of Scotland:** National art gallery of Scotland located in Edinburgh. The gallery first opened to the public in 1859.

**Nazi:** Member of the National Socialist German Worker's party which controlled Germany from 1933 to 1945. Nazism under Adolf Hitler advocated totalitarian government, territorial expansion, anti-Semitism and Aryan supremacy, all these leading directly to World War II and the Holocaust.

**Notre Dame Cathedral (France):** Gothic cathedral located in the fourth arrondissement of Paris, France.

**Nuremberg Trials:** Series of military tribunals held after World War II in Nuremberg (also spelled Nürnberg) Germany by the Allied forces under the international law of war crimes. These tribunals were held to bring war criminals to justice.

**Old Masters:** Refers to painters of skill who worked in Europe before about 1800.

**Optical Microscope:** Designed for the magnification of a sample, typically using light reflected from the surface of an object.

**Palette:** Term originally referring to a flat and rigid surface on which a painter arranges and mixes paints. The term may also refer to the range of colors that artists use in producing their artwork.

**Palette-knife:** Blunt tool with a flexible steel blade that is used for mixing or applying paint to a support.

**Pentimenti:** Changes to an earlier painting beneath a layer or layers of paint. These changes are identified through the reappearance of earlier traces or sketches showing details that have been modified and painted over by the artist. Originates from the Italian word *pentire* meaning 'to repent'.

**Perón, Juan Domingo:** President of Argentina elected three times (1946–1952, 1952–1955 and 1973–1974). Founder and leader of the Peronist political movement.

**Phthalocyanines:** Intensely blue-green colored organic compounds used extensively in dyeing. Phthalocyanine pigments were developed around the 1930s.

**Picasso, Pablo (1881–1973):** One of the greatest and most influential artists of the 20th century; co-founder of the Cubist movement.

**Pigments:** Chemical compounds (including some minerals and synthetic compounds) used as colorants. They transmit only selected wavelengths of visible light, which makes them appear colorful.

**Plasma:** Ionized gas in which electrons and ions coexist in an overall electrically neutral medium. It is considered the fourth state of matter.

**Polarized Light Microscope (PLM):** Microscope designed to observe and photograph samples that are visible primarily due to their anisotropic nature (exhibiting properties with different values when measured in different directions of light, such as *refractive index*). It is a contrast enhancing technique.

**Poussin, Nicolas (1594–1665):** French painter who led the French Baroque Classicism despite spending virtually all of his working life in Rome where he died in the Papal States. The classically trained Poussin specialized in painting scenes from the Bible, ancient history, and mythology. Early in his career, his works notable for their coloristic richness were beholden to Venetian art and most especially to Titian. In his later years, Poussin had rejected this overtly glamorous approach in favor of a more rational and disciplined Classicism of Raphael where he gave growing prominence to line over color and emphasized clarity, rationality and order in a much more deliberate manner.

**Proteinaceous Materials:** Any material pertaining to, or of, the nature of a protein.

**Proton-induced or Particle-induced X-ray Emission (PIXE):** A non-destructive elemental analysis technique that determines the elemental composition of a sample, through exposure to a proton beam that causes excitation of inner shell electrons. X-rays specific to the component elements are subsequently emitted.

**Provenance:** Record of the documented historical record of a work of art, typically used as a guide to authenticity or quality.

**Pyrolysis:** Thermal decomposition of materials under vacuum or in an inert atmosphere.

**Pyrolysis-Gas Chromatography-Mass Spectrometry (Py-GC-MS):** An analytical technique in which the sample is heated under vacuum to 600–1000 °C, causing large molecules to break down into smaller, more volatile fragments that can be separated by gas chromatography. The data can be used either to identify the material or to obtain some structural information.

**Radiocarbon Dating:** Scientific technique for determining the age of a carbon containing object that is based on the measurement of its radiocarbon ($^{14}$C) content.

**Raking Light:** Light source set at a very acute angle which is nearly parallel to the surface of the object. Raking light is useful for the examination of the surface topography of works of art and archaeological pieces.

**Raman Spectroscopy:** Non-invasive spectroscopic technique typically used to determine vibrational modes of molecules and to provide a structural fingerprint by which molecules can be identified.

**Raphael, or Raffaello Santi (1483–1520):** Master painter and architect of the Italian High Renaissance. Best known for his Madonnas and for his large figure compositions in the Vatican.

**Renaissance:** Period in European history marking a cultural, artistic, political and economic uprising, which transitioned the Old Continent from the middle ages to modernity. This period is typically thought to cover the period between the 15th and 17th centuries.

**Retouch:** Highlights to a painting in order to produce a more desirable appearance, to add new touches.

***Rhapsodie Moderne (1957):*** A surrealistic painting by Salvador Dalí where the woman pictured is surprisingly reminiscent of the heroine personifying progress in the painting *American Progress (1872)* by John Gast. One interpretation of the symbolism of this painting by Dalí is a criticism of US expansion policy to the west, where he makes the woman defenseless in the face of a technological monster, blinded with a beam directed from the searchlight eye and entwining with telephone wires growing instead of eyelashes.

**Richelieu (1585–1642):** Generally referred to as Cardinal Richelieu. He dominated the history of France from 1624 to his death as Louis XIII's chief minister. He is considered one of the greatest politicians in French history.

**Royal Academy of Arts:** Founded in 1768 by King George III, the Royal Academy of Arts has a mission to promote the arts of design in the UK through education and exhibition. Situated in the heart of London's West End on Piccadilly, it is the oldest fine arts institution in Britain and one of the most prestigious in the world.

**Rubens, Peter Paul (1577–1640):** Flemish born artist, who made a name for himself not only in the art world, but also through the diplomatic reign. He was known for his Baroque style, and much of his work focused on diplomatic and religious figures.

**Sapwood (or alburnum):** The younger, outermost wood; in a growing tree. It is living wood, and and its principal functions are to conduct water from the roots to the leaves and to store up and give back according to the season the reserves prepared in the leaves.

**Scanning Electron Microscopy:** Technique that produces images of a sample by scanning its surface with a focused beam of electrons. It gives information about the sample's surface topography.

**Stereomicroscope:** Microscope that provides a three-dimensional view of the specimen. It does this with separate objective lenses and eyepieces for each eye.

***Still Life with Meadow Flowers and Roses* (1886):** Painting created in 1886 by Vincent van Gogh in Realism style. It had been executed on top of a rendering of two wrestlers, visible with synchrotron X-rays.

**Surrealistic Painting Style:** 20th-century avant-garde movement in art that sought to release the creative potential of the unconscious mind by the irrational juxtaposition of images.

**Synchrotron:** A synchrotron is a particle accelerator in which a charged particle — typically an electron or a proton — is accelerated to very high energies while confined to a constant circular orbit by a magnetic field.

**Tabby Weave:** Plain weave known as the most basic of three fundamental types of textile weaves. In this type of weave, the warp and weft threads cross at right angles providing strength and durability.

**Tate Gallery:** Network of four art galleries in London (founded in 1897 by the sugar tycoon Henry Tate). These are known as Tate Modern, Tate Britain, Tate Liverpool and Tate St Ives. Tate Britain displays a collection of British art from the 1500s to the present while the rest of the gallery network focuses on modern and contemporary art from the 1900s to the present.

**Technical Art History:** Novel field of endeavor combining expertise from art historians, conservators and scientists.

**Tempera:** Also known as egg tempera, is a permanent, fast-drying painting medium consisting of colored pigments mixed with egg yolk.

**Terahertz Spectroscopy:** THz spectroscopy is a method that utilizes radiation in the region between the microwave and infrared in the electromagnetic spectrum for the elucidation and structure determination of matter.

***The Accommodation of Desire (1929):*** Painted in the summer of 1929 by Salvador Dalí, the picture depicts Dalí's sexual anxieties over a love affair with an older, married woman. The woman, Gala, then the wife of the Surrealist poet Paul Éluard, became Dalí's life-long muse and mate.

***The Bedroom (1888–1889):*** Vincent van Gogh produced this painting of his bedroom in October 1888, a month after he moved into his 'Yellow House' in Arles, France. Van Gogh loved this painting so much that he made three distinct versions of it. The first is now in the collection of the Van Gogh Museum in Amsterdam; the second, belonging to the Art Institute of Chicago, was painted a year later on the same scale and an almost identical composition; and a third, smaller canvas is in the collection of the Musée d'Orsay in Paris, which he made as a gift for his mother and sister.

***The Birdnester (1568)*:** Also known as 'The Peasant and the Nest Robber' is an oil-on-panel painting by Pieter Bruegel the Elder. It is in the collection of the Kunsthistorisches Museum in Vienna.

***The Coachman (1920–1923)*:** Kustodiev is known to have produced four versions of this composition. Three watercolor versions (1920) and an oil on canvas (1923). The composition of each differs slightly, through the details in the background, the coachman's belt and mitten as well as the number on the droshky. This series received major accolades while on display at the 1924 Russian Art Exhibition in New York. The oil on canvas version was purchased by Peter Leonidovich Kapitza (1894–1984), the only member of the presidium of the Soviet Academy of Sciences who was not a member of the Communist Party and more famously, the recipient of the 1978 Nobel Prize for Physics.

***The Flight into Egypt (1657–1658)*:** Oil on canvas picture by Nicolas Poussin, that depicts the flight of the Holy Family, guided by an angel directing them to safety from Judea to Egypt. This theme is depicted in several paintings, and at times under the exact same name by Old Masters including, Titian, Giotto, Rembrandt and Peter Paul Rubens.

***The Gloomy Day (1565)*:** Oil on wood painting by Pieter Bruegel the Elder as part of a series of six works depicting common Netherlandish activities at different times of the year. The painting is currently in the collection of the Kunsthistorisches Museum, located in Vienna, Austria.

***The Harvesters (1565)*:** Oil on wood painting by Pieter Bruegel the Elder as part of a series of six works depicting common Netherlandish activities at different times of the year. The painting is currently in the collection of the Metropolitan Museum of Art in New York.

**The Holy Family:** Name given to the family unit of Jesus: Jesus, his mother the Virgin Mary and his foster-father Joseph.

***The Hunters in the Snow (1565)* also known as *The Return of the Hunters*:** Oil on wood painting by Pieter Bruegel the Elder as part of a series of six works depicting common Netherlandish activities at different times of the year. The painting is currently in the collection of the Kunsthistorisches Museum, located in Vienna, Austria.

***The Man with the Head of the Blue Hortensias (1936):*** In this relatively small canvas, Salvador Dalí places a lone figure sitting by a roadside which initially appears to be leaning with his head down propped on his arm, as if deep in thought. However, above the head a strategically placed opening in the rock makes it appear that the blue distant landscape in the opening could also be the head looking out from the work. The stylistic freedom of using double images, which is evident in this painting, something he would do more often in his classic period, is possibly the result of Dalí's time in Italy.

***The Return of the Herd (1565):*** Oil on wood painting by Pieter Bruegel the Elder as part of a series of six works depicting common Netherlandish activities at different times of the year. The painting is currently in the collection of the Kunsthistorisches Museum, located in Vienna, Austria.

***The Virgin Adoring the Sleeping Christ Child (ca. 1485):*** Picture by Botticelli depicting the Virgin Mary adoring her son, the Christ Child, who lies on the ground enwrapped in a cloth.

**Turner, Joseph Mallord William (1775–1851):** British landscape painter, whose legacy include some 300 oil paintings and thousands of watercolors and drawings. At age 14, Turner, the son of a barber and a wig-maker, was able to secure admission to the prestigious Royal Academy of Arts, where at 21 he was the youngest-ever painter to be featured in the Academy's annual exhibition. He became an associate member of the Academy at age 24, and by 26 he had achieved the institution's terminal rank of Royal Academician — again the youngest in its history. Turner was commercially successful and was much in demand as a painter of castles and countryseats for their owners.

He was described as 'the painter of light' because of his propensity for brilliant colors but was also famed for his often turbulent, sometimes violent marine paintings. In 2016, the Bank of England selected Turner as the first artist to grace the £20 note.

**Ultramarine:** Deep blue color pigment, which was originally made by grinding the mineral lapis lazuli into a powder.

**Ultraviolet Fluorescence (UVF) Imaging:** Technique that detects organic compounds that are typically easily observed under UV light. This effective tool can detect recent restorations to paintings that would appear darker than the aged original varnish layers. UVF can also reveal the presence of natural resin varnishes, as these often fluoresce under UV light.

**Ultraviolet Light:** Electromagnetic radiation with wavelength from 10 nm to 400 nm, shorter than that of visible light but longer than X-rays.

**Underdrawings:** Preparative drawings done typically on a painting ground layer before paint is applied.

**US District Court:** General trial court of the United States Federal Judiciary. Both civil and criminal cases are filed in US district courts.

**UV-Induced Infrared Fluorescence:** A longwave UV light source causes painting materials to fluoresce in the visible and infrared regions of the electromagnetic spectrum. As a technique, UV–induced infrared fluorescence is more selective than UV-visible fluorescence and occurs in a limited range of materials.

**Van Gogh Museum:** Dutch art museum dedicated to the works of Vincent van Gogh and his contemporaries in Amsterdam.

**Van Gogh, Theo (1857–1891):** Younger brother of the famed Dutch painter Vincent van Gogh. Theo was an art dealer and the financial supporter of his older brother Vincent. He died at the age of 33, six months after his brother committed suicide at the age of 37.

**Van Gogh, Vincent (1853–1890):** Vincent Willem van Gogh was a Dutch post-impressionist painter who was and still is among the most famous and influential figures in the history of Western art. He was a prolific painter, especially during the last two years of his life. Over his career, he produced over 2000 works of art including around 860 oil paintings of varied subjects including landscapes, still lifes, portraits and self-portraits. His vivid works, which contributed to the foundations of modern art, are full of bold colors and expressive brushwork. Van Gogh was not commercially successful. He committed suicide at 37 after years of battle with mental illness, depression and poverty.

**Varnish:** A layer that protects the painting from dirt, dust and atmospheric ravages. It evens out the surface of the painting, making it equally glossy or matte. Most varnishes are a blend of resin, drying oil and volatile solvent.

**Verdigris:** Bright bluish-green pigment of copper acetate. The low stability of this pigment causes the formation of byproducts by means of atmospheric oxidation. This pigment was used from antiquity until the 19th century. Nowadays, verdigris is rarely used as a pigment due to its toxic nature.

**Veridian Green:** Chromium-based green pigment composed of chromium oxide dihydrate produced initially by Pannetier, a color maker in Paris, starting in 1838.

**Vermilion:** The name 'vermilion' comes from Latin vermiculus (small worm, cochineal) from which the natural red dye carmine is derived. Vermilion, however, is a mercury sulfide mineral (cinnabar) used from the 8th century until the manufacture of its synthetic replacement, cadmium red in 1919.

**X-ray Diffraction (XRD):** It refers to the scattering of X-rays by a solid producing a pattern that gives information about the structure and nature of the crystal.

**X-ray Fluorescence (XRF):** It is a non-invasive technique that causes the emission of characteristic X-rays from a material that has been excited by being bombarded with a source of high-energy X-rays.

**X-ray Radiography (XRR):** It is a non-destructive testing method that uses X-ray radiation to penetrate the solid object (such as a painting) and produce a radiograph (or image). In the case of paintings, the thickness and density of the pigments affect the amount of radiation reaching a detector. Images of underdrawings which are not in charcoal can be observed.

**X-ray Synchrotron Imaging:** When a moving electron changes direction, it emits energy. In a synchrotron, the emitted energy due to a change in direction is of high energy at X-ray wavelength. Using this X-ray radiation, it is possible to record depth-selective, element-selective or species-selective images of entire paintings.

# Index